JULIAN McDOUGALL

THE MEDIA TEACHER'S BOOK

Hodder Arnold

A MEMBER OF THE HODDER HEADLINE GROUP

First published in Great Britain in 2006 by
Hodder Education, a member of the Hodder Headline Group,
338 Euston Road, London NW1 3BH

www.hoddereducation.com

Distributed in the United States of America by
Oxford University Press Inc.
198 Madison Avenue, New York, NY10016

British Library Cataloguing in Publication Data
A catalogue record for this book is available from the British Library

Library of Congress Cataloging-in-Publication Data
A catalog record for this book is available from the Library of Congress

ISBN-10 0 340 90516 6
ISBN-13 978 0 340 90516 6

1 2 3 4 5 6 7 8 9 10

Typeset in 10/13 Adobe Garamond by Servis Filmsetting Ltd, Manchester
Printed and bound in Malta

What do you think about this book? Or any other Hodder
Education title? Please send your comments to the feedback
section on www.hoddereducation.com.

Contents

Acknowledgements

This book is dedicated to Mike McDougall, and would not have been possible without the love and support of Lydia, Alex and Jan.

For the personal experiences which have formed the approaches described in this book I am indebted to the FE students I have worked with at Runshaw College and Halesowen College in particular.

I would also like to thank Pete Fraser, Nick Peim, Adrian Stokes, Mark Reid, Nicky North, David Buckingham, Joanna Bailey, Julian Coultas, Stuart McConnell, Julie Goodwin, Wayne O'Brien, Hilary Dunphy and Dave Trotman for modelling the kinds of good practice in learning and teaching that I am hoping to pass on.

Having achieved little at school, I am indebted to Dave Plowright who led the National Diploma in Media at South Notts FE College that got me motivated and into Sheffield Polytechnic, where the late Tessa Perkins and her colleagues had created a degree course that gave equal value to Althusser and *Pop Will Eat Itself*.

A flick through the further reading sections will reveal three sources that I have heavily relied upon. I would like to express my respect for Len Masterman, whose work I regularly return to throughout (and start from, in some ways), and my gratitude for the support and inspiration offered since I started teaching Media by Roy Stafford and Jenny Grahame. Anyone with a serious interest in Media education should read Masterman, and support both *In the Picture* and *Media Magazine*.

The courtesy of the following is also acknowledged for permission to reproduce copyright material:

Scopitones (the record label of Cinerama and The Wedding Present) for use of an image from their website; Stuart McConnell at Halesowen College for permission to use images from students' production work, Guardian newspapers for permission to reproduce 'Turn on, tune in, blog out' by Stephen Pritchard; Pete Dadds for use of an image from *Shameless*; John Sandwell and students at Long Road Sixth Form College for permission to photograph them in the classroom and use the images in the book; David Nock for a still image from his film *The Golden Sphere*; BBC/Film Council/The Kobal Collection for a still from *In this World*; EA Games for an image from *Medal of Honor* and News International for a front cover of *The Sun*.

My thanks also to Steve Archer for help finding an elusive page number.

Preface: How to Take this Book

'I see a progressive story: mass culture growing more sophisticated, demanding more cognitive engagement with each passing year. Think of it as a kind of positive brainwashing: the popular media steadily, but almost imperceptibly, making our minds sharper, as we soak in entertainment usually dismissed as so much lowbrow fluff'. (Johnson: 2005: pxi)

Let's read this as a kind of 'establishing shot'. To teach Media Studies well, I think you have to have this kind of enthusiasm for popular culture, and its rapid proliferation through technology. You need to be happy to learn from your students, and cautious about imposing your own cultural preferences in the classroom. And you ought to feel privileged to have access to young people's tastes and proximity to their creative practices.

This book aims to offer a wide range of suggestions for good practice in Media teaching. It makes no assumptions about either the course you are teaching or the kind of institution you teach in. It is not geared to any one awarding body or level of study.

In 2004 there were almost 40,000 GCSE Media students in England, alongside 30,000 at AS and 23,000 at A2. In 2005, 1500 students took GNVQ Media, with a total of 3000 following the VCE. As for National Diploma, altogether 4500 were entered in 2005 for courses at all levels (source of data: QCA, 2005). So if we combine all these courses, we can say that at any one time about 115,000 people are studying the Media in a formal, mainstream educational setting, most often set up for 14–19 year olds.

So you might be teaching GCSE or A Level Media Studies in a school or sixth form, or a vocational course such as a National Diploma in a further education college. You might be fortunate enough to be teaching in one of the 37 specialist Media Arts Schools. Or you could be teaching Media within English at Key Stage 3 and 4 or using media as a base for Citizenship or extra-curricular enrichment activities. Perhaps you are dealing with aspects of media in prison education or for work-based training. My hope is that by taking a generic approach to content and pedagogy my suggestions for dealing with creative production tasks and theoretical analysis will be adaptable to all these learning settings and contexts.

I have a primary objective, which is to offer an update to and also a shift in approach from Len Masterman's *Teaching the Media* (1985). Masterman's book remains a comprehensive presentation of strategies for the (A Level) Media teacher and indeed a compelling *raison d'etre* for the subject. However, it is my view that the Media learner twenty years on operates within a different set of cultural and technological discourses, and equally the Media teacher resides in a very different educational paradigm. It is difficult to remember the world now before the framing agendas imposed by the National Curriculum, Ofsted and the QCA, and Masterman was writing before such prescription.

Media Studies is taught formally from age 14 and as such, it will be significantly affected by the pending changes to 14–19 provision, in particular the renegotiation of what it means to learn in a 'vocational' or an 'academic' context. For this reason, this book adopts a holistic approach and does not separate its pedagogic content in terms of A Level, VCE and so on. In the new 14–19 landscape, we might see a change in this academic division of labour (the status of Media Studies is up for grabs at the time of writing), so it is important that a book such as this deals with Media education as a whole, as opposed to particular specifications (out of date as they inevitably become). So the use of generic types of lesson as chapter headings allows for adaptation to more specific content and learning objectives.

The 'project'

'I absolutely, in fact increasingly, believe in the crucial importance of Media Studies; they should be at the heart of any educational system which claims to equip its citizens to deal with the complexities of life in the 21st century'. (Lord Puttnam, quoted in QCA, 2005: 4.)

What is the role of the Media teacher in contemporary English society? Is it merely as deliverer of a prescribed curriculum that is either academic (with claims to 'critical autonomy') or vocational (a more technical preparation for work or at least the acquisition of creative and technical skills for a variety of contexts, not necessarily Media-related)? Or is Media teaching a social practice? Undoubtedly, the latter makes more sense, as Media learning is a dynamic, creative and highly reflexive endeavour providing the teacher allows it to be so. Media teaching is certainly political, but I would suggest that this no longer translates into lecturing about ideology. It might now be more micro-political, in the sense that students designing websites or constructing computer game narratives might be engaging in new literacy practices that renegotiate their socio-cultural identities. Ultimately, all Media learning is to do with discourse, whether practical or theoretical, visual or written. With this sense of the world, the Media teacher, despite the ongoing public derision levelled at her, has a pretty important job.

There was a time when Media learning could look like an annex to English, and the distinction between academic and vocational media activities were clearly marked. In this era, the Media teacher would navigate a primarily 'critical' curriculum, focusing on messages, meanings and language (for GCSE and A Level) or she would operate within a highly technicist agenda, in order to 'train' students in specialist skills within a workplace paradigm.

It is clear that digital technology has ushered us into a new (perhaps postmodern) place, where new forms of creativity and literacy, which foster critical thinking, are available through technological means. This changes two things: on the academic side (if we believe these distinctions can be maintained), Media learners are engaging with reflective analysis of citizenship and power through the use of MP3 for example, while on vocational courses digital editing and web design software is allowing more creativity with less training in the traditional sense. I believe that our traditional models and 'handed down' conceptual framework for Media learning must adapt or perhaps even be challenged by new approaches, in the wake of these technological sea-changes.

So this book intends to retain Masterman's focus on audience and the study of popular culture while offering a more directly applicable set of suggestions for facilitating Media learning in a digital era. In addition, it provides guidance for teaching Media in the context of inspection and firmly locates its pedagogic suggestions within an inclusivity agenda. In other words, it aims to equip the reader with an approach to teaching Media which is at once supportive of all learners and demonstrative of 'good practice' as it is defined by the current inspectoral context. Fundamentally this book is concerned with *how* to teach Media successfully, as opposed to *what* to teach, and for this reason I hope it will be of equal value to all Media practitioners, regardless of the specification you are using. To this end, each chapter offers strategies for constructing lessons (for any Media course) that are inclusive, offer differentiated routes to clear learning goals accompanied by suggestions for classroom management, research support and formative assessment for learning.

Media Studies is taught within both academic and vocational boundaries, and suffers from many misconceptions as a result. It is derided for its failure to lead to employment in the Media (in a way that, say, History would never be), and it is criticized for its apparent 'lightweight' academic nature because of the accessibility of its subject matter. This book seeks to offer guidance for teaching on both types of courses, and to avoid labelling learners in either way. Each chapter is of equal value for teaching on theory or production based courses. The book makes no political claims, there is no grand narrative of empowerment or emancipation residing here. And there are no value judgements to be made about the purposes of various forms of Media learning. The guidance offered relates to the specifications used by students on GCSE, A/AS and vocational Media courses, and offers strategies for raising achievement and managing learning toward assessment objectives as configured by awarding bodies (of which I have had considerable 'inside' experience). Particular attention is paid to digital technologies, and how best to teach both through and about them.

The suggestions made here are in many cases examples of successful practice in the colleges in which I have taught Media. At Halesowen College in the West Midlands, the Media department I worked in has been transformed from an environment in which pass rates were always at or near 100 per cent (but nobody got an A) to one in which higher grades are now the norm (on both A/AS and vocational courses). This has been achieved through a shift in culture and approach. This involved course planning (in particular the strategic integration of schemes of work and assessments) combined with a profound philosophical change in attitudes and approaches to student support and motivation, ultimately leading to an Ofsted Grade One award for outstanding practice in February 2005 (six months after I moved to another institution, I should add!). I have for several years offered INSET courses and conference workshops to try to share the kinds of practice I was involved in at the college, and this book includes some of the ideas discussed at such events.

Media Studies has passed through the 'relevance boom'. As a National Diploma student in the 1980s (at the time Masterman was writing) I was excited and motivated on a daily basis by access to video cameras in a way that we cannot expect our current students to be. The technology young people use these days in their out-of-school/college contexts will often be more sophisticated than what we are offering, and they may find our interventions into their everyday digital culture clumsy and awkward, rather than inspiring and empowering. Equally, we cannot assume a political response to the media when we are teaching a post-Thatcher generation of students (and why should we?). So, we need new ways of exploring technology, creativity, politics and culture. We cannot (for better or worse) rely on the models in currency in the 1980s.

So this book tries to offer some suggestions based on these cultural shifts and on my experiences of successful Media teaching. It is very much a teacher's book, as opposed to an overview of the 'zeitgeist', and as such, it is intended to directly aid those teaching Media, about to teach Media or intending to do so. According to the QCA's statistics, only 22 per cent of Media teachers have a degree in the subject, and in the absence of a PGCE course in Media alone, each year a plethora of training courses are provided to compensate and to offer resources and approaches. In addition, there is a wonderful range of resources available commercially and for free to support teaching for particular units. These are all of value, and I recommend some of these in each chapter, but I hope this book can offer an everyday range of support in a way that such 'days out' from school or college or specific resources cannot, and thus it will complement these existing opportunities and materials.

This book is not explicitly based on classroom research (see Buckingham, 2003 for such a perspective on Media education), nor is it purely a theoretical overview (though I suggest it is impossible to be 'untheoretical' in a pedagogic context). Rather, it offers a broad range of ideas for approaching concepts, texts, technologies and research with students and I hope these will reaffirm your reasons for teaching Media in creative and inspiring ways.

My biggest challenge is to try to offer strategies for a progressive form of learning and teaching within the constraints of the qualifications framework you are working with. Buckingham suggests that digital technologies present a challenge or an 'other' to traditional boundaries placed between critical analysis and creative production. Consequently, there are different opportunities for more 'playful' forms of pedagogic practice. In this sense, he asserts, the classroom reduces in significance and thus we need to pay attention to (and value) learning taking place in other locations and at other times.

Our obligations

Quite a daunting prospect, then, to foster these new learning practices at the same time as pleasing the inspectors and maintaining a healthy position in the league tables and the value-added profiles. But it is to these various demands and discourses that we must turn our attention if we are to successfully update our practice and add to the conceptual/ideological approach suggested in Masterman's *Teaching the Media*. To this end, here at the outset is a series of ten framing statements (or a 'vow of chastity' for the Media teacher, to borrow the *Dogme* term, with a pinch of salt):

The Media teacher's 'vow of chastity'

1. The primary value of technology in the Media classroom is to enable creativity.
2. Creativity need not necessarily be challenging or alternative (and these ideas might need a rethink).
3. No theory is 'too hard' for any learners.
4. The distinction between theory and production is a false binary opposition. In fact, much theory is practical and much production is in itself highly theorizing.
5. Media learning should be free of all value judgements and notions of enrichment or cultural worth. All texts are of equal interest.
6. Media learning is not automatically inclusive: great efforts must be made to make it so. The subject matter of Media lessons is not automatically of any greater interest than other subjects.
7. The study of the media and the acquisition of media literacy is of cultural importance but it is not a political project.
8. Media learning is reflective in the sense that its starting point is audience and learners are readers, but all reading is socio-culturally framed.
9. Media Studies is primarily the study and practice of discourse.
10. No Media lesson should be taught in the same way two years running.

Strategies for inclusive Media Learning

Much attention is (rightly) paid these days on teacher training courses and in professional development to the variety of learning styles at work in the educational encounter. The most sensible approach to inclusive learning is simply to ensure that any group of students will have access to a range of learning contexts which incorporate visual, auditory and kinaesthetic application. Equally, collaborative classroom activity or production work can guarantee differentiation, so long as careful attention is paid to resources and content. And equality of opportunity must be understood in its holistic entirety – the consideration of the learning experience from curriculum choices to learning materials and both cultural and physical access.

With this inclusion agenda in mind, this book focuses (as already stated) on the 'how' rather than the 'what' of Media learning. Towards this end, a wide range of strategies for creative class activities is described, linked chapter by chapter to a different type of Media lesson in each case. They are listed below, with the chapter in which they appear, so that you have the option to use the book in this way if you wish. The idea is that you can adapt any of the strategies to any topic, unit, course or level, but they appear in the context of the subject matter of the chapter in each case.

Further reading

Buckingham, D., 2003, *Media Education: Literacy, Learning and Contemporary Culture*, London: Polity.

Johnson, S., 2005, *Everything Bad is Good for You*, London: Penguin.

Masterman, L., 1985, *Teaching the Media*, London: Routledge.

QCA, 2005, 'Media Matters: a review of Media Studies in schools and colleges', London: QCA.

chapter one

Helping Media Learning

A history of the present

Some narratives of the history of Media Studies have emerged, most notably in documents produced by Buckingham (2003) and in a report (2005) by the Qualifications and Curriculum Authority (QCA). Buckingham's account is the result of his many years at the heart of the subject's development, and as such is a very useful, reflective account based on a wealth of experience. The QCA report is the product of a research exercise conducted with the help of The English and Media Centre, and is very clear and helpful in a factual, quantitative sense (though somewhat less critically informed, in my opinion).

Trying to make my own sense of 'where we've been', as part of a broader research project (McDougall, 2004a), I interviewed (by email) a range of 'key players' in Media education: those involved over a period of time in curriculum design and reform for the subject, and some of the key authors in the emerging canon of work about the subject, as well as a large group of examiners (who are, of course, also teachers of the subject). I asked questions about the development of Media Studies as a formal, institutionalised subject in schools and colleges. I called this official form 'Subject Media', from Peim's critique of 'Subject English' (1995). I was also interested in their ideas about the separation of academic and vocational versions of Media education, and how they could be justified, or at least conceptually understood, in a shared way.

In summary, the moments of *consensus* from my research were as follows:

- The distinction between academic and vocational courses is that academic courses are more concerned with theory than production; with analysis rather than skills; with assessment through examinations rather than portfolio moderation; with prescribed content rather than briefs set within centres; and with deconstruction through concepts and critical theory rather than construction through technical competence.

- The development of A Level Media Studies represented a watershed moment in the professional status of Media teachers and the resources available for the subject, and it also led to a marginalization of vocational Media education.

- Film Studies has existed in various forms for longer, and Media teaching has a long tradition, especially in London, within other courses in a liberal/humanities tradition, and within English.

- Media Studies as a subject has a set of key 'stakeholder' groups that are concerned with shaping its institutional agendas through policy and through training and developing Media teachers and influencing their practice. These groups' roles are given further import due to the lack of a formal teacher training course in Media Studies, and as a result, the need for in-service training of new Media teachers, many of whom are from an English background.

There were moments of *disagreement* over the following issues:

- The role of the BFI in the history of the subject.
- The academic value of some kinds of vocational courses.
- The importance and/or purpose of practical work within Media Studies.
- The distinction between Media Studies as a formal academic subject and Media education as a more general term, or a term for cross-curricular teaching.
- The relationship of Film Studies to Media Studies (interestingly, the respondents were not asked to include Film Studies in their historical narratives, but all did).

Media Studies today

Media teachers come from a variety of backgrounds. This is a strength, in so much as it maintains the subject's status as a 'horizontal discourse' (Bernstein, 1990), a set of practices informed by a spread of contexts in the outside world (rather than a more closed and 'handed down' vertical discourse, perhaps). However, it can also be a reason for anxiety, if the lack of an established pedagogic 'rule book' results in more variability in the quality of teaching or practitioner 'expertise.' Working at Newman College in Birmingham with a group of English students preparing to teach in the 14–19 sector, I asked them to map the insides and outsides of Media Studies specifications from the English teacher's perspective (the insides being the bits that overlap with English). Their particular responses suggested that technical aspects of production, teaching about technologies, technical analysis of visual texts and politics and institutions resided on the outside (this was drawn as a wall, with these bits being on the other side), while on the

Communication of meaning   Technical aspects of production

Teaching about technologies   *Critical evaluation*

Layout conventions   *Identity/culture*

Language   Technical analysis of visual texts

Politics and institutions   *Print texts*

Representation   *Written coursework*

Advertising

Visual representation of the insides (in italics) and outsides (in boxes) of Media Studies from trainee English teachers' perspectives (Newman College, 2004).

wall itself were critical evaluation, layout conventions, language, written coursework, representation, advertising, print texts, communication of meaning and identity/culture.

My own view is that ideally we would 'do' Textual Studies and move away from academic boundaries which separate poems, paintings, websites and films from one another. This would, for example, create a parity between creative writing and video production, as well as Shakespeare and *The Sopranos*. Peim (2000) suggests that we should consider opportunities to read *Much Ado about Nothing* in terms of gender politics alongside *EastEnders*, for example. This would allow us to scrutinise and challenge the cultural authority of Shakespeare as a 'naturally superior form of fiction'. Literature as a whole might become unstable as a category as a result of such practice.

However, in the 'state we're in' it is useful to declare at the outset that there are many important distinctions between 'doing Media' and teaching English as these subjects are currently configured. Three clear distinctions are these: audience study as a starting point; the importance of theoretical engagement with digital technologies (from students' perspectives); and the constant attention to commercial context. It would still be relatively surprising to encounter an English literature lesson in which the commercial imperatives of an author's publisher and the promotion of the novel as a product were given significant attention in terms of the coded meanings of the text itself. Nor is the arena of negotiated readings of texts afforded much attention.

> 'On the one hand, there is the discipline which we can now call "traditional" media and cultural studies, where television programmes and films are discussed as "texts" by isolated scholars. This approach makes no reference to what actual audiences might think – based on the model of English literature, where no-one ever thought it was particularly relevant to hang around in Stratford asking punters what Macbeth *meant to them*. While English has traditionally got away with this by having a range of interesting people to write about some complex, beautiful and writerly texts, this has always been shaky ground for media studies. While the philosophical justification for why media scholars could do to telly what literary hacks had done with books was solid enough, it just never seemed right to be told about the Catholic-death wish subtext in an episode of *EastEnders*, when you suspected that not one of the sixteen million viewers at the time has spotted it. It is probably this element of media studies – whether real or imagined – which led, more than any other, to innumerable teenage media students having the piss taken out of them mercilessly by their mums and dads.' (Gauntlett, 1997: 9)

Other subject areas provide a basis for Media Studies teaching, but again, there are clear shifts in focus. The sociologist may need to adopt a more fluid sense of the relationship between media and society, while the art teacher may experience some tension when confronted with work that may seem derivative rather than inspired. The vocational teacher with industry experience needs to develop the craft of teaching and find ways to motivate learners within an environment that is 'always-already' artificial. After all, why should students on vocational courses be any more ready for accepting the rule-governed pressure of the workplace than other learners? Again, we must remember that a National Diploma course is highly theoretical and reflective, despite attempts to present it as otherwise.

Pleasure

Personally, teaching Media Studies has given me enormous privileges, despite the derision I have encountered (from the 'just showing videos' banter to more prejudicial asides based on intellectual snobbery and ignorance). I have been able to work with students on their terms, and genuinely learn from their interests and their consumption. I would not be so adept at downloading music, for example, if I had earned my living a different way. But I started to enjoy it all the more once I (pretty quickly) rethought my own identity and stopped concerning myself with what I should be 'teaching' them, or what they should be interested in (say, the funding of the BBC) and started paying more attention to the ways in which students weave mediated identities and communicate creatively through creativity and through consumption. Adopting a more reflexive, perhaps postmodern approach to media theory and research remains abstract if the teacher refuses to shift to a more reflexive approach to the 'educational encounter' itself.

The remainder of this introduction offers an 'establishing shot' for each of the major concepts, theories and technological areas covered in the chapters that follow. However, the mode of address is very much for teachers here, and the intention is to provide a contemporary 'spin' on each of the major concepts and theories. It is not my intention to suggest that the kinds of theory mentioned should be accessed by students in a traditional 'scholarly' way. Indeed, it may be the case that the teacher's approach is theoretically informed, but learners are not explicitly aware of names or terms.

The 'big concepts'

All kinds of Media learning tend to adopt a conceptual framework. Whether the concept is foregrounded (i.e. for learning about the concept itself) or used as a vehicle for creativity and theoretical reflection, most students will become familiar with audience, representation, narrative and genre along the way. The most pedestrian work reveals assumptions about how these areas are 'used' by producers and for analysis, while the more interesting activities offer a critique of the concepts themselves, or at least a renegotiation of their application.

Audience

Audience should be the starting point for Media learning, and audience theory now includes attempts to conceptualize such notions as interactivity and new conceptions of audiences in computer gaming, for example (in which the audience member is also an active participant). Traditional models describing a linear flow of media information in terms of sender – message – receiver are outdated, as is the over-used 'Uses and Gratifications' model. Seemingly common-sense notions of how audiences are targeted, and how they respond to texts, should be critically reviewed by learners, in dialogue with reflection on how they exist inside and outside of various audience groups. The social-cultural construction of pleasure and the suggestion that audience is increasingly fragmented in the digital world are two key themes.

As subscription and consumer choice become the norm, and the internet offers a myriad of ways of consuming media, our analysis of active media readers needs to adapt to this changing scene. Generally, audience study has moved to a more critical framework in which the reader's cultural positioning is key (a phenomenological approach), as opposed to a referential approach in which the media representation is treated as fixed and stable. Gauntlett's work (2004) on the internet and also on gender and identity (2002) offer two useful examples of the kind of theory that challenges previous notions of audience and meaning. His response to the effects model is a clear starting point for student work on the active reader. Gee's work (2003) on computer games and literacy is essential in terms of the question of whether existing models and concepts (such as literacy itself) can survive in the digital era, or whether the technological advances require us to create new ways of analysing meaning and identity. Students on vocational courses should not be reduced in their learning to 'common-sense' notions of target audience and audience research. Clearly, the commercial context of media production demands great attention to market segmentation and audience profiling, but this activity in itself is theoretical and should be approached through critical reflection. Where do existing ideas about audience groups come from? Were these notions of difference between people already there, or are they in some way media-constructed? How are audiences changing and how is production adapting? The 'bedrock' of all this is the agreement that audiences make meaning and that media-constructed identities are negotiated and fluid. The potential interpretations of media texts are subject to a matrix of cultural and symbolic determinants and Media learning is to do with bearing witness to this plurality of meaning, whether the vehicle is web design or critical research.

Representation

While this concept is also omnipresent in Media learning, it is useful only when called into question. That is, Media learning is reductive when students describe how texts represent 'reality' and is interesting when the distinction between reality and media construction is challenged. Baudrillard's work (1988) on 'hyper-reality' is useful, for example, in the context of the recent proliferation of reality TV programmes, in which we might say that reality is 'fetishized' (perhaps due to the difficulty in pinning it down in our mediated society?). Learning about representation is best facilitated through creativity and play – that is, students engaging with this concept through experimentation, by representing themselves and constructing others. Vocational learners will get more chance to do this as their course will afford them more sustained time for creative activities, so in this sense we might expect them to be the most 'theoretical' learners. The study of (and practice of) representation ranges from analysis of the selection and construction of news to prevailing images of asylum seekers in British cinema. It is concerned with competing notions of reality or realism, with the study of who is under-represented in any culture and with reflection on how our own sense of the world is mediated. A useful starting point for students is a critique early on of the representation of Media Studies itself, as it brings forth for discussion a range of discourses of derision and notions of cultural value which can be returned to throughout a course.

Narrative

In my opinion, the worst examples of regurgitated 'theory without thinking' tend to involve the application of Todorov (1971) and Propp (1968) to students' own creative work, or the assumption, for example, that Tarantino 'used' Todorov's model in the development of *Kill Bill*. This desire to 'do theory' by clumsily applying a formalist model in this way does little in terms of understanding our roles in constructing narratives, and how narratives carry discourses that appear natural. Certainly, in an instrumental sense, there is a need to teach students how to use conventions and technical opportunities to construct meaningful narratives, and to explore where our dominant narrative patterns and themes come from in cultural terms. But the most interesting Media learning leads us to consider everything as narrative – from Reality TV to our understanding of science and history, for example (as opposed to the other way around where the structure of narrative is learned, as though a science in itself). Considering narrative as operating to frame our experiences in both micro and macro ways enables Media learners to reflect on the interrelatedness of their personal narratives with public media narratives. In this sense, I think narrative is the concept that must be handled with the most care if Media learning is to thrive beyond a variant of English.

Genre

A limitation of Media learning can be the uncritical acceptance of genre as a 'natural' means of categorizing texts which then, it is assumed, acts as a contract between producer and audience. More attention to ideas of audience pleasure can allow us to be more flexible in our analysis of conventions. All specifications, for academic or vocational courses, offer choices of genres to be studied and clearly, there is a shortcut route to this that reinforces existing versions of a genre's history, codes and conventions, key players and the reasons for its popularity. This kind of study usually progresses to a consideration of hybrid texts and texts that extend, or in some way parody their genre. Creative production will usually be accompanied by a 'log' or similar written account, which explains to the audience the use of genre conventions. On vocational courses this may well be linked to studies of the marketing context of particular genre products. But the key interplay for interesting Media learning is that between reader, text and socio-cultural context. In this arena students can investigate the construction of taste along generic lines in dialogue with other ways of understanding media pleasure (Mark Reid of the BFI has offered at conferences an interesting, but unpublished, approach to this area, based on Altman, 1982).

Digital technologies

Fraser and Oram's book on digital video editing (2004) is an excellent resource, not only for technical and pedagogical guidance but also in its presentation of a 'spirit' to help us understand creativity and social learning. Fraser and Oram support and reinforce the view articulated in Reid, Burn and Parker's report on the BECTA video project (2002) that Media learning is most usefully conceptualized as a 'creative apprenticeship' and that a degree of derivative production is a necessary starting point for more radical or playful creative departure.

Proliferating discourses around the use of digital video editing, in particular, tend to involve creativity, engagement of learners who have 'switched off' from the traditional curriculum, and assumptions about vocational education and the importance of skills in the modern economy. More fundamental is the consideration of digital literacy, which, if taken seriously by the teacher, can offer the most compelling justification of all for Media education. It is my view that digital technology ought to harnessed as often as is possible in Media learning, and that there should be as little separation as possible between production and theory. Successful integration of the curriculum can enable this, so that students studying media industries can be digitally creative. More strikingly, perhaps, the existence of digital technologies in the home necessitates a shift in how we think about learning. Undoubtedly, the stigmatised teenager playing *Grand Theft Auto* in her bedroom is constantly learning, and becoming increasingly literate, but it may take great efforts from the parent culture to understand this. Indeed we may have to learn a great deal from our students in this respect. To clarify, then, digital technology in the Media curriculum includes the use of (for creative ends) and the study of (in terms of ownership, ethics, citizenship, democracy and textual analysis) the following (at the time of writing): Convergence; mobile phones; video and sound editing; image manipulation and desk-top publishing; web use, design and streaming; MP3 and file sharing; digital and 'interactive' television and radio, digital film production and screening and computer gaming.

Discourse

The suggestions for learning and teaching in this book assume a consensus that Media learning resides in a kind of postmodern paradigm in which identities are shifted and negotiated and the analysis of discourse is paramount. Thus theories like ideology start to look more problematic, especially if they assume an original truth hidden behind false consciousness or media illusion. It is therefore more sensible, in our contemporary context, to allude to discourse as presented by Foucault (1988), who suggests that discourses 'define, describe and delimit what is possible to say and not possible to say . . . about a given area.' Far from being an abstract, philosophical idea, as it may seem at first, this is actually of enormous direct use for the Media learner, since media texts are disseminators of ideas that are interpreted by audiences through socially constructed discourses that are intertextually coded. So the 'common-sense' statements produced through media or about the media are, in fact, examples of discourses seeking to gain the power that comes from appearing 'natural'. But where this approach differs to the study of ideology is in its refusal to suggest that there is a truth to be found behind the discourse of the ruling group. All discourse in this sense is seen as a 'claim to power' and it is the job of the Media learner to deconstruct texts in order to expose the discourses at work (and no more). In production terms, it is an enabling concept, as it offers a 'way in' to notions about targeting and mode of address that is applicable and at the same time critical and reflective, and it goes beyond notions of whether your production is challenging the dominant ideology or not (usually too blunt a question).

Practice/theory

The chapters that follow explore in more detail how we can use the principles discussed here to inform creative Media learning, whether theoretical or practical. It seems most appropriate to conclude this series of opening gambits with the words of a Media student I taught who is also a practising film-maker:

> 'Inspiration can come from many places, but my main area of reflection was my Media Studies course. I had studied cultural representation, characterisation and the basis of narrative structure. Anyone hoping to form a coherent screenplay, or one that deals with a strand of themes, would be doing themselves a favour by doing a Media course. After all, the bulk of our crew came from academic backgrounds related to the medium. It certainly provided us with an edge when it came to planning the shoot.' (Nock, 2004)

I know what label David's course was given, but I'm not sure where the academic ends and the vocational begins, or vice versa, in this case. What I can say for certain is that theory and practice were never far apart in his Media learning.

Further reading

Baudrillard, J. (ed. Poster, M.), 1988, *Selected Writings*, Cambridge: Polity.
For the theory of 'hyper-reality', which I suggest Media Education needs to engage with (or is itself a product of).

Bernstein, B., 1990, *The Structuring of Pedagogic Discourse*, London: Routledge.
For a theoretical analysis of horizontal and vertical discourses, which I used in my research to investigate the institutionalised form of contemporary Media Studies.

Buckingham, D., 2003, *Media Education: Literacy, Learning and Contemporary Culture*, London: Polity.
A comprehensive theoretical overview of the history of Media education and a range of contemporary issues in classroom practice.

Fraser, P. and Oram, B., 2004, *Teaching Digital Video Production*. London: BFI.
A manual for creative production work in video which takes a stance on media literacy and creativity which I hope this book shares.

Gauntlett, D., 1997, 'Another crisis for Media Studies' in *In the Picture*, 31. Keighley: itp Publications.

Gee, J., 2003, *What Video Games have to teach us about Learning and Literacy*, New York: Palgrave Macmillan.

Horrocks, C. and Jetvic, Z., 1999, *Introducing Foucault*, Cambridge: Icon.
A handy, concise introduction to the theories of discourse and knowledge/power which I am suggesting as framing ideas for Media learning.

Masterman, L., 1985, *Teaching the Media*, London: Routledge.
The original 'blueprint' for Media Studies pedagogy.

McDougall, J., 2004, 'Subject Media: A Study in the Sociocultural Framing of Discourse.' Unpublished PhD thesis, Birmingham: University of Birmingham.

Nock, D., 2004, 'Confessions of a B-Movie Writer' in *Media Magazine* 8, London: English and Media Centre.

Stafford, R. and Branston, G., 2004, *The Media Student's Book*, London: Routledge.
This is, in my opinion, the most useful book for Media students and offers a range of excellent case studies through which key concepts and theories can be explored.

Watson, J. and Hill, A., 2003, *Dictionary of Media and Communication Studies*, London: Arnold.

See also the 'Top 40 websites' section.

chapter two

The 'Grade One' Theory Lesson

Introduction

The QCA's 2005 report on Media Studies includes findings from some research with students. Predictably, one of the 'turn-offs' they described about their Media learning was 'lecture-based teaching of theory' (p. 39). Tellingly, among the positives, students identified 'deconstruction and analysis'. Proof then, if we need it, that theory in itself is not dry, boring or pointless. Indeed, working with texts is seen as active, engaging and essential. But the medium through which it is facilitated is crucial.

Class strategy – Icebreaker

By constructing an amusing, reflective and media-related activity for the first meeting of a group, we can set a comfortable, productive but enquiring tone for the duration of a course or a unit of study. Here is an example.

1. Using a 'reveal' OHT or PowerPoint, go through 10–15 questions that are all structured as: 'If you were a. . ., what. . .would you be?' (Examples include: mode of public transport, pop group, breakfast cereal, TV programme, electrical device. If resources allow, include 'inanimate object in college' and ask them to take a digital photograph of it – it is useful to get students using kit as early as possible.)
2. Students write down their responses.
3. Take in the responses and then provide time for all the students to pair up with each other (so that everyone meets everyone) and have a strictly timed one or two minute discussion, during which they have to exchange names and likes and dislikes. While this is taking place, read their answers to your questions and choose one example of each category for a short quiz (e.g. who do you think would be a hair-dryer, who do you think would be a knackered old bus, and so on).
4. Award a prize to the student who gets the most right (probably only two or three).

> At this point, explain that they have been working on a semiotic presentation and give a brief, visual introduction to the study of signs, with reference to how this will figure in the course. Keep the answers and a month later, construct another quiz and go through the same exercise. You will find that students get more answers correct second time round and that there is much more knowing laughter when the right answers are revealed.

To clarify, the 'Grade One' reference in the title of this chapter is to the current inspectorate and thus could perhaps be read as a reductive framing for what follows. On the other hand, having been involved in a Media department which went through a change of strategy resulting in an Ofsted grade one award, there will clearly be some immediately useful practical suggestions in what follows. Another problem with my chapter heading might be that it reinforces a binary between theory and production, a demarcation that I have suggested avoiding. Thus, it is important to state that what follows are suggestions for offering energized, creative learning in areas traditionally marked as 'theoretical'. They are, however, presented within a safety net, in the sense that the ideas signpost some key quality buzzwords: inclusivity and differentiation, learning technology, promotion of diversity and active participation. First, we need some working definitions for these.

Inclusivity and differentiation

All learners must have, in terms of their human rights to education, equal access to the curriculum and to the learning environment. For the teacher, this means careful consideration of specification, unit, text and topic choices. Choices should be made on the basis of student interests and profiles, as opposed to teacher preference (for example, resisting the temptation to take the easy option by dusting down the *film noir* resource box for the fifteenth year running, when the students might find more currency in Bollywood). Inclusivity extends to the accommodation of a variety of learning preferences, and to the provision of variety in learning outcomes and their assessment. An inclusive classroom will be an arena in which a calm atmosphere pervades and learners feel safe, so there is a classroom management element also.

Differentiation should be a given in learning and teaching (it is alarming, in my opinion, that some institutions treat it as an adjunct to classroom practice: it appears as an extra column on schemes of work, separate to 'lesson content', for example). Whilst it may appear on the surface that teachers of creative arts subjects can rely on their subject itself guaranteeing differentiation, the fact is that Media teachers have to work just as hard as Mathematicians to make sure their planning caters for a range of learning preferences and needs. A differentiated learning space is one in which students collaborate in their exploration of subject matter, skills and concepts and flexibility is constant, in task and assignment setting, in the rhythm and pace of the work done, in resource allocation, in opportunities to succeed and in feedback.

Learning technology

It is really important to use a value judgement when observing teachers making use of technology in their work with learners. Put simply, technology is of no particular use if it does not lead to the enhancement of the learning opportunities provided for students. When using the smartboard, ask yourself: 'Could I do the same thing on a whiteboard?' If the answer is 'Yes', then there is nothing wrong with the use of technology, but you cannot stake a claim about learning. Similarly, if students are not equipped with selection and processing skills, then sending them to use the internet will be of no greater value than 'library work'. And if your teaching is becoming regressive as a result of using technology (i.e. if students are hiding behind monitors where you cannot see them or if your lesson collapses because the network crashes and you have no alternatives) then we are very far away from the enhancement of learning! On the other hand, technology can aid learning in very clear and exciting ways. Students can use smartboard technology to explain to their peers how they constructed their digital photography by drawing on the still frame. Email and message boards can be used to extend learning beyond the timetable, and digital editing, image manipulation and computer gaming can take us into the exploration of new forms of literacy. In theory work, the question will always be about enhancement of creative theoretical practice (e.g. building a website and e-forum to explore ideas about censorship) rather than the mere presence of computers.

Promotion of diversity

Sometimes misunderstood as another phrase to describe Equal Opportunities, the promotion of diversity is a requirement for the project of education for citizenship in our multicultural society. Put simply, throughout a scheme of work on any area of the curriculum, learners should encounter a diverse range of resources from a variety of positions so that their learning hinges not only on subject matter and skills but also on an awareness of the diversity of our culture. This is another area where it is tempting for Media teachers to claim that the subject somehow does this automatically, if compared to, say, Physics. But while representation will undoubtedly be high on the agenda and this indeed guarantees an awareness of cultural bias, scrutiny is still needed, of textual choice in particular. Good practice in this area simply involves attention to texts, theories and case studies from a variety of cultural positions to include ethnicity, gender, sexuality and disability, so that respect for diversity is integrated into the literacy practices of the subject.

Active participation

You will, I am sure, teach students who do very well in their written work but remain reticent when in public. I always struggle when explaining to parents that their daughter's coursework is superb but she really ought to contribute more in class discussions. The challenge to this is often: 'If she is doing so well, then why?' But the 'quality' agenda asserts that a success measure for a lesson is that *every* student contributes, so we need to find ways of making this safe for students who do not comfortably take centre stage. There are a variety of strategies for this, most often through group work, which enforces collaboration but offers anonymity in presentation.

The crucial 'task' for our pedagogic practice is that we should do as little talking as possible and students should reflect and express themselves in a variety of ways as often as we can enable.

Creative theory

The starting point for any Media theory teaching should be demystification. Theory as social practice is of great value, and we should encourage young people to be critical, but regurgitation of learned theories without application or any personal narrative is of no particular value, other than to gain cultural capital (Bourdieu and Passeron, 1977) through acquiring an 'elaborated code'. So, we are going to assume that being theoretical means thinking reflectively about taking for granted common-sense notions that are in circulation around us; whether this means that we analyse the common use of sports co-commentators (to add 'expert' punditry), while adopting the convention in our own production work; or that we question the extent to which MP3 and peer-to-peer file-sharing of music on the internet is really threatening the music industry. In any case, the emphasis is on using theory in a new way for the students' own ends, questioning the theory in terms of its validity in specific contexts, and always aiming to create *new* theory. In this sense, we move from a transmission model of knowledge (teacher tells students about news values and they tell the examiner how they work) to an autonomous, reflective model of learning (student develops theoretical approach to inform her own creative interventions).

Most of the time you will want to use group work to foster collaborative learning for theory tasks, but you should never just allow groups to develop without a purpose. Over a period of time, any class should experience friendship groups, mixed-ability groups based on 'cold data' such as target grades, mixed-ability groups based on specific aptitude in a particular kind of learning, randomly chosen groups, groups based on personal interests and 'jigsawing' (described fully as a strategy in Chapter Six). Depending on what is at stake and the kind of collaborative learning taking place, you should always have a *strategic* reason for the construction of groups.

Another ground rule for theory is that it should not be taken too seriously. Students should be discouraged from having unconditional reverence for the writers of theories, and it is useful and amusing to remind them that most 'theorists' are teachers who are no different from yourself. In other words, ideas are important, but status is not.

Class strategy – Invent a theory

1. Arrange students in groups of three and ask them to find some common ground in terms of a media genre or type of text that they feel strongly about, in one way or another. Each group needs a chair (to keep order), a scribe (to make notes and then produce the display material) and an oracle (to present verbally at the end).
2. Groups discuss aspects of such texts that account for audience pleasure, popularity, controversy or dwindling success. Whatever they discuss, they need to get into the *reasons* why media texts have particular sets of meanings. For example, they might choose the obvious example that

people like horror movies because there is a security attached to being scared by fantasy or fiction rather than by lived experience.

3. Next, they swap with other groups and the second task is to provide a range of everyday words to summarise the first group's discussions. So, for the horror example these might be: comfort, safety, security or distance (from real horror). Each group should arrive at about five words.

4. The key words are then given back to the first group, who then select one of the words and use a thesaurus to find a 'posh' academic-sounding word to stand in for the everyday one. This then becomes the name of their theory, and the outcome is a large display-sized representation with the name of the theory, the surnames of the group members, the year and a one-sentence summary of the central idea they started out with. For our horror example, this might be the 'palliation' theory. Palliation means to ease away pain, so we could understand this in terms of the horror genre providing the comfort of easing our states of anxiety by reminding us that our world is relatively stable when compared with the events of the fictional texts.

5. Display the outcomes on the class wall immediately. The scribes stay next to the outcomes and the rest of the students move around freely, asking the scribes to explain their theory to them.

6. Ask for verbal summaries of what has been learned, and congratulate the students on becoming media theorists!

7. For a follow-up activity, give students 'real' theories: either big concepts, such as ideology, postmodernism and feminism, or more specific examples, such as news values, realism or narrative, then help them to work back so they end up with some everyday words and ideas which the theorists probably started out from.

Reasons to be theoretical

There is a balance to be struck here, as we want to celebrate critical thinking at the same time as demystifying and deconstructing the idea of alienating language and big ideas. The Media learner can end up with a profoundly radical perspective on contemporary life. Here are ten justifications for theory work, or active uses of theory, for students to suggest as a starting point:

1. Theory informs production – the most important selling point is that you will make better films if you know how they are made by the experts.

2. Theory gives you critical power – we can enjoy media texts all the more if we can develop a sense of how they are constructed.

3. Theory is useful for citizenship – we can become more aware of representation and who is being excluded through a theoretical understanding of texts.

4. Theory gives us cultural capital – far from thinking of Media Studies as a trivial pursuit,

students' parents will be impressed when they are treated to an analysis of how current affairs are presented according to news agendas, for example.

5. Theory is relevant – Media students get to understand how technology works and to take some of the claims about it with a pinch of salt – so they are 'digitally informed' consumers.

6. Media theory is all about people – for example, audience theory is just stories about people and how they use media in their lives in creative ways.

7. Theory is reflective – most Media theory is about you and your opinions (e.g. whether *Big Brother* is mindless trash or interactive democracy in action): the Media student will have a developed spin on their response.

8. Media theory is 'interdisciplinary' – Media Studies is pioneering in the sense that whether you realise it or not, you are studying History, Politics, Sociology and Art: a '*massala curriculum*', even!

9. Media theory reminds you that things are not real – getting a grip on the space between media reality and whether or not there is another reality to be grasped is a 'life skill'. Better to be aware that you are being manipulated, then you can enjoy it more!

10. Media theory demystifies the world – many people have some idea that behind rhetoric about the global village there are big companies making a lot of money. The Media student knows who they are and how they operate.

Class strategy – Writing frames for theory

If you ask students to do a small research exercise and then report back (whether in written form or not) you are making a whole range of assumptions about their skills in framing information and selecting and presenting it for an audience. A writing frame helps students with this. As you move through a course you can provide more or less elements of the frame for different students, and eventually some students will not require such a resource at all.

Example: Research into the use of interactive television

I interviewed a group of people who have digital television in their homes.

The purpose of this research was to find out:

The sample I chose had the following demographic features:

In quantitative terms (looking at the simple facts about who is using what), I discovered that:

The qualitative data I gathered was interesting because it shows that:

My conclusions from this small piece of research are that:

For the research to be more valid I would need to:

By using such a tool you can ensure that learners do not miss out a section of the report, and be confident that each learner will be aware of the requirements of the piece of work. They will also be able to ask you for clarification during the task, or before they start. In this particular case, you get to flag up two important issues in research – the demographics of the sample selected and the limitations of any research. It is likely that they would be neglected otherwise.

Specifications

What kinds of theory are required? Scanning specifications for GCSE, A and AS, Vocational A Level and National Diploma, the range of prescribed theory includes the key concepts (audience, genre, narrative and representation) and then a number of different varieties in the study of media language or literacy (or textual analysis). There tends to be a distinction maintained between still and moving images, but they are usually studied using semiotics to theorize the construction of meaning through signs and symbols. A more vocational approach to this might well go into more technical detail about, for example, shot composition through consideration of lens choice. The analysis of audio media tends to be neglected on A Level courses (although there are usually options available in this area). Vocational courses will often have at least one unit on radio, audio or sound and thus significant attention to the study of broadcast radio, formats and schedules, ownership and digital shifts is more likely on an ND course, for example.

Film is hugely popular across the range of Media education environments, and one reason for this is the plethora of resources produced by Film Education, *In the Picture* and the BFI (the latter have a specific remit for moving image education) across the curriculum. There are a range of ways of studying film. Analysis of narrative, genre and representation dominates, with units on film language, the concept of genre or specific genres across all the specifications. Separate topics include auteurship, women and film, censorship and studies of the film industry. Vocational courses tend to separate Film Studies from institutional work on the industry and marketing, and from film production. On 'academic courses' magazines are often theorized in relation to gender or audience, and newspapers tend to be discussed in terms of news values. Vocational learning often leans towards the production of news, desktop publishing and journalism. Television genres proliferate, and there is often a realism context (soap opera, documentary, sitcom and documentary appear consistently). In some cases, television is studied institutionally in terms of its funding and changes in regulation (such as the birth of Ofcom). All specifications, despite appearances perhaps, provide opportunities for the study of new media and computer games and the likelihood is that these topic areas will become much more central to the curriculum.

Integration

My central suggestion for all theory teaching is that it should be integrated into production or creative work at all times. Complex though it may seem at first, there are enormous benefits for both students and teachers if certain principles can be accommodated.

Reduce the content of the course to the bare minimum by combining units and projects. For example, students might be given the topic 'Media Representations of Britain' and study this for the whole year. The theoretical prism would be the ways in which the changing demographics of the UK are negotiated on screen. Within this, they could produce a trailer for a new British film, study new British Cinema (including films like *Last Resort* which deal with asylum, and more conventional text such as *Bend it Like Beckham* and *Anita and Me*), Soap Opera and Sitcom (looking at changing representations of class, gender and ethnicity) and conduct some research into British directors' use of digital video for low-budget production. These areas would, on either an A Level or a vocational course, cross unit boundaries in order to develop a deeper theoretical understanding of this area. The textual analysis at the heart of this topic is best managed through application in creative tasks. Students would be creating ideas and small chunks of their own soap opera and sitcom sequences (for theoretical ends) alongside the production of their trailer.

If you work at an institution that offers vocational courses as well as 'academic' ones, then timetable students together to remove these boundaries. Avoid creating territorial distinctions by having different rooms and resources for these learners. Get your A Level students working collaboratively on aspects of production with the National Diploma group, for example. They could analyse the video work of their fellow students using semiotics. And if the A Level students are studying media ownership and regulation, why not give them a research project on Ofcom that they can present to the vocational group to inform their production research for their next project?

Your aim through these kinds of strategies is to reduce all boundaries. The worst examples are the use of the words 'theory' and 'production' to describe lessons. If the unit on 'Media Industries' seems dry compared to 'Web Design', then the teacher needs to work twice as hard to make it dynamic, creative and active. If possible, creative timetabling can mobilise a culture shift, by avoiding housing a theory lesson on Friday afternoon, for example. A Media Industries workshop, with visiting speakers, a short placement, internet research and video conferencing can 'transmit' the same content for the same assessment ends, but the journey is a far more exciting one. Impression management of the curriculum itself is what is at stake. Your ultimate goal is to create a course where all lessons are practical and there is a buzz of collaborative energy, indeed where the notion of the 'lesson' in its traditional sense is obscured.

So, what does this 'Grade One' theory lesson look like? Here is an example. The lesson is to introduce 'Representation of Gender'. One approach to this would be to use PowerPoint or OHTs to describe concepts of representation and perhaps to move into notions of ideology and feminist theory. This would be a 'theory first' approach. I favour the 'text first' alternative, which this lesson demonstrates.

Class strategy – Geezers and Birds

1. Distribute a range of birthday cards for Mum and for Dad and gendered 'New baby' cards (ideally, ask students to bring these in at the end of the previous session). Spend some time on structured small group discussions on nature/nurture (each group has chair, scribe and presenter), followed by the presenters sharing the group views as a whole and describing any disagreement, without using names. The way in to this big area is to ask some groups to describe the differences they can see that are reinforced by the cards, and ask other groups to consider the extent to which the cards just represent the 'Venus and Mars' thing, or whether such images actually create ideas of difference in our heads as we grow up.

2. Next, play 'Geezers Need Excitement' by The Streets (from the album Original Pirate Material). The narrative of this song (like all of The Streets' material) is operatic in form, as it follows its central character, Mike Skinner, on a night out which involves drugs, clubbing, fast food, moral dilemmas about infidelity (and double standards in that area) and the ever-present undercurrent of violence. Play the song once without any context and clarify the narrative in case the lyrics are unclear (it is best to offer a printed transcript at the end of the exercise).

3. For the main activity, play the song three more times, but ask each student to cross-gender by taking on the role of female (if they are male) and vice versa. Ask them to note down every reference to their gender they hear during the song.

4. After they have listened three times, pair the students (male/female) to share their responses and facilitate a discussion about the representation of gender in the song. At this stage, avoid all critique; the task is simply to describe how each gender is portrayed. Manage this process by first grouping the pairs into teams of four, and then asking for the group's overall outcomes in each case. You may wish to ask for visual representation of this as well. It is important here that you pick different presenters from the first exercise, so that you increase the scope of verbal participation.

5. For homework, or as a follow-up task, students work in groups to produce a version of the song that does not use gender stereotypes. The work of Bernard Right-On might be useful here as they will be using the same technique. (Bernard Right-On is a comedian who begins jokes in

the style of Bernard Manning and then completes them in a politically correct fashion.)

Note: Clearly, the song used here can be substituted for another in which the demarcation of gender roles is not so obvious. What is particularly useful about The Streets' material, in my opinion, is that it attempts to tell a story using characterization, hinging on self-reflection and morality. You will need to hear the song to see what I mean (and decide whether or not you agree!).

Let's take another example of Media theory and consider a range of practical methods for making learning inclusive.

Most Media courses include a practical element and a heavy emphasis on textual analysis, but in their organization there is often a separation of technical theory (essentially instructions for using equipment) and analysis of existing texts. We might facilitate learning about the construction of meaning if we remove that distinction (and any subsequent physical boundaries, as mentioned previously). In this way, we could create a lesson on realism that is both practical and theoretical, and both instrumental ('how to') and reflective ('with what assumptions?').

Students might (depending on the content of the course) consider this matrix of subject matter through the prism of understanding documentary as a genre or textual form.

Class strategy – Collaborative theory/practice

1. This lesson might begin (after the stating of learning outcomes) with a genre-mapping exercise in which the whole class participates through group sharing. The outcome is a visual representation of the genre, its sub-genres and its overlaps. At this early point there will probably be some reflection on the status of documentary as a genre or as an approach (which may inform a variety of genres, given that we are now thinking about this in the context of reality TV).
2. From this starting point, a group might be divided up (see page 13 for guidance on group work and ideas about how to do this) for the purposes of collaborative learning.

One group of students will use the internet during the lesson to research definitions of documentary film and its origins and history. This assumes a lesson or workshop on searching skills has taken place and a guidance sheet on URLs is provided (for example, the very useful Film Education website has a section on documentary films). A time limit and presentation brief must be clear for this purpose – students must present their findings in the form of a three-minute presentation with three bullet points, for example.

Another group will either plan or (and this is highly preferable) film a short documentary about the lesson itself, in the context of clear decisions about target audience, purpose and style, as well as point of view (most likely from the students' perspective). This group will require technical support, either from a technician, from the teacher or ideally from a student from another group or year who is technically adept with non-fiction video work. They will need guidance on shot composition and editing considerations within the documentary style.

A third group will view two extracts from documentaries about 'ordinary people'. One should be something like *We are the Lambeth Boys* – the Free Cinema movement's study of working-class males at a youth club in London discussing capital punishment and other topics of the day, edited with a voiceover that might be considered highly patronizing. Any documentary film or television programme from the 1950s is likely to be useful for considering the notion of people as objects for scrutiny. Alongside this, they will consider an extract from any recent docu-soap (*Wife Swap* is always fun). They will need to prepare a comparative presentation with three bullet points, and the teacher will encourage reflection on the style of each programme, its shared conventions and its function in terms of citizenship (putting ordinary people on the screen, but on what terms and for whom).

3. Depending on time, the outcomes will be shared either at the conclusion of this lesson or at another meeting and they will constitute the screening of the rough cut of the documentary and two presentations – one on received notions of documentary and its history and the other on documentaries from different eras.

In each case the feedback should be provided by a spokesperson, speaking to a prepared group offering. All other students are required to pose a further question to one of the groups and the answer is given by a group member other than the spokesperson. (This is the opportunity to evaluate the learning.)

The 'old fashioned lecture'

Looking at the activities in the lesson on documentary from a 'quality' perspective, we would find a highly active, participative lesson in which tasks are differentiated. The discussion on the purpose of documentary will throw up questions of diversity, and by being given time constraints and clear structures for summary and selection, you can signpost Key Skills in Communication, Working With Others and Problem Solving. Technology is being used in the lesson in a way that genuinely aids learning (provided sufficient guidance is provided for effective searching and selecting within the time allowed – this kind of attention to detail is vital). More important in terms of Media pedagogy, though, we have avoided demarcating this as either a theory or a practical lesson; and we have managed to link textual analysis, some of the received conventional 'body of knowledge' and technical production. But contrary though this might sound, there is nothing wrong with a good, old-fashioned lecture every now and again. Students intending to apply for higher education will need to engage with a sustained argument, illustrated with quotations and examples. As long as a calm but stimulating environment is provided, there is no reason why students on any type of Media course should not experience a lecture model of delivery on occasion (this might even be a joint lecture, where several groups are put together – after all, this is what you get for your money when you take students to revision conferences). Indeed, one might argue that if we *never* teach students in this way, then we disadvantage them (and even patronise them) by assuming their attention spans or intellectual capabilities are insufficient for such an undertaking.

So if we accept that one lecture is reasonable on any scheme of work, and might even be a stimulating adjunct to our more participative norms, then how should we approach it? Certainly not by transmitting the published ideas of an established writer (for example, Marx on ideology, or Mulvey on 'the Male Gaze'). Rather, we should put together an entertaining argument that draws together ideas about audience, institution and Media theory. We should always use visual stimulus such as PowerPoint and DVD (preferably integrated, to avoid the need for remote controls to alter the source). However, we shouldn't simply read from PowerPoint, or provide handouts with all the information and then just run through it – the balance is right when this presentation method is used for key headings rather than all the content.

The following class strategy gives an example. During the study of British Cinema, leading to an analysis of how changing notions of Britishness are renegotiated on screen to provide a voice for asylum seekers as well as 'settled' ethic minority groups (for which *Anita and Me, Bend it Like Beckham, In this World* and *Last Resort* will be our key texts), we are to offer a lecture on the conventions of British Social Realism. This will pay particular attention to films depicting the North of England (as opposed to 'Swinging London' in the 1960s), often referred to as 'Kitchen Sink Drama'.

Class strategy – Lecture (90 minutes)

1. PowerPoint slides – Learning outcomes, continuity.
2. Clip – 'Money marries money, lad', from *Room at the Top*.
3. Exploration of themes – *North and South*, escape from background, the constraints of the British class system.
4. Clip – *Saturday Night and Sunday Morning*: first 10 minutes.
5. Exploration of themes. The main character works in a factory and escapes at weekends (hence the title) through drink and sex. He has an understanding of exploitation but is he still powerless? Or is understanding power an escape from False Consciousness? Throughout the film, Arthur rejects commodities such as television sets and new houses and the conventions of marriage – all of which he associates with entrapment and 'letting the bastards grind you down'.
6. Clips – *The Full Monty* and *Brassed Off*: Brass Band performance/dance routines and comedic clips hinging on banter and camaraderie.
7. Exploration of themes. A 'good life' – the extended family, community and belonging.

8. PowerPoint – two co-existing depictions of working-class people in Britain in these films: romantic view of community and sharing alongside harsh, impoverished environment from which the aim is to escape.

9. PowerPoint – summary of theory: Higson (1996) on romanticism and claustrophobia in British films.

10. Question and answer (insist on three questions before close of play).

Follow-up screening – *Billy Elliot* (or students view independently, if practical).

Task for next lesson – (small group seminars). What elements of the film's narrative do you think present the community as romantic and claustrophobic?

Follow up individual task:

1. Identify a British film which breaks this mould by being exclusively romantic or claustrophobic.

2. Find another British film which is neither.

I suggest that the material above lends itself to a lecture style, in the sense that you are presenting a view on British cinema and illustrating it with examples. Good practice is maintained because the 'official' theory comes in after the exploration of less alienating themes (so we are considering the theory through the lens of the clips, rather than the other way around). The discussion or testing of Medhurst's hypothesis will be housed in a seminar context, of course, as would be more kinaesthetic material, such as matching British films to the BFI's categories for doing so in order to explore the increasing difficulty of actually defining a British film. This would be best done through a sorting exercise in groups, where information about films (I suggest from *Sight & Sound* or the Internet Movie Database) can be matched to the categories as a result of discussion. Clearly, this material could not be the subject of a lecture.

Setting up debate

At the opposite end of the spectrum is a strategy such as role-play for debate. The teacher can become completely redundant (apart from planning) if this works. However, there is some essential groundwork to be undertaken for this to be successful. Role play is not a 'given' in terms of skills and confidence, so some rehearsal and exemplar material helps. Also, you need to have reached a point towards the end of a topic because, essentially, you are in the realm of discourse analysis with such an activity: in order for students to be 'in character' they need a developed understanding of the points of view they will need to 'act out'.

Class strategy – Role play for debate

A combination of prepared script and creative application is required and in this sense, differentiation can be achieved through controlling the amount of each that particular groups of students are asked to do.

1. To explore the censorship debate, students are allocated a particular discourse from these four: Protection, Moral Panic, 'Responsible' Liberal, Freedom.

2. Through differentiated approaches, they will each arrive at the debate with a clear sense of their character (it can be entertaining to ask them to dress as their character and it can reveal some interesting semiotic assumptions if the 'protector' wears a suit and the 'free thinker' is scruffy, for example) and how they will respond to predictable questions from the Chair. (The Chair could be the teacher or a student, or a student from another group such as Sociology or Art if this is productive, to shift the discursive dynamics slightly and offer a different view.) The first half of the debate involves a traditional chaired discussion (recorded on video) and then a video extract is introduced (this must be a clip that has not been scrutinised previously) as an example. The 'higher order' thinking skill now required is to apply the character's predisposition to this stimulus, while maintaining the discourse. Here it is useful for the chair to be more sensitive to confidence levels and degrees of adaptability, so in some cases it may be useful for the teacher to take over this second phase.

3. If an exam answer, coursework essay or portfolio report on film and censorship is the endgame (in other words if students have no alternative but to apply a written academic register when showing their learning on this theme), then the homework should be an immediate translation of this inclusive, active experience into a traditional written exploration, such as 'Describe the competing discourses at work in debates over film and censorship' (or substitute discourses for opinions or points of view). Encourage students to think of their peers in character as personifications of these discourses.

The approach to the censorship debate described above directly addresses the study of discourse. During the study of such a contested area, students should be introduced (after a letter has been sent home informing parents) to a range of texts which have been censored, alongside others that were not, but were controversial because they were not. It is important to address the political dimensions of such arguments. For example, films that were seen as shocking when the novels on which they were based were not; films that are of concern not because of the violence itself but because of the moral framework (or lack of) surrounding it; and films in which language and/or politics are more important than images in their potential to 'shock'. While there tends to be an assumption that in Liberal Humanities, the path to enlightenment is to do with understanding competing arguments and then forming opinion, I think in the case of Media theory it is paramount to devote most time to the 'understanding' bit but to emphasize the socio-political underpinnings of arguments in order to deconstruct them. What we will find, then, is that we are not so much deconstructing texts but deconstructing the interplay of text, audience and society. In particular we are scrutinising the unequal distribution of cultural capital: who is the censor, who do they assume they are protecting, who is a subject and who is an object in these debates?

A staggered approach

However 'technical' a programme of study might appear on the surface (for example, a unit on the film industry on a vocational course), we must not ever assume that such crucial lines of enquiry about who has a stake in deciding who can see what are not of interest to certain students. Theory tends to take on greater immediacy when it can be related to lived experience. For this reason I favour an approach that starts with texts and/or games (as we have seen with the class strategy 'Geezers and Birds') and then builds received theory onto this preliminary engagement. The three lesson ideas that follow link together to introduce theory in such ways.

Class strategy – My life as a . . .

1. An easy way to make genre work 'come alive' is to establish the idea that conventions are paramount in genre pleasure rather than subject matter (this, of course, is an assertion that is contestable, but it presents a particular reading of genre that is helpful initially).
2. To show this in action, ask students to consider the mundane aspects of their own life (there must be a ground rule that sensitive or overly personal elements are to be excluded) as the subject matter of a genre text (a sitcom, for example). This can be presented orally, via a trailer storyboard, a poster or in written 'treatment' format.
3. In the following lesson, you can ask students to adapt it to a second genre, or to introduce 'hybridity' by combining the original idea with another set of conventions.

Class strategy – Vote for the project

A simple strategy for collaborative learning, which works particularly v genre work (in this case, thinking about the conventions of the sitcom gei

1. For homework or preparatory work, ask students to develop an idea for a sitcom (for example, the 'My life as a sitcom' idea (see above)) and then in the lesson to adapt this to a 60-second pitch (the 'way in' to this is: 'Which of these would you put money into?').
2. Arrange students tactically in groups and ask them to pitch to one another, leaving time for every student to ask a question to each of the other 'pitchers' at the end of each presentation (so that everyone participates).
3. Each group must then vote (through a secret ballot) for the best idea to carry forward to the next stage. Each student must then prepare to pitch that idea to others.

4. Jigsaw the groups (see Chapter 6, pages 100–101) and you get a 'Champions League' of each group pitching the four or five best ideas, as voted for by the original groups. At the end of this phase, continue the secret ballot in each group and hopefully, once the votes are counted, you will have a clear winner. This is the project the whole class will work on.

5. Next, count the students in the whole class and subtract one from this figure. Ask the class collaboratively to come up with that number of conventions for this particular genre, and use the smartboard or other means to display these (the advantage of smartboard technology is that you can write these up, whiteboard style, but then save it to an intranet area for students to print out to: a) avoid 'copying from the board' and b) remove excuses for non-attenders!).

6. The student whose project is carried forward is rewarded with no homework.

7. The rest of the class take one convention each and, after hearing the original pitch again for clarification, develop this convention for the first episode of this specific programme for the next lesson.

Class strategy – Chinese whispers

1. Students come prepared for this lesson with their developed conv for the first episode of the programme they voted for earlier. Clear. these ideas will not fit together, as they have been developed in isolation from one another.

2. Now you construct a game of 'Chinese whispers' in which students (in a circle or square, with tables) pass their convention on in a clockwise direction. On receipt of a different convention, they adapt what they find to fit with their idea, until they have seen every convention and are presented with their own homework defaced many times.

3. In my experience, students find this frustrating and amusing in equal measure, but they develop an illustrated understanding of the stock conventions of a particular genre, and their inter-relatedness to one another.

Having established a set of agreed notions about genre, at this stage I would introduce genre theory (for example, Hartley's model (1999) of the contract between producer and audience) alongside the assertion that genre is one way of thinking about texts but not the only one, and thus its 'use value' as a means of conceptualizing textual meaning is very much 'up for grabs'. (Mark Reid's approach to genre, as demonstrated in his INSET workshops, is a great example of such a questioning strategy.)

Digital theory

Let's reassert that it is not in the gift of this book to provide content for lessons. Instead, the intention is to suggest a 'spirit' and a range of strategies you might try (in order, of course, to develop your own ways of operating). Nor is it possible to cover all kinds of theory for all kinds of courses, or to go far beneath the surface (hence it is easier to suggest ideas for lessons fairly early on in a scheme of work rather than later). At the end of this chapter, it is prudent to devote some space to the specialized kinds of theory that are negotiated on vocational courses. One such example is a unit on Web Authoring for an E-Media specification, for which students must work in HTML, explore a variety of tools and features, and go on to produce a 'media-rich website'.

This is as seemingly removed from traditional Media theory or concepts as could be, and yet clearly, a learner cannot demonstrate imaginative use of technology and its tools without a theoretical foundation. But the vocational learner on this kind of course has the same entitlement to reflective, conceptual study as the GCSE student analysing gender representation in Science Fiction, for example. Rather than suggesting the vocational student 'learns by doing' I am arguing that all students should work in this way. For this example, the teacher should facilitate analysis of HTML as a language and develop in students the ability to operate metalinguistically – that is, to talk about the language as well as work in it. They will also work towards theoretical consensus on what constitutes a media-rich website, and if they are to demonstrate understanding of vocational practice, this inevitably takes them into discussion of professional discourse in terms of hierarchy, team work and different understandings of management, so essentially, a range of political discussions will take place.

Usually, vocational specifications insist on an evaluation, and yet many teachers underplay this as a skill. Evaluative discourses need to be exposed and discussed: they are an institutional language game rather than a natural, common sense 'after the event' inevitability and students will operate much more effectively within this discourse if they understand it as such.

Class strategy – Technical peer instruction

This lesson only works if your course organization is creative enough. Or are to use a student from a different group who has already excelled in thi. or to identify prior learning in this area. You may have a student working as a technician in some way, which would be ideal. The peer element is important.

1. Taking the example of site management, the peer instructor enables students to access their site and asks them to judge it in comparison to a range of other sites, in terms of navigation and ease of use.
2. In small groups, students are then asked to produce criteria for deciding on the success of a site in this context (this is in consumer/user guise).
3. Next, the instructor describes their site management processes in accessible language and students are asked to match these criteria to their

judgements about ease of use. If there is a mismatch, the teacher intervenes to suggest that site management may not make the site accessible in equal measure for every user, because of the inevitability of difference in cognition and learner preference (highly theoretical concerns), but what is at stake is a 'best fit' mapping of the one to the other.

4. Finally, students in different small groups access a website of their choice and attempt (preferably through annotation of screen grabs) to 'second guess' the site management decisions made by the web team behind the site.

5. For homework, students individually produce a paper design for a badly managed site, and present them in the next lesson.

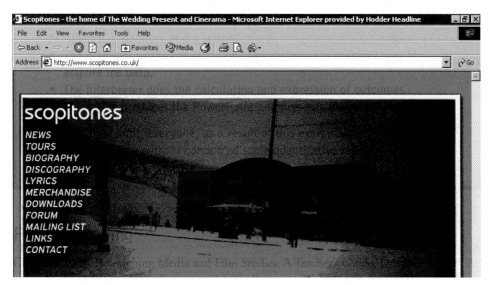

A homepage is the outcome of an array of site management decisions

For a more developed approach to analysing websites as media texts, see Burn and Parker (2003), who set up this kind of study around the following themes:

'We will begin by looking at the organisational function of the texts and what this organisation allows their users to do; but we will also consider how they present ideas, narratives and representations of their subject, as well as how they address their audience. We want to consider how the visual elements of the design, written language, and the nodes and links of hypertext combine to offer multiple-user pathways. How do these structures represent the content areas central to the sites; how do they construct relations between text and audience'? (2003: 29)

The lesson idea on site management demonstrates a broader principle, which I hope this chapter has explored in some depth. In short, we should be looking to theorize the practical and energize the theoretical so that all Media students are 'learning by doing'. If we do this, then our teaching is inclusive and we start to erode some of the divisive and unnecessary boundaries placed between different so-called 'types' of learners.

Further reading

Altman, R., 1982, *Genre: The Musical,* London: Routledge.
A useful 'way in' to a view of genre which does not take it for granted as a categorical device. Mark Reid's approach is influenced by Altman.

Burn, A., and Parker, D., 2003, *Analysing Media Texts,* London: Continuum.
Very useful contemporary focus for multimodal textual analysis, including example analyses of websites and computer games.

Creeber, G., (ed.), 2001, *The Television Genre Book.* London: BFI.
Useful for establishing a theoretical overview of specific genres.

Gauntlett, D., 2004, *Web Studies,* London: Arnold.
Very interesting, and at times, contentious, range of approaches to theorizing the internet. Equally useful for vocational production exercises as for more conceptual analysis.

Hartley, J., 1999, *Uses of Television,* London: Routledge.
For an elaboration of the idea of genre as a contract.

Higson, A., 1995, *Dissolving Views,* London: Cassell.
Referred to in the suggestions for a lecture on British cinema.

Musburger, R., and Kindem, G., 2004, *Introduction to Media Production: The Path to Digital Media Production,* Oxford: Focal Press.
Very useful contemporary overview of theoretical foundations for digital production work.

Ofsted, 2001, *Common Inspection Framework,* London: HMI.
Self-explanatory. Sobering, but essential reading.

O'Brien, W., 2003, 'Key Media Concepts Courtesy of Big Brother 4', in *Media Magazine,* 6, London: English and Media Centre.
Written for students, a very clear analysis of this reality TV show through the prism of the key concepts for Media learning.

QCA, 2005, 'Media Matters: a review of Media Studies in schools and colleges', London: QCA.

Stafford, R., 2003, 'Ofcom is Off and Running', in *In the Picture,* 47, Keighley: itp Publications.
A simple, clear, one-page summary of the debates surrounding the inception of this new regulator.

See also the 'Top 40 Websites' section.

chapter three

The 'Grade One' Production Class

Introduction

To return to the 'Grade One' label, clearly, good teaching is generic in many of its qualities. However, there are certain elements of good practice that are specific to the practical lesson, and in my experience, many production teachers dislike the inspection process because they feel that the criteria do not fit the kinds of pedagogic interactions they facilitate. So I will offer in this chapter a range of strategies primarily for the organization of production work that will, I hope, enable you to operate creatively and as far as possible within a vocational paradigm but at the same time hit the right notes in terms of inclusivity and differentiation, learning technology, promotion of diversity and active participation (see Chapter Two for a working definition of each of these 'buzzword' terms).

Class strategy – Visiting speaker

Education as a whole is under increasing pressure to increase employer engagement. This is one of the most difficult aspects of the Media teacher's role. Employers are reluctant to take on large numbers of students on placements, and sadly, some can be negative about Media courses (ironic, as vocational education is in some ways a response to employer needs). Asking an industry practitioner to come in and speak to students is relatively easy but being in control of the 'script' needs preparation.

For a visit at the start of a unit of work on Photography, using a professional with experience of working on a contract and as a freelancer is useful. Rather than offering a 'cold' talk with no preparation, the following guidelines might be adopted:

1. Present the unit in terms of its content and assessment outcomes. Then ask students in pairs to translate it into their own language: What do we need to know? What do we need to do? How will we know if it is any good?
2. Ask students to draft a letter to the visiting speaker, making clear what the students' needs are and what the format should be like.

3. Peer assess the letters and construct an agreed whole-class version, using highlights from each.
4. Make attendance at the session compulsory and agree on a set of questions to ask (the teacher can then be responsible for the supplementary questions that arise during the talk).
5. Ask a group of students to film the session and edit it for other groups who are not invited to watch, or for use as an independent study resource.
6. Persuade the visiting speaker to set the assignment for the unit (using the correct criteria) and ask her/him to act as an external examiner/moderator of the work.

These simple strategies should do three things:

1. Prepare the students so they know the value of the session before it happens (ideally, circulate a CV beforehand to avoid the 'some bloke' syndrome).
2. Give students a stake in the activity as it takes place, to avoid making them passive.
3. Make the rest of the unit 'come alive' in the vocational sense, as you can refer to the speaker in every session as you take students through the production process (even more so if s/he will be involved in assessment at the end of the process).

Production takes many forms, but for the purposes of this chapter we are dealing with lessons that take place outside of traditional classroom settings. These settings might be edit suites, computer rooms, studios or various outside locations. These lessons will not involve 'teacher-talk and student-listen'. Instead, the teacher will be spending her time with smaller groups, working on specific creative projects in progress. While the lesson is taking place, other students may be operating in an open-plan environment, students from other courses might be taking or returning equipment, and there may be technicians working with groups of students on independent study outside of lesson time. Indeed, lessons might be taking place in a workplace setting or in a specialist location hired by the school or college (or a partner institution, if this is a 14–16 initiative course). Or, the lesson might be part of a vocational trip.

Complex interactions

All of these interesting, creative environments of learning and expression cause a problem for the 'Grade One' teacher, which is that these lessons do not seem to fit the inspection brief. Crisp, three-phase lessons with clear objectives and a starter, a development activity and a plenary, are so much harder to present to an outside audience if the lesson is actually 90 minutes on the timetable but the second of three in a row on the same day (often the case for vocational learners, in which case the notions of starts and ends becomes artificial).

Equally, what might be clear good practice to Media teachers in terms of independent creative endeavour (for example, a student entering the room to use an edit suite in their own time) might be considered an interruption within the fairly one-dimensional quality framework.

However, there are a number of strategies we can use to manage this complex set of interactions.

Class strategy – Creative buddying

Every group of students will either arrive with or emerge with a variety of specialist skills, which may not be apparent until coaxed out. Assuming (on a vocational course perhaps) students are working on a number of practical briefs at once, it is possible to pair them so as to give each person two roles – one as 'expert' and one as 'novice' in the same pairing. So, if we call our two students who are going to buddy one another Alex and Lydia, we might end up with Alex mentoring Lydia on a web design project and Lydia supporting Alex on animation (we could go further and integrate learner styles if appropriate). If the timetable is flexible enough (and I always argue that if it is not, you should make it so), these pairings could be across different teaching groups, courses or even subjects (Music Technology students and Video students are an obvious mutually beneficial combination). The teacher's interventions are threefold:

1. Create the pairings and sell the idea, agreeing some ground rules in the form of a contract of mutual support and exchange. This can easily be related to workplace schemes – you may have a peer observation initiative in your school or college that will provide a similar context to reflect on.
2. Arrange a regular opportunity for the buddying to take place.
3. Integrate this process into the assessment criteria by insisting on some reflection on the encounter in either an evaluation or presentation. There is also an opportunity here to signpost wider Key Skills, such as Improving own learning and performance, Working with others and Problem solving. Indeed, the buddying relationship could generate all the evidence for these areas, if it helps.

Flexibility

Sefton-Green (1999) warns us against making assumptions about students' prior access to digital technologies, which may be an issue for production work (and one that the buddying approach would address). He describes a youth project in which it became abundantly clear that the degree of prior access to web design software and computer games related significantly to levels of engagement on the course. I have encountered a huge amount of misguided assumption about 16-year-olds choosing Media courses in terms of their levels of enthusiasm and competence in the domain of risky creative activity. Sometimes we have to remind ourselves, especially in FE, that Media courses attract a large number of disengaged learners who are seeking a second chance, some of whom might have misconceptions about the course being an easy option (see Irvine (2004) for a fuller picture of this issue in FE, albeit a perspective I do not share).

Any Media production activity can harness enthusiasm and ownership of learning if it is less about a transmission model of technical skills and more about self-expression and collaboration. During a long-term project, it is vital for us not to be tempted by the 'work in progress' model of learning and inject each lesson with its own flavour and set of objectives. One easy way of doing this is to alter the brief at a strategic point.

Class strategy – Raise the production stakes

To inject some pace and energy at a mid-point in a long-term project, suddenly introduce a problem and insist that it is solved within the duration of the lesson.

Examples include:

- reducing or extending the required length of a piece of video or radio
- reducing the budget for a production
- introducing a legislative or regulatory problem from the client's perspective
- extending or amending the target audience
- bringing forward the client's deadline
- requesting an additional element to the production.

It is important that you plan this lesson so that a physical, creative solution can be attempted. As a paper exercise (planning to make changes), it is of limited value if we accept an experiential model for production work.

This can work equally well for GCSE and A Level projects if you want to differentiate and extend the groups who are making the most progress. While this is not a specific assessment requirement, if groups are ahead of the game and possibly 'treading water' while you crisis-manage others, this can be a nice extension task to reflect on in their logs or critical evaluations, providing the changes you insist on do not deviate from the original brief too much, where these are set by the board.

A great example of a production team having to respond to a change of plan was the promotional campaign for the film *Spiderman*. After September 11, the original promotional images of the World Trade Centre were no longer viable, so an alternative set of persuasive texts had to be created pretty quickly. The original trailer featured Spiderman building a web between the twin towers to catch his enemies, and a poster showed the towers reflected in Spiderman's shades.

At about the same time, on US television a scene in which Chandler makes a joke about going through airport security was cut from *Friends*, and in *The Ellen Show* a character's line about a collapsing building was deleted. It is worth reminding students doing production of the inevitable artificiality of the educational version of media work. They need to accept, whether for reasons of future ability to be employed in media industries, or just for information, that creativity rarely takes place in a smooth, planned, timetabled manner. The ability to respond to the unforeseen is a valuable skill.

Team teaching

A potential but often under-deployed resource for really helping students with production work is team teaching. Using this approach gives students a live, tangible understanding of the way in which media professionals collaborate. Just as putting students from different creative courses together works to extend their repertoire of skills, so does working with practitioners from other subject areas.

Class strategy – Team teaching: Media Arts

I have found the boundaries between Art teaching and Media Studies really interesting, especially in terms of debates around originality and aesthetics. Working with Art teachers in the Media classroom is a really dynamic move: On one level students get more expert creative advice in terms of conception, process and interpretation, and on another level they can see the pedagogic relation between the Media teacher and the Art teacher in action. Students are also given an opportunity to ask some questions about subject identity and vocational issues, for example: what is the relationship between cinematographer and director on a film?

But as always, this needs a framework for it to be successful, which might take one of these forms (all of which will involve the Art and Media departments working together):

- Art department input to one specific element of a production.
- Art department commission brief for a project and assess it.
- One department sets a brief and the other assesses it.
- Multimedia project in which artists work with some students (on graphics work, perhaps) while Media staff work with electronic aspects. This works very well for an art installation, in my experience.
- Art and Media departments work together with students to design a show or exhibition that can be used as assessment evidence for both Media and Art units. In this way, students and staff are collaborating – an example of this is an exhibition about media imagery.

> What the Media department can offer in return in all of these cases is a focus on the commercial and cultural context for aesthetic and creative production. In terms of theorizing production, students can reflect on the different contexts of creativity they encounter and discuss the differences between art and media.

Work in progress

The worst kind of production in school and colleges is the model in which students are free to work unaided for long periods of time without support or critique along the way. (For this kind of work, the scheme of work is likely to feature a single phrase such as 'build websites' cut and pasted on many successive rows under 'content'.) The best kind is the opposite, where a project has a scheme of work just as detailed as a theory topic. In this good-practice model, differentiation and inclusivity will be taken seriously lesson by lesson, as the learning will be facilitated by a series of activities, rather than by just 'carrying on'. (One way of looking at it would be to ask: How long would it take to explain the lesson if I were not in class? If the answer is that you would just say: 'Carry on with project work', then there is a problem.)

It can, however, be difficult without adequate resources to find ways of monitoring the progress of project work (see Chapter Nine) with a large group. The simple opportunities created by interactive whiteboards are ideal for this.

Class strategy – Smartboard image annotation for work in progress

Where students have taken digital images that they intend to manipulate with software and use within a particular text or production, it is useful to stop at an early stage and focus on the importance of the image. Otherwise, the danger is that you get to the end of a larger project and much of the hard work is undone by the poor quality of the primary images.

However user-friendly technology becomes, image creation and manipulation are skills that require cultural knowledge, intertextual understanding, sensitivity to context and audience and no small amount of aesthetic competence.

Whatever the wider project, students can download their images and use the smartboard notebook tools to present their image and use one colour pen to annotate the image to show intended cropping, enlargement, further manipulation and text. Then other students in the group, offering critique and further suggestions, can use another colour to annotate the work on screen further. These ideas, visual representations of feedback as they are, can be saved and printed out for evidence of the creative process in the context of peer review, which will be useful for any assessment purpose on a vocational course, an A/AS or GCSE.

Equipment

One question I have often been asked at INSET courses concerns the level of technical evidence required, so it may be useful to set out my views here. (However, please note that you should always check that your procedures meet with the requirements of your awarding body.)

I do not acknowledge any difference in the technical specification of production work on any Media courses. The difference will be purely one of time and access: for example, students doing a National Diploma in moving image production will need more sustained access to Final Cut Pro (at the time of writing, an industry standard editing software) than students producing one piece of video for AS. However, in my opinion it would be a nonsense to expect AS students to work on outdated linear editing kit just because their course is not 'vocational'. For all Media courses, students need to demonstrate experience, whether it is technical or not, of the specific kinds of production that 'real' media practitioners are working with at the time they take the course. It is your duty to the students to find out, and this is why I suggest you make links with people working in the media. If students are working with outdated technology or in ways that are vocationally unrealistic, then there is little point in the work. This is equally true for the practical elements of academic courses. Some educational institutions arrange work placements for staff: I would advise any Media teacher to take this opportunity and to develop a scheme of work for students out of the experience. In my view, using outdated equipment or ways of working is as problematic as ignoring recent theoretical developments in your subject area.

It is not advisable to list specific technologies at the time of writing, due to the time between writing and publication.

Practical work

Another personal view is that all practical coursework should *be* practical, and as such, involve digital technology. This means I do not accept storyboarding, planning or drafting in itself to be a production task. This certainly was the case in A Level Media Studies in the mid-1990s, largely because of resource problems, but also because it was deemed acceptable when the digital world was emerging. Now, however, it is the 'zeitgeist' of our students. The Media teacher can no longer work within a purely theoretical, textual environment without sufficient attention to digital production, consumption and culture. The simple reason for this is that there *is* no longer any textual meaning, culture or activity to be critiqued outside of the interventions of digital worlds. To be clear, so as to acknowledge that there remains an enormous digital divide, I mean that even non-digital media production and consumption is situated in its status as *other* to digital work.

Attention to detail

Practical media learning, when successful, operates on a set of principles which I call 'disciplined creativity'. Teachers from Creative Arts backgrounds will agree with me, I am sure, that the most inspired creative output arises from the most disciplined, rigorous application, and thus the stereotype of the 'laid-back', disorganised Art or Media teacher is deceptive. Pete Fraser has an outstanding track record, at Long Road Sixth Form College in Cambridge, of supporting highly original, industry-standard production work (again, it is interesting to question whether doing A Level on his course is academic or vocational) and I encourage readers to access Long Road's Media Studies website for examples of good practice. His published suggestions (2002) for laying foundations for successful creative work are sensible and applicable to all production work on all Media courses. To summarize (and group his many suggestions into a few 'bedrock' principles) he argues that students must start from research into real media texts, audience awareness and planning deadlines. Following this initial research and planning, the generation of simple ideas is more sensible than great ambition. A combination of simplicity and originality is the key to a creative project, alongside rigorous attention to detail. In the case of video, he points to planning the minute details of each shoot meticulously to avoid wasting time on location, testing batteries, lighting and microphones before setting off, and planning to improvize when group members are absent. I mention these points, mundane as they might seem, for an important reason. No matter what advice I give you about the creative or technical exchange between you and your students, if you do not accept that your primary objective with production work is a combination of motivation and organization, the students will not fulfil their potential. Once you and your teaching group have established this rigorous attention to detail, planning, health and safety and time management, then creativity will flourish. Or as Fraser says:

Production work from Halesowen College. Using user-friendly technology to set a high standard for media learning.

'Treat your project with professionalism and organisation and you will not go far wrong! Enjoy your work. Being creative is brilliant – but you can't beat being organised.' (2002: 42)

Stuart McConnell, at Halesowen College, gets results from the same attention to organization and detail. Students do not embark on production work until they have gained approval, and their progress is monitored frequently against agreed planning objectives. Fraser and McConnell both believe that creativity emerges from discipline (see Chapter Nine for set of strategies for managing production projects).

Class strategy – Production troubleshooting

If you can make solving problems as they arise part of the process (and assessment) of a creative project, then you might be able to prepare students better for this eventuality and reduce stress levels in the classroom. One method for doing this is to take them through an exercise early on, when they try problem-solving in response to a real dilemma faced by a group in a previous year. Clearly, this needs forward planning. A classic scenario is the breakdown of the group dynamic: for example, on a filming session one week before the deadline (so the film needs editing) one of the actors fails to turn up. The exercise might be as follows:

1. Show the students the rushes (or the edited version) of the filming up to this point.
2. Give them the original storyboard.
3. Give them 20 minutes to provide a solution (which might involve recasting, rewriting the script or even cutting short the film).
4. Discuss the solutions through jigsawing or group-sharing, and vote for the most sensible answer (you might differentiate between creative and practically sensible).
5. For homework, students should write a mock-up evaluation section describing the problem and solution in terms of: a) decision-making, b) group dynamics, c) problem solving.

Note that these are not obviously theoretical or creative areas, but the point you are trying to make is that it is out of these practical skills of organization, crisis management and practical thinking that creative production work arises.

Writing skills

In addition to this focus on management of time, resources and group roles, another vital underpinning area is the development of writing skills, whether for evaluative purposes (almost all media production work has to be accompanied by a written piece, needlessly in my opinion) or for generating text, a script, treatment or pitch. Theory teaching revolves around the support of writing skills, but strangely, many production projects are allowed to progress with little attention to language use. There are three writing modes of production within which students need to operate: commercial writing (to sell an idea); conventional writing (a script in a particular genre or style, for example); and vocational writing (describing, analysing and evaluating the project in terms of its relationship to real industry output). Sometimes (especially on A/AS courses) there is in addition a requirement to write conceptually (analysing your own text using genre, narrative and representation). If we accept that all media production is writing and all media consumption is reading (in the broader sense of textual encoding and decoding) then we must realise that students with developing linguistic confidence will need support on a Media production course, despite appearances to the contrary (that it is vocational or technical and these things are to do with hands, rather than minds).

Class strategy – Writing frames for production/production frames

These are two versions of the same principle. It is useful to differentiate them. All students should use them at the outset and then the more able can use less detailed versions and ultimately, work without them.

Writing frames for production

These can be used to:

- provide the opening sentence of each paragraph for a treatment
- provide a framework of sentences for an evaluation
- provide a template for the organization of a script
- offer a statement bank for dialogue
- provide the opening and final sentence of each text area of a webpage.

Note that these are different to templates for storyboards or radio scripts, which are to do with conventions and presentation. These frames are to encourage the use of conventional language by disciplining the range of content used and framing the flow of language in each paragraph. In other words, they 'force' students into working in the idioms of the language game in question. Again, you are establishing discipline, from which creativity will flow.

Production frames

Examples of these are:

- a mapping chart for a soap opera episode (four interweaving storylines to be inter-connected)
- a website navigation map from the user's point of view, with some of the links defined

- a set of rules for an animation (number of drawings or images, length, plot structure)
- a pop video storyboard with the first five shots included.

Note that these are intended to avoid the 'blank sheet of paper' syndrome where students spend several planning lessons achieving very little. They serve to get the ball rolling, to discipline the creative energy and to provide a safety net, a starting point. Clearly, your intention is to gradually reduce the need for these, but they help us to avoid making assumptions about our students' levels of confidence in throwing themselves into using media language.

Jacks of all trades

Irvine (2004) offers a nice illustration that I think serves to demonstrate the need for the contemporary Media teacher to be less an expert in everything than a master of resources and organization:

'On the same day, a Media teacher might start with a class doing quite sophisticated work in Quark Express and Photoshop (i.e. things some people do full time) followed by a lesson on silent cinema and then a session of TV soap operas and representation and a final lesson on more production work but this time on radio script techniques. Few subjects demand such a range of expertise. It makes accusations of being a "Mickey Mouse" subject even less tolerable'. (Irvine, 2004:24)

I have avoided giving guidance on specific technical skills in this chapter, and I am sorry if you had hoped for more of a 'what to teach' angle. My reasons are simple: first, I do not want to offer a lot of technical tips that will be outdated within a year, and second, I believe principles are more useful than content. While it is clear that a Media teacher needs an array of digital production skills, these are relatively easy to acquire for teaching at Levels 2 and 3, especially if you have technician support and 'savvy' students to help you with the tricky stuff while you concentrate on organizing the learning.

Further reading

Beetlestone, F., 1998, *Creative Children, Imaginative Teaching*, Buckingham: Open University Press.
A range of research evidence and general strategies for teachers who are engaged in the imaginative life worlds of their pupils/students.

Buckingham, D., 2003, *Media Education: Literacy, Learning and Contemporary Culture*, London: Polity.
Chapter 8, on creativity, is an excellent overview of the changing context for Media production work and is relevant as a 'state of play' for all Media teachers.

Burn, A., *et al.*, 2001, 'The Rush of Images: a research report into digital editing and the moving image' in *English in Education*, 35 (2): Sheffield: Nate.

Edwards, C., 2001, *Radio for Media Studies,* London: Auteur.
Radio, as usual, is under-represented in this book. Clive Edwards' book offers a range of ideas for working in the medium that is actually the most realistic destination for students with a Media qualification in the first instance.

Fraser, P., 2002, 'Production Work Tips' in *Media Magazine,* 1, London: English and Media Centre.

Grahame, J., 1994, *Production Practices,* London: English and Media Centre.
Among a range of other excellent resources from this author, this remains relevant as a set of principles for production work with students.

Irvine, S., 2004, 'Media in FE: How Things Stand Today' in *In the Picture*, 50, Keighley: itp Publications.
Rather a pessimistic account, in my view, but doubtless an interesting and eye-opening statement on the life of the contemporary Media teacher in the post-16 sector.

Sefton-Greene, J., 1999, 'Media Education, but not as we know it; digital technology and the end of Media Studies', in *English and Media Magazine*, 40, London: English and Media Centre.
Provocative set of questions posed for Media teachers in the digital world.

Sefton-Greene, J., and Sinker, R., (eds.), 2000, *Evaluating Creativity: Making and Learning by Young People,* London: Routledge.
Engaging research into creative practices and their relationship with formal education.

See also the 'Top 40 Websites' section.

chapter four

Teaching Technologies

Introduction

Is television a collective experience? It shows how far we have come, perhaps, that a medium still derided for its provision of sinful anti-social and passive delights is now heralded in some quarters as a bastion of collective experience. In this argument, the shared mass viewing experience is set against solitary internet use and the fragmented alienation of the TV downloader who watches programmes when she wants to (free from the broadcasting 'moment': still defined in relation to the Coronation in 1953).

These notions, of course, have always been to do with myth and moral panic. Many people watch TV alone, but using technology is almost always an act of communication, even if your friend in Africa doesn't reply for a couple of weeks, or if none of your virtual community know what you look like.

Julian Sefton-Green speaking in 2005 at a conference organized by *The Guardian* and *Media Magazine*, summarized some key themes for Media teachers arising from new technologies by dividing the issues into two areas: the individual and the wider, institutional public world. For the individual in the 'digital world', students and teachers need to engage with questions of audience, consumption and production (the one and the other converging, so that a web user also provides content) and how the dynamic of, and between, each are changing. These sender/receiver interplays might lead students to reflect on possibilities for creativity and new media literacies.

Meanwhile, media institutions are responding to the advent of digital technologies in ways that might constitute a shift in our understanding of the state, political economy and the social world more widely. In this arena, concerns about the 'digital divide' and competing claims and counterclaims for media access need to be discussed.

So, in this section I would like to argue from the outset that teaching about technology or through technology is never abstracted from other Media learning. We are never *just* playing and being creative. These activities are always bound up, however subtly, with ideas about identity, society, communication and culture. We may just need new models for dealing with these now.

Tackling digital technology

This chapter presents some approaches to teaching about technology and also teaching through technology. In keeping with the spirit of this book, my desire is to reduce the boundaries between 'thinking' and 'doing' so that the use of technology aids learning *about* it, and thus becomes reflective.

It is impossible to make credible any form of Media education in these times without paying a great deal of attention to digital technology. For some Media teachers, this seems to be a source of some anxiety. I think this response is often based on the fear of the unknown. It is also ironic, given that the greatest gift digital technology has brought to education has been to liberate us from the need to be technical experts.

When I began teaching Media I worked in what was called (laughably, in retrospect) 'Studio 1' which consisted of an old toilet block converted into a classroom. In this room, which had the capacity for a maximum of 25 students, I taught around 30. In two corners there were a 'crash edit' suite and an early form of non-linear editing called 'Video Machine Lite'. We mostly had to use crash editing (literally pressing play on one VCR and record on the other) because neither the college technician nor any of the Media staff could work out how to solve any of the many problems the digital suite provided (which were to do with the interface between digital editing and mechanical video recording). This was a pretty typical situation. We had no designated Media technician and we were, on reflection, partly duped by a technical sales pitch into buying equipment that was intended for professional use by a small team of experts, as opposed to hundreds of 16-year-olds learning by trial and error.

Educationally-geared companies now sell cheap equipment that is designed for your needs, and although in reality you can teach yourself how to use the kit in a couple of hours (or the students can teach you), you can go on a day course run by Media teachers where they will take you through not only the basics but also how to manage student projects through the technology.

We are in an 'invisibility paradigm' in Media teaching, where (thankfully) you do not really need to know in any detail how all the technology works to use it effectively. Hence, we are liberated from the technical and can operate more in aesthetic and conventional domains, in production terms. But we also need to teach students about digital technology in sociological terms. What difference has the digital world made to producers and consumers? What is convergence and what is its impact? What are the limitations, both technically and socially, of digital environments? Are we living in a postmodern, hyperreal state, or is all this technology just 'old wine in new bottles'?

Transformative technologies?

'There's a funny thing about the fusion of technology and culture. It has been part of human experience since the first cave painter, but we've had a hard time seeing it until now. When James Joyce published Ulysses in 1922 and revolutionised all of our expectations about how books should work. . .he was a highly skilled technician, tinkering around with a book-machine, making it do things it had never done before... Technology used to advance in slower, more differentiated stages. The book reigned as the mass medium of choice for several centuries; newspapers had a couple of hundred years to innovate, even film ruled the roost for thirty years before the rapid-fire succession of radio, then television, then the personal computer. With each innovation, the gap that kept the past at bay grew shorter, more attenuated. This meant little in the centuries-long increments of the book or the newspaper – not to mention the millennial scale of the cave painter – but as the stages grew more abbreviated, they began to interrupt the life cycles of individual humans... The explosion of media types in the twentieth century makes it possible for the first time to grasp the relationship of form to content, medium to message, engineering to artistry.' (Johnson, 1997: 3–4)

So, for the Media teacher in the early twenty-first century, the key question is this: Can we adapt our old models to the new technology (can we incorporate these digital interactions into our existing conceptual paradigm), or does the technology ask us questions about our traditional ways of thinking about texts and audiences? Do we need to adapt to change in a fundamental, theoretical way? As always, the best people to ask are your students.

Class strategy – Presentations

After a lecture on convergence, with as many interesting examples as you can provide (this is one area where students can actually be encouraged to use mobile phones in your lesson!) set students a research task within the school or college itself. They need to select a sample of students and find out what converged media they are using, and how.

In the interests of time, narrow down the number of presentations you will have by putting students into groups of three (these should be strategically chosen, as always). In this case, I suggest putting 'techno-phobes' with the opposite. Give them these problem-solving tasks:

- Decide on a method for analysing the shared data.
- Decide on three significant conclusions.

Next, give each of the groups a different focus to use as a 'prism' for their conclusions. If there are five groups, these might be:

- In reality, what difference is convergence making?
- Is there a digital divide economically?
- Is there a digital gender divide?
- Is convergence enhancing or reducing social life?
- Is convergence enhancing or reducing communication?

Ask each group to prepare a PowerPoint presentation of five minutes' duration, with these *crucial* ground-rules:

1. Students cannot use existing PowerPoint templates for the background. They need to either provide or resource suitable images related to the subject matter and use them as a design template for the presentation.
2. The maximum number of slides is five (one minute each). PowerPoint slides must ONLY contain bullet point headings.
3. Each bullet point must be explained orally, in detail, while other students make notes.

In the next lesson, agree some criteria with the students to enable them to peer-assess. There is absolutely no need (in fact it would be detrimental) for you to mark these presentations, as long as you are happy with the assessed criteria.

Film the presentations so you can play them back for whole-class feedback. This also gives you the opportunity to use them as content when discussing convergence with other groups.

If we find ourselves in the midst of a paradigm shift in terms of the relationship between technology and society, it is only in the sense that we are always in one. Try to think of a time when we were not at the 'edge' of a shift from one mode of techno-existence to another. It is difficult to do so. History tells us that all shifts in communication through technology, from the telephone to the television to the internet and mobile phones foster moral panics and over-stated anxiety. For Media teachers, there is the accompanying angst about finding the time to use all the technology we ought to be expert in (on my list at the time of writing is subscribing to more music download sites, getting further into blogging and video logging (V-logging) and researching options for making my home wireless). The crisis point at the change from one techno-zeitgeist to another, we are told, is of great interest to sociologists and psychologists, as well as media institutions. The point I want to make is that we are already in this crisis: it is a permanent 'status anxiety' and as such, we are engaged in a history of the present – the future is already here.

Class strategy – Arranging a showcase

School or college productions are regular, established events in the annual calendar but surprisingly, very few institutions showcase their Media students' work in the same way. For me, this is a missed opportunity, since arranging such an event helps with motivation while it is in production, offers a heartening reward for everyone involved at the end-point and raises the stakes hugely in terms of students' learning about text and audience. There is no need for great amounts of detail here since the idea is pretty self-explanatory, but suffice to say, students need to be responsible for:

- arranging a date for the showcase that corresponds with deadlines and institutional considerations
- selecting a venue (some colleges have access to a local cinema)
- establishing format criteria for production groups

- gathering the material and preparing it for exhibition (a single showreel is sensible) – here, technician support is needed for the best results
- marketing the event, selling tickets (and lobbying for the funds to go towards something in the department)
- risk assessments, insurance and ease of access for all.

The benefits of 'going the extra mile' and arranging such an event are obvious in terms of motivation and reward (your parents and friends seeing your video work in a cinema) but they also extend learning about technologies as preparing material for exhibition in another domain. If such an event can become a regular feature, you will find that previous students get interested in returning to help out and that the local media may be interested. The latter awareness can lead to work-placement opportunities and all sorts of other vocational spin-offs. You might consider putting students into vocational roles each year, by appointing a showcase manager each time.

What's new?

Let us engage with a few examples of technological innovations that have 'caught on' at the time of writing, and I dare predict will have sufficient longevity to be of interest at the time of reading.

Web studies

Class strategy – Surfing skills workshop

Never assume that students can use the internet routinely in the way that you can. If you list the skills you use every time you need to access information quickly on the web, and then prepare a workshop to share these, you will enable your students to safely overcome any anxieties they may have. (It is becoming taboo to 'come out' as a technophobe or an entry level user.)

Your list of skills might look something like this:

- Choosing a search engine or gateway.
- Using advanced searching techniques – key words, phrases, names and combinations.
- Narrowing scope (UK or world sites, for example).
- Speed-evaluating content and credentials.
- Distinguishing content (promotion, information, opinion, analysis).
- Following links and navigating between sites.
- Selecting, copying and adapting (to avoid plagiarism).

A workshop (preferably with expert students helping you), where students work on a carousel of activities in which they work on one of these skills in isolation from the others, will raise confidence levels and allow you to diagnose needs on an individual basis, before you set independent internet research as a part of the learning.

The dangers of assuming that students have already acquired these skills are that you may end up treating students harshly when they produce swathes of printouts without any selection criteria, when this may be what they thought you wanted.

There is certainly an immense proliferation of content on the internet which is of interest for theory topics on news as well as for learning about internet consumption and its socio-cultural implications. Blogging, online news (and online news filtering services such as the ever-expanding *Google* empire) and 'wall-less' online encyclopaedias (such as *Wikipaedia*) are used by millions worldwide and even the most web-cynical would concede that these constitute a threat to traditional models of news consumption and production. In short, users become authors with ease (in a sense, we can argue that a 'punk' ethos pervades) and it is very easy for students to set up blogs in order to investigate this facility through direct action as opposed to passive instruction. A number of HE institutions are encouraging students to use blogging as a general learning practice, and a number of Media departments are helping students set up blogs (and 'podcasts') as a Media learning facility (visit Long Road Sixth Form College's Media site; and see Luhrs, 2005). By the time you read this, therefore, this may be standard practice as opposed to an innovation. Opportunities exist in abundance to become at once consumer and producer in the realms of popular music (where you can produce a playlist from downloaded material or produce your own music using software like Garageband and broadcast it as a radio show across the internet). Again, these facilities offer you easy projects that afford consideration of theory and practice entwined. The key issue to keep in mind is this: all learning about technology is really learning about people, their choices, changing habits and behaviours. This can be done at micro level (local consumer research and activity) or at macro level (consideration of cultural differences in internet behaviour, for example).

Class strategy – Collaborative question and answer

This idea allows for knowledge building and critical thinking about online news provision. The ratio of the latter to the former can be adapted with differentiation in mind.

Students are divided into four groups (strategically, as always – in this case this might be related to the relative degree of news awareness demonstrated).

The four groups are given a task each, from:

- reading a piece of journalism on the state of online news in the UK and answering two comprehension questions
- reading an academic piece of online news and answering two comprehension questions
- visiting two online news sites and answering two comprehension questions (to do with what is offered in comparison to other news formats)
- carrying out a micro consumer research exercise around the institution with staff and students (within the time allowed for the other tasks).

Students then jigsaw (see Chapter Six) and make notes from one another so they can complete the writing frame provided (which has the six comprehension questions part-completed, and two openings of statements about consumer usage) for homework.

So, in the space of one lesson and one homework activity, students have covered this topic at an introductory level, learning about:

- what online news looks like in comparison to 'traditional' modes
- who is using it and who isn't
- information from popular sources
- academic perspectives.

For the remainder of the topic, different groups can work on each of these areas to much greater depth in a 'carousel' arrangement.

We return to this question later, in the sections dealing with the 'classic' theory topics, but when considering online news it is important to consider the issue of threat with an informed view of the complexities. For example, if *The Guardian* has more readers from the USA than the UK (as the web version is so successful globally), does this change the readership rather than threaten its existence? And what does the interplay between the press and other news providers look like? Does the press still set the agenda, so that the internet, rolling TV news and digital radio merely repeat the stories created by and for the morning papers? Or is this changing? In other words, does the technology provide new forms for the same, or fundamentally shift the sand? I think a real paradigm shift would have to involve the latter, so that news as a commodity and service would be a different entity in a digital world than it was before.

Blogging and politics

Blogs played a significant part in the 2005 UK election campaign. Blogging gives us an opportunity to do work with students, through a study of technology, that might otherwise be alienating (if we accept that our audience is 'depoliticised', as we are encouraged to by the middle-class establishment). Labour politician Tom Watson set himself up as the first MP to start a blog, and a number of sites offered advice on strategic and tactical voting in marginal areas. Billy Bragg set up 'Voting valentine' blog-forums on the internet to encourage tactical voting to keep the Tories out of Dorset (it didn't work). Of equal significance to the democratic process, a host of sites set up by members of the public offered live scrutiny of the politicians' moves during a particularly negative and ideologically bankrupt campaign season. My personal favourites were *theyworkforyou.com*, offering information about every MP and their activities in Parliament, and *writetothem.com*, a communication facility from which the web user emails their opinion and the website faxes it to any elected official.

Narrowcasting?

Another domain for engaging with this 'chicken and egg' debate is television genre, a subject traditionally housed within the confines of the theory curriculum. Those that lament the deregularised world of formatting over genre suggest that the successes of reality TV and other forms of 'event television' have led to an era of 'narrowcasting', in which producers, in ever-increasing anxiety about competition from more and more channels fighting for smaller audiences, play safer than ever before. If fragmented audiences have influenced producers into commissioning less of a range of programmes, is this a commercial issue, or is it to do with technology leading content? In other words, is the interactive, online nature of *Big Brother* an agent in this revolution, for better or worse, or is it a red herring when placed in the context of commercial imperatives?

Digital TV

Digital television (and interactive services made possible by it) is an arena for dispute and debate. Some would have us believe that scheduling as we know it is doomed, as we will all be watching programmes downloaded and played back at our convenience. If this is the case, and programme guide information on our televisions becomes ever more sophisticated at leading us to our preferences, then the notion of channel will erode, so we do not really know the origin of what we are watching, let alone when it was 'broadcast'. Others take a more sceptical view (the 'old wine, new bottles' argument) and say that the 'watercooler' moment will always remain, as human beings will always enjoy the guilty pleasure of passivity (just 'watching what is on') as opposed to the planned, work-like itinerary viewing created by SkyPlus and TIVO. Evidence (from Guy Winter, the BBC's expert in viewer behaviour, speaking at *The Guardian's* 2005 conference) shows that people who use this more organized, downloaded choice of consumption actually watch 15 per cent more television as a result, but this viewing is planned as opposed to random. Based on Winter's data, 90 per cent of the programmes recorded are actually watched (far higher a ratio than VCR recording, which we all use to record things we think we ought to watch but don't get round to it). So here is a debate which your students are well equipped to converse within. A project in which they produce a futuristic content guide and various search tools for a world of television in which consumers are 'channel-blind' will be at once creative and theoretical.

A further area for research and debate is the forthcoming 'switch-off' of the analogue signal by the Government at some point at the end of this decade. Some argue that this in an ill-judged plan, which only retains its mobility because the powers that be are committed to it. This argument is based on evidence that many older people and those with social disadvantage are simply not aware of the deadline and thus have no intention of transferring to digital voluntarily, which begs the question – who pays for the future?

Some more 'paradigm-shift' considerations for your students are as follows:

- How is radio changing because of software for digital consumption? New platforms or new conventions?

- Is TV on your mobile bound to catch on?

- Are the younger generation more relaxed about commodity ownership? In other words, is it an 'adult thing' to want a CD or DVD collection, as opposed to a portable hard drive full of films and music?

It is important, I think, to remind students regularly about the need to be precise when dealing with technology and social activity. For example, we might agree that we are dealing with an 'information economy', in which the ownership and transference of information is the most valuable commodity (as opposed to the means to produce commodities from raw materials), at least in the advanced world. But this is still specific to the internet at the time of writing, I would argue, in an era when television is still predominately about entertainment. In a few years, this book will possibly seem terribly out of date since we are still future-gazing when it comes to convergence, still in a developmental state. I still watch my TV, then go into a different room to check emails and make a phone call on yet another piece of hardware. And though I do my food shopping online, my fridge doesn't yet order things I have run out of for me.

So when we deal with downloaded TV and other forms of convergence, the mantra question for students at the present time is still: 'What can we do differently: who wins and who loses?'

And, since I am arguing that we are always in a state of transformation from technology to technology, albeit more or less pronounced at key times, it seems prudent to suggest that we will never *not* be asking these questions.

Throughout this book I return often to the assertion that it is not my intention to provide guidance on content that will be out of date by the time you read it. Thus, it would not be wise to explain convergence through specific examples (I could talk about MP4 but no doubt MP5 will be here by the time your scheme of work takes shape!). However, it is more straightforward to deal with the key learning principles you should embed into your work with students.

MP5?

Starting with music downloading, you can (unless you are considerably younger than me) use yourself as a case study. In my case, I still own large quantities of vinyl (in a former life, when CDs did not exist, I was a DJ at a nightclub and worked in a record shop). At the same time, I have an iPod and enthusiastically download CDs into playlists. I am not a confident internet downloader though, so for me there is still a clear demarcation between the products and formats I consume. Things that are on my MP3 player are also in my collection in a tangible 'hard copy' presence. So for me, the iPod is a glorified Walkman. For my students, MP3 players are more like portable hard drives for music they never intend to 'own'. They are amused by my romantic nostalgia for 'record sleeves'. They find my reluctant, gradual selling of some of the rarer bits of my vinyl horde on eBay at best quaint, but usually dull. They inhabit a different world in terms of what music is, how it is used and its semiotic boundaries.

Let's spend a minute on the technological chronology and detail. At the time of writing, *Crazy Frog* is the first ring-tone to have achieved the Number 1 singles chart position. (This really makes me feel old: when young people's tastes don't just bewilder you but really annoy you too, you've arrived at middle age, for sure.) Compact Discs arrived in 1980, followed by digital audio discs for computers in 1982. It wasn't until 1989 that CD sales overtook vinyl. Meanwhile, DAT was introduced in 1987, and in 1992 mini-discs were on sale. DAB arrived, courtesy of the BBC, in 1995. In the decade to 2005, there was an intensity of proliferation in terms of hardware. In 1996, enhanced CDs were introduced, and from 1997, MP3 transformed from emerging technology to Year Zero for the music industry, via Napster. Broadband appeared from 2000, the iPod changed everything a year later, and in 2003, CD sales started to decline in the face of the Mac iTunes music store and its rivals.

On 17 April 2005, downloads featured in the charts for the first time, at a time when legal downloads alone were recorded at 4.5 million. As you read this, your youngest students will have little or no experience of consuming music without the option of downloading. The detail above is now history.

Chris Walker (2004) researched the question of whether digital downloading is really a threat to big business, and suggested that for the community of 'serious' downloaders (as opposed to casual users of MP3 who also buy CDs, or novices like myself who really only copy what has been purchased) there is a political element to the activity:

'A reason why record companies are disliked is that they are seen as being responsible for blocking creativity and innovation. Downloading is seen as the 'holy grail' of independent artists – bands and musicians being free to share and to distribute freely through the net. In some ways, file-sharing is seen as resisting commodification.' (2004: 27)

Walker's findings are useful in two key ways. First, his thesis provides some evidence that amongst the 'hardcore' users of this technology, we can locate a form of micro-politics in which a concern about corporations and their actions emerges through the specific consumption of music (as opposed to party politics). If this is the case, then the so-called 'slacker generation' might be more of a politically and socially engaged community than they are given credit for. Second, Walker used the internet to access this community and found that asking questions on e-forums generated a vast amount of qualitative, discursive data for him to interpret. This method is equally accessible for your students. If you can identify students who are more 'savvy' in terms of downloading and either membership of or awareness of subcultural groups (in Walker's case he accessed *Kerrang!* readers), and group them with other students who have less experience, you can easily mobilise a number of interesting research projects within a scheme of work on digital music.

Class strategy – Text conference

To get students thinking theoretically about their mobile phones, it is necessary to 'bite the bullet' and break one of your most fundamental ground rules. You need the students to get their phones out and start texting. (Given that some are probably already doing this while you hope they are listening to you, you should encounter little credible reluctance to reduce their credit.) After sessions in which you cover some of the historical context, from the emergence of WAP to MP4 and beyond, a straw poll of consumer usage and the obvious socio-cultural issues (pros and cons, quality of communication, safety versus surveillance), I suggest the following activity.

Everyone in the group sets up a group list for texting, so they can text-conference each other throughout the lesson. Let the students arrange this as they may be more adept than you at managing groups.

Introduce the film *Enemy of the State* by presenting two questions for students to consider as they view the film:

1. Which of these fictional examples of technology are plausible and which are not (i.e. they could not happen)?
2. When is the technology helping 'the people' and when is it helping 'the man' (or: When is it liberating ordinary folk and when is it oppressing them)?

The rules are that every student must offer at least one text contribution, but they are restricted to a maximum of three.

Two students act as scribes, either by saving the messages to transcribe later or by making notes as the conference progresses.

The outcome (for homework) is a report covering these two areas:

1. The content of the messages – a summary of what opinions were expressed by the group and the ratio of agreement to disagreement.
2. An evaluation of how useful the text-conference facility was. What were the pros and cons of this set-up in comparison to watching the film, making notes and then having a discussion?

This lesson works if it fits into the scheme of the work at the right point. The students will have covered issues of functionality, sociology, consumption and commerce. The novelty value is part of the exercise, of course, but it must act as a resource for further discussion.

Theory/practice and technology

The traditional Media concepts that are usually associated with theory and production (such as genre, narrative, representation, audience and ideology) are, in some minds, separated from teaching about institutions and technologies. So, a false boundary between bits of courses becomes established and a notion develops that there is conceptual thinking (which is learned and then demonstrated through creative work) in one place, and that in another place there is a largely factual body of knowledge about history, companies and gadgets which is best acquired through a transmission model (the teacher learns it all and then, through case studies, presents it to the learners).

This works, up to a point, but a more coherent strategy for Media learning can be adopted if these boundaries are removed. An example might be the teaching of visual literacy or image analysis. Rather than teach about semiotics first and then require students to consider their own production in relation to the theory at the end-point, why not teach semiotics through digital image manipulation? This can be done by giving students a simple brief in which they present themselves on the cover of a magazine of their choice, situating themselves as an actor, musician, comedian, sports personality, presenter or other form of celebrity. Students need to carefully consider clothing, facial expression (and general 'performance') and location ('studio' or external background), in the first instance. After selecting a still image for editing (I suggest you use the smartboard annotation facility explained in Chapter Three), students might then use Photoshop and Quark Express or equivalent image editing and desk-top publishing software to create the cover mock-up.

To present semiotics as a working model for reflecting on meaning, simply pair the students and give them two exercises to be carried out at the same time without cross-referencing. First, they present a descriptive account of their own work (you will later use the terms 'signifier' and 'denotation'). Next, they respond to another student's images in terms of the representational devices at work ('a summary of what you think when you look at this magazine cover').

The images and the reports should then be displayed around the room. After a lecture (remember, we sometimes do owe it to the students to present theory in this way as long as it is bracketed within more active sessions on either side) where you give an introduction to signifier/signified, types of signs (iconic, indexical and arbitrary), degrees of motivation and anchorage, the students spend a lesson simply moving around the room collecting examples of each type of sign from their fellow students' digital production work.

Class strategy – E-seminar

This works easily if you have an intranet and a virtual learning environment. I am basing this on WebCT as a platform.

It is not productive at all if you merely set up the activity and expect action. Two things must happen first. You need to run a session on access and protocols that assumes no prior understanding. Just think of the variability in 'netiquette' in your institution, and the tensions that may have arisen in the workplace as a result of insensitive emailing. (I once had a manager who would regularly reply to very long, heartfelt requests for staffing or resources with the letters 'n' and 'o' in upper case. Looking back, this was a breakdown in communication arising from polarised ideas of what email is for.)

So you need to cover technical confidence and then protocols, but more importantly, you must recognize that to send an email to the whole year-group is no less daunting for students than offering a verbal contribution. Students are easily embarrassed and equally concerned about a) appearing arrogant and b) appearing 'stupid'. The trick is to identify three or four students and encourage them to get the ball rolling, with some help in terms of wording and content.

In this example, students are spending time on work experience in a variety of settings broadly related to Media employment. The teacher is concerned about the students' ability to relate this experience to the content of the scheme of work, which is to do with media employment and how the advent of new digital technologies has affected the sector in question.

WebCT gives them (and you) the opportunity to reflect and learn experientially by responding to discussion postings that you facilitate. Over a five day placement, the structure might be:

Day 1:
Information: introduce yourself, where are you, what have you been doing today?
Question: about how this experience will help understanding of employment and technology.

Day 2:
Information: give one example of some new knowledge in relation to the unit.
Response: respond to one other person's question from yesterday.

Days 3 and 4:
Same as Day 2.

Day 5:
Summary and list of three issues/questions to discuss further in school/college.

If the placement is longer, simply expand each stage.

This activity does many things that help with your teaching 'back at the ranch' and another technology which you can discuss the merits of (there is lots of scope for talking about face-to-face communication versus 24/7 multi-user interfaces; concepts of e-learning; 'Will we need schools in the future?').

Second, the students are into a dialectical exchange and some knowledge-building, as long as they stick to the protocols of exchange: information, question and response.

Third, you keep the theory-practice relationship in their minds for the whole placement. They are encouraged to constantly reflect and collaborate (hopefully they won't come back and say they just made tea and surfed the internet!).

What can go wrong? Unfortunately, many things can, and in my experience this has been a barrier to people trying out this kind of work. The obvious sticking points are:

- students not using the facility, so you get a hardcore few who dominate
- students breaking protocols and using the facility to gossip about people they encounter on placement
- the teacher's anxiety leading her to dominate the forum with questions that go unanswered
- technical problems meaning students can't access the forum
- students who do not have computers feeling alienated.

You can avoid the last problem by writing to the employers and making it clear that students need access to the internet daily throughout the experience. Clearly, you need an intranet system that can be accessed externally with a user name and password. And you can avoid some of the others by making use of the forum (though not necessarily quality of postings) mandatory and assessing it: building into assessment criteria for the higher grades 'daily use of the e-seminar facility.'

But you cannot avoid all the problems. If you think about it, there are no greater risks or pedagogic dilemmas here than are present in every 'traditional' lesson you teach (disengaged students, absence, breaking ground rules, lack of confidence and so on). Often, I think teachers' reluctance to experiment with unusual methods including technology is predicated on a misrepresentation of how well things normally work!

Keeping it real

It is important to take a 'reality check' when exploring institutional and social issues that arise from digital technologies. You might want to explore notions of hyper-reality and virtual worlds but be careful to constrain 'future claims' sensitively. At the time of writing, 12.7 per cent of the world are described as internet users, so clearly we need to remind our students that we are dealing with developed world phenomena. Indeed, all ideas about the postmodern condition should be placed in this context (I am sure there are still some grand narratives worth fighting for in Africa and Afghanistan). There are a set of key celebratory claims made regularly about the internet in social and political terms, and here there are some obvious links with other subjects such as Sociology and Citizenship, and some opportunities for Key Skills coverage. These are to do with:

- democracy (in terms of access to publishing, and the rise of blogging)
- interactivity (this is often articulated as a form of empowerment, access or as an example of the amplification of the ordinary citizen's voice)
- erosion of boundaries (the reduction of limits in terms of time and space, within a larger positive discourse about globalization)
- convergence (the coming together of telecommunications, mass media and information technology).

The internet is best understood in Media Studies as a 'nexus' for a range of digital media, which are now made and consumed in new ways. This change in production and consumption is at the heart of our interest, and it separates Media Studies from Sociology, in particular. In audience terms, the vast increase in participation in the media (on whatever terms we define participation) is revolutionary in the sense that it is far greater and quicker than any previous technology. Certainly, most of our students use the internet and a great number (and more by the time of publication) will have built a website. This last point calls for a change in our teaching practices. With the increasing use of digital film, we may very soon be teaching Film Studies to large groups of film-makers, a profound shift in learning and teaching dynamics: Who is the expert?

A still from The Golden Sphere, a film made by Media student David Nock, which can be viewed through broadband at www.thegoldensphere.org

Returning to our 'reality check' statistic, we should be working with students on the agreement that 'global' means developed. Within this definition, students should consider the degree of internet use in the UK compared to other countries and the demographics of this use. The increasing adoption of broadband is a research topic in itself, for instance. The key issue is constantly to relate these knowledge building and research areas to questions about media production and consumption as well as socio-cultural questions. While the claims made for the internet's transformative potential are great, the use of online strategy by the mass media might be considered predictable and mundane in many cases, in the sense that the internet is a vast commercial tool, rather than an empowering vehicle for freedom.

Student research

Let's consider a few examples of specific technologies that students on any Media course might get into. Questions to ask about digital television include consumer use of interactive features and their views on the value of this; the nature of television web access (at present a 'walled garden' rather than a genuine opportunity for unlimited surfing); and huge questions about institutions, the future of the BBC and debates over choice and 'quality'. I have successfully used a Peter Bazalgette (of Endemol) lecture on video in which he challenges some assumptions about quality and range of programming and makes a spirited case for *Big Brother* as inclusive democracy in action (for example, the nation has voted for a gay male and a transsexual). His *Billion Dollar Game* (2005) includes some nice, provocative and spirited defences for this contested example of popular culture, too. You will be able to find interesting and accessible examples of the case for subscription TV and I have found it easier to provide examples of this side and then discuss the alternatives (public service ethos, taxation, the traditional Reith argument) than the other way around. My view is that if you start with inform, educate and entertain, and end up looking at *I'm a Celebrity. . .* later, you have set up a straw man. While I would not want to undermine the political importance of asking the big questions about public service broadcasting, I think there are more interesting ways of approaching these issues, starting with audience views and working back.

Class strategy – Thinking hats

This strategy is a very crude appropriation of the work of Edward de Bono (2000), which works well if you want to make visible the difference between description, analysis, critique and opinion. It is certainly worth doing this fairly early on, because doubtless you will return to these terms often when giving students feedback on their work, and it is wrong to assume that these nuances (for example between describing an argument rather than factual material) are clear for students.

In de Bono's model, the hats work as follows:

- the White Hat: information only
- the Black Hat: judgement/devil's advocate

- the Green Hat: creativity, new ideas
- the Red Hat: feelings, hunches and intuition
- the Yellow Hat: brightness and optimism
- the Blue Hat: managing the thinking process.

I prefer to switch the colours in order to move away from connotations of black/white. Regardless, taking the subject matter of digital television, choice and quality, I suggest the following use of the 'thinking hats' idea.

First, give a presentation on the history and political context of deregulation. This is essential, as we cannot expect students to have an understanding of the debate without some factual background.

Next, provide resources that illustrate the arguments in a popular, accessible way. Germaine Greer's ambiguous relationship with reality TV is one good example, and you will easily find a variety of examples of the 'dumbing down' thesis in the broadsheet press. For the counter-argument, I suggest using Peter Bazalgette's (2005) compelling rhetoric about choice and quality in the digital world and the various arguments for a post-licence TV world.

Then hold a fairly informal debate without a clear structure, in order to get raw opinion out into the open and recognize it as such.

When you are happy with students' working knowledge of the arguments, choose three programmes as examples (in consultation with the group) and take these as case study 'micros' through which you will explore the complexities of the issues.

Divide the class into six and give each student a hat colour (if you can actually provide headgear it works better, of course). Chair a debate, structured so that discussion moves from raw information, through argument, counter-argument and opinion through eventually to new ideas being generated.

Crucially, the students have two tasks here. First, they must reflect on the content of the discussion to upgrade their understanding and critical thinking skills, but equally they need to report on the nature of the thinking that is articulated, so they develop a keener sense of how idea-generation is formed dialectically.

The outcome of this unusual approach should be that students start to recognize the difference between information, argument, opinion and creative thinking. This is a clear, user-friendly translation of assessment criteria that you can refer to again and again in the future.

Digital film-making has made a big difference to the production process. Put simply, many films are now in circulation that would not have been previously. At the time of writing, the question of consumption is more difficult. Much will depend on the take-up of broadband in the home, and the increasing convergence of television and the internet. Film downloading often takes place in the relatively less comfortable space of the home computer, while the major film channels send blockbusters via cable or satellite into the luxurious space of the living-room TV. On the one hand, there is the 'democratising' impulse to consider, which will almost certainly include student film-makers in your classroom. Alongside this, there is the increasing use of digital production by 'big players' (for example, Michael Mann's use of the digital camera to capture a particular Los Angeles aesthetic in *Collateral*).

At the opposite end of the spectrum, the video-log (or 'v-log') offers anyone the cheap, easy option of uploading video images to a host website (just like adding images to a weblog), for about £5 per month. At the time of writing, there are a number of fledgling sites that students could use to set up vlogs, and many young people have made themselves the subject of home-made reality TV shows. (In my opinion the most fascinating is *The Carol and Steve Show*, where we get to see the Garfields washing their car.)

Music downloading, mentioned earlier in this chapter, offers the chance for students to consider the complexities of media consumption: does downloading constitute a major threat to the music industry as we know it, or is it a 'blip'? Remember the phrase 'Home Taping is Killing Music'? At the time of writing, CD burning (the digital equivalent of taping your mate's albums) is more of an issue in terms of copyright for the music industry than online downloading. Against this 'don't believe the hype' factor, we might set the opportunities for new bands to avoid the hassle of a deal with a label and use the internet for exposure to interested audiences. This factor might threaten record companies in the future.

There is an array of very interesting research into the use of computer games, much of which serves to dismantle myths about the antisocial and anti-literacy implications of this technology. Many students (and they are not exclusively male) have a great deal of knowledge about this area which it seems a waste not to tap into. Equally, the fact that gaming is the largest commercial market in contemporary mass media, alongside its resonance with debates about audience effects that you will want to deal with in the 'theory' parts of your course, make it (in my view) pretty mandatory as an area for study. Depending on resources and confidence, you may be teaching game design, in which case, as always, the theory and knowledge will develop through the creative practice, or you may link audience research with some promotional production work rather than design and programming itself. Either way, the obvious questions are to do with convergence, in particular with film. For example what kind of text is *The Matrix*? We might argue that Warner Brothers have actually constructed a commercial and technological matrix of products, which seamlessly converge. For the study of media institutions, the games market is increasingly dominated by multinational corporations such as Sony and Microsoft. Also, there are the social factors mentioned earlier, for which I suggest reference to James Paul Gee's work (2003) on computer games, and learning and literacy and research carried out by Caroline Pelletier and Diane Carr at the Institute of Education (see Carr *et al.*, 2005). These need to be considered alongside more 'popular' examples of moral panic from the print media in particular. It may seem like this last suggestion is departing into the more theoretical, social areas of Media Studies and away from considerations of technology itself. However, the research mentioned raised questions about the relationship between the technology, the game-player interface, cognition and learning that challenge many of the assumptions about social development and literacy that the 'anti-games' discourse elaborates.

Class strategy – 90-minute film-making

This lesson is a risk, but it usually works. You need a digital video camera and a firewire connection to an iMac computer or iBook (or the PC equivalents). Ideally, you need these in the same room. This lesson is useful for 'setting the scene' and establishing an approach to digital video production in your department which will be less about technical factors (as the new software does all that for you) and more about conventions, aesthetics and storytelling. Thus this lesson should give you confidence in the fact that (perhaps ironically) the digital technology actually means we can spend *less* time worrying about technology and more time on creativity.

The first stage is for your department to make a short film within a time limit, where you all act. Try to maintain a balance between making the students laugh and getting them to realise that even a bunch of old failures ('. . .those that can't. . .' and all that) like us can produce a half-decent film with music and titles, a readable narrative and some convincing generic conventions now that we can use digital kit. This movie is to be played after the students have had a go, rather than before.

The exercise is as follows:

1. Provide a script template for the opening 30 seconds, with titles, of a thriller. The script involves a group of characters who each arrive in turn at a destination (easy examples are waiting rooms of various kinds) to receive information that creates an enigma. This could be that they all have an appointment for the same time, and that none of the characters knows the reason for their being summoned. Or your students may come up with more interesting variations on this theme.
2. Limit the group to a maximum of five shots, and in the 90-minute time limit, they must plan, briefly rehearse, film the shots, capture the images in iMovie, edit the sequence with basic shot transitions, add titles (actors' names – usually these appear as the characters enter the scene), fade to black after the fifth shot for the film title and fade from black at the stare, out of the director's name (for example, a Ned Kendall film) into the first shot in the sequence. Finally, add suitable music over the film title.
3. At the end of the lesson, save the project and download it to DVD if necessary. Devote the whole of the next meeting with the group to a playback and critique. The outcome should be between five and ten 'don'ts' for the real thing. These tend to involve shaky hand-held camera, laughing when acting, poor lighting, poor sound and hasty scripting.

The benefit of this exercise in terms of the longer-term creative process is that the students will have confidence in the technology before they start — after all, if they can do this in 90 minutes, what can they achieve in three months?

Equally, if you show them the staff's efforts ('. . .and here is one we made earlier'), you will create a collaborative ethos and gain respect in the sense that you are prepared to set yourself up for ridicule and also that you can create something pretty good using the same processes. And most important, students should recall the mistakes they made in this safe, experimental context when they are under the pressures of deadlines on external location film-making. The objective of the exercise is to learn from mistakes.

Some tips on resources

Systems

While it would not be prudent to offer a long list of tips in terms of equipment (as these would soon be out of date), it is worthwhile covering a few strategic suggestions. Regardless of which course or specification is in question, the OCR Media email forum regularly hosts lengthy discussion threads on the merits of various specific types of hardware and software, which can be accessed through the archive facility. One such debate is around the relative merits of PCs and Macintosh computers. Generally speaking, one can avoid the specificities of these platforms and operating systems by discussing software, which tends to be available for either system. However, one exception which I think cannot be neglected is iMovie. The reason for this is that iMovie has transformed my experience of video production from one of nervous enthusiasm to fairly confident second-nature. This does not mean my skills have improved, or that I am considering a career in film-making. Instead, it simply means that filming and editing for me now is as easy a resource as using PowerPoint, downloading a PDF file or sending an email. Teachers with industry background teaching on National Diploma courses may prefer working with software like Final Cut Pro or Adobe Premier, as these are industry standard at present, but even vocational students will benefit from the basic expertise afforded by iMovie.

iMovie comes free with eMacs or Mac G4 machines, and as a result the connection between the camera and the software is built in to the logic of the machine. The software is incredibly straightforward, and the all-important Firewire connection is pretty robust. The Mac itself will have enough storage space for several groups to store their work in progress (the 'project') at the same time. A crucial tip is to buy cameras with a DV-in facility, as this means the work can easily be recorded back on to digital video tape once completed, freeing up memory from the machines while you transfer the final images to DVD from the tapes, which can then be used over again.

There are pros and cons of networked computer systems over stand-alone machines. I have had experience of both and found that the server option (where every student has a user area where there work is stored and password protected) are better for ease of access (it doesn't matter which machine you work on) but can cause tremendous problems if the server is vulnerable (whole days lost when nobody can access their work, which awarding bodies are understandably less than sympathetic to when the deadline comes around). Having a number of computers (enough for a student-console ratio of 1:2 in any one session), each with a scanner and a zip drive (alternatively, using high spec. memory sticks gives you the same portability) connected to a printer is a good compromise, but is clearly more expensive in terms of peripherals.

One of the most positive shifts for the Media teacher in recent years has been to do with the liberation of space. Whereas previously, Media departments needed to manage rooms with names like 'edit suite' and 'radio studio', a single computer can now act as both of those, with a darkroom as well. Managing students' use of these machines (ensuring the use of zip or memory stick storage, sensible file use and using high spec. headphones when editing) allows you to use open-access areas where students can progress with a range of editing activities, preferably with a technician/instructor available for more complex tasks. If managed well, this makes the awful edit suite bottleneck close to deadlines a thing of the past.

Audio

Straightforward audio editing is made possible, at the time of writing, by software such as Cool Edit Pro, Soundforge, Cubase or Sound Edit. Connecting a minidisk player to the computer and downloading sound enables the user then to edit the sound working in layers in turn. Again, like with video editing where the ease of technical use allows for greater attention to visual language and narrative, so with audio 'the theory of sound' can be foregrounded now that the student is liberated from the problem of reconnecting endless leads into the mixer.

Class strategy – The 'no homework incentive'

Sometimes, not having to do something may be more exciting for a teenager than an active outcome. Here is one example.

This lesson on game design does not involve any technology. However, it works only if students have had some experience of playing games in lessons, so that the whole class has a working knowledge of gaming, ease of use, complexity of problem solving, game narratives and graphics. This must not be restricted to the hardcore gamers in the group. Equally, if you are using this approach within a more technically focused course (perhaps on a Games Development or Narrative in Games unit) then you could 'step up' the technical elements and move from planning to actual origination.

The idea is simple – students form groups and are given a particular games genre to work in, and within a time limit they 'idea shower' and make notes on the following points:

- the narrative (depending on the group, you will provide more or less structure and content for them at this point)
- character identification – who are the player(s)?

The term 'avatar' describes the player's representation in the verisimilitude of the game. Here, students might think about the degree of control or agency the player will have, whether or not the avatar will evolve or develop during the game, and the nature of the journey in terms of any history or extra-textual cultural mythology.

And on:

- the rule-based system the game will operate within (again, this could be very basic or you could get into some basic programming ideas) and the nature of competition (player to player, player to machine).

Here students will consider the nature of machine-player dialogue, and how to get the right balance between frustration and achievement for the player (an interesting psycho-social area in itself).

And, finally, on:

- the sub-generic elements, intertextual meanings and primary audience for the game.

Here it is useful to group the gamers with the non-initiated, but intertextuality might well be to do with film, music or television as opposed to other games, so a general contemporary media knowledge will suffice.

By using this set of criteria, you are spanning traditional modes of studying Media through concepts such as genre, narrative and audience, as well as more postmodern thinking in terms of intertextual references and identity-shifting. Equally, you are in a position to focus more or less on programming and game design in a technical sense (but I don't want to make assumptions and stipulate by age or course, as students always surprise us in terms of their technical competence). Representation in its wider sense is deliberately neglected at this point to avoid confusion. Students are in game designer role here. They can be in social/analytical mode later.

A whole lesson and some directed time/homework should be given to this exercise so that students are confident when they come to present their idea in the form of a pitch (you can use jigsawing, presentation or web-posting for this exercise but it must be peer-peer rather than to the teacher).

After the presentations, a secret ballot should take place where students have to vote for another group's idea. The winning group's game idea is then adopted by the whole class, and you set a homework task in which different groups of students take different elements of the idea to the next level, so they can come together in the next meeting and cross-reference these extended ideas.

The group whose original pitch was successful are removed from this equation – no homework. I have found it helps to set up this reward at the start of the exercise. While students tend to be enthused by this task once it develops, it does help to get them started if they have this extrinsic negative in sights!

Authoring

Web design and multimedia production can be easily picked up with software such as (again, at the time of writing) Dreamweaver and Macromedia Director, in connection with desk-top publishing resources such as Photoshop, Quark Express or Pagemaker and video-editing software as mentioned above. As we head further towards an 'invisibility paradigm' the user-end will become ever more obvious and students will need less understanding of HTML. Assuming the institution has a broadband connection and an intranet, the relationship between simulated and 'live' work in this area will be of concern to senior management. My view is that persuading the powers that be to allow students' websites to 'go live' is a battle worth fighting. The reason is that the interactive elements of websites cannot easily be reproduced artificially, and experience shows that the most effective assessment and evaluation of site design is through real audience interaction, which is fundamentally different in nature to a film or television programme. So, while it is possible for a teacher or group of students to evaluate a piece of video without the need for an actual broadcast, the same is not strictly true of websites.

Class strategy – Must/should/could

Strangely, there is a tendency for all the good differentiation practice that is evident in analytical Media learning to be forgotten in the domain of production work. So while a student deconstructing a website might be given a range of tasks to choose from or a degree of expectation in outcome relative to their ability or progress, students working on creative outcomes tend to be given a 'one size fits all' experience.

This strategy offers a simple approach to this issue, by dividing a web design exercise related to music downloading into three elements: a mandatory level (the must), a suggested task (the should – that most students will manage) and an optional, higher level activity (the could – for the most able).

The task is to design, in small groups, an interactive website that will harness the liberating potential of both the internet and peer to peer music sharing (as opposed to the commercial use of the internet for copyright music distribution). The type of software used is left open, but the demands of the task are differentiated as follows:

You *must*:

- develop an original design for a website. This site must offer the user the opportunity to download and upload music; be free from commercial imperatives and advertising; and must break even financially. The homepage and three linked pages must be produced, including the pages from which uploading and downloading would be available.

You *should*:

- develop one interactive element (for example, a discussion forum) and provide hyperlinks to other sites.

You *could*:

- develop the uploading and downloading facility for real 'live' use.

While Media Studies is distinct from IT pedagogically, in so much as IT is used in Media as a tool for projects designed to attract mass media audiences in particular, sometimes it is essential to borrow practice from the 'sister' subject. Students will have little chance of producing a credible website if there is no input from expert web-builders. Just as one would naturally talk to Art teachers about an animation project, so you should approach the IT people in your institution about principles of designing internet materials.

Steve Krug (2000) suggests, in his useful 'common sense' guidance on ensuring web usability, that there are four questions users ask when stumbling across new territory on the internet. They ask what the site is, what the designers have to offer, what the user can do there and why they should be there and not somewhere else. I suggest using Krug's questions as a mantra throughout a web-building project as they are more fundamental than discussions about frames, cascading and HTML. Krug's last point, about luring the user to linger rather than escape or link to elsewhere, connects us to Gauntlett's (2004) thesis on internet disappointment. In the second edition of Gauntlett's seminal *Web Studies*, he shares his sadness that the radical ability for the internet to be an open tapestry, in which site designers would resist the temptation to build walls to keep the user within their domain, has been undermined by the 'walled garden' approach in which sites only offer internal links, apart from the obligatory links page. Gauntlett refers to the inventor of the world wide web (and he reminds us that www and the internet are not the same thing, of course), Tim Berners-Lee, who hoped that the web would be energised by collaboration, and this spirit would allow users to browse and then edit and ultimately rewrite content. Clearly, either something in human nature or the commercialisation of the web has obstructed this Utopia. Perhaps we might return to the Masterman (1985) idea that students should produce media products which challenge the dominant ideology and create projects for students to experiment with this collaborative ethos?

Animation

Animation is usually very popular with students and yet sadly, it is an under-developed area of Media learning. Colleges where Media is housed with Art and Design rather than English may be better situated for such work, but again, this is an area where software has allowed for more confident beginner play. Clearly, there is a time factor in terms of image origination (twenty-four frames per second!), but as always, digital technology provides a few short cuts that may offend the purist, but get the job done in terms of creativity. Macromedia Flash and Adobe After Effects are ideal for linking with the kinds of video editing software mentioned before (in particular, Adobe's two packages work very well together). In some cases, students can only work in two dimensions with computer-animation, and compared to the other technologies we have discussed, these are more complicated operations. However, the modification process and the opportunity to import images from a variety of sources are advantages of the non-linear experience.

Class strategy – Cross-department teaching

This idea assumes it is possible to persuade an Art teacher to take your students through an animation project. The strategy relates to how you manage the relationship, brief, support, outcomes and assessment. Here are three alternative approaches.

1. Meet with the Art teacher before the conception of the project. Be very clear about the outcomes in terms of the assessment criteria, which will usually differ from Art in that the institutional, commercial and mass media audience contexts will be equal (for better or worse) in value to originality, development of ideas and realization in artistic terms. A key shift may be around the issue of derivative work. If a Media student works within generic conventions at the expense of 'originality', there is no special concern or attention paid to this. Once this is clear, and you have worked together on the brief, your role is to set up the project and be available throughout the process for content guidance, as opposed to aesthetic or technical input.

2. If you need more direct input to the process, but lack the technical confidence to teach animation, organize a scheme of work so that you take the first two sessions, to introduce animation as a media form, analyse real animations and adopt a critical approach with students, and introduce the brief and the mass media context. Then your Art colleague can take the next three or four sessions to take the students through the animation software. Following that, you then return for the remainder of the course to take them through the implementation of their learned techniques in terms of the media-related brief.

3. You arrange some staff development whereby you are 'trained' by your Art colleague in animation, in order for you to teach the unit yourself.

Each of these approaches has merits. The first model (more common practice in HE and on vocational courses) sends some nice messages to students about collaboration, cross-discipline work and the importance of aesthetics in Media, perhaps at the risk of the project departing into other domains which might be interesting in practice but cause some anxiety for the Media department when it comes to assessment.

The second approach liberates you from the technical aspects, while allowing you to give students more contact and support throughout the process (to 'keep it Media', I suppose), but you run the risk of having to fetch the Art teacher every time things get tricky towards the end of the project.

The third model is ideal in terms of your own confidence, credibility and 'control' of the project, but it is time-consuming and, of course, goes against the grain of collaboration and reinforces academic boundaries.

Games

Games design is a developing area in Media Studies and, hopefully, at the time of publication there will be more evidence of it 'on the ground'. At the time of writing, there are some wonderful opportunities on vocational Media courses to work in the province, not only of design but also of narrative, identity-play and representation. In my view, here is yet another example of the enhanced 'theorization' of learning which, despite appearances to the contrary, is more evident on National Diploma courses than on A Level, where so far very few institutions have taken up the chance to teach about computer games instead of film and TV.

The OCR Media teachers' email community recently had a long, detailed and at times passionate debate about the distinction between theory and practice. One of the questions raised was to do with 'active' theory, but (perhaps due to the domination of the list by A Level teachers) there was little interest in looking at the nature of theory in vocational settings, as contributors preferred to distinguish between the 'theoretical' and 'practical' elements of the A Level courses they teach on. I think it is worth having a look at a particular vocational example to raise some important issues in this area.

The Level 3 Edexcel Unit on Games Design features assessment criteria that includes: 'write a fully justified analysis of the features that are considered to make a successful game', while another unit on Digital Communication requires learners to: 'demonstrate sophisticated understanding of differences between digital and non-digital communication critically evaluating conventions and with fully justified analysis of examples'. In a decade of Media teaching, I have yet to encounter an argument to convince me that this kind of work is not critical or theoretical. During my research degree, where I focused on assessment, subject identity and discourses about academic and vocational Media learning, I gathered data from teachers, examiners and 'key players' in the development of 'Subject Media' (the official, exam board determined version of the subject) and found little in the way of consensus or credible definitions in this area (McDougall, 2004a). And yet, there still exists a dominant myth that one type of learning is critical and the other is practical. My hope is that the necessity of engaging with digital production in order to be theoretical in new ways will eventually erode these needless boundaries, which are little more, in my view, than renegotiated versions of age-old social class divisions.

Class strategy – Radio soap

Digital audio has revolutionised editing radio far more even than non-linear editing has done for video. The old 'chalk and razor blade' techniques seem even more prehistoric now than vinyl and Betamax.

This idea can be used in order to teach about technology (the practice of editing in this way) and about genre, realism, representation and audience. In particular, comparison of radio to TV soap takes you into deeper areas about the nature of realism and how the lack of visuals places greater emphasis on representation (and perhaps stereotyping) through pitch, accent and dialect.

The brief is to create and produce the opening five minutes of a new radio soap which will be broadcast on a digital radio channel only (taking you into the study of institutions, commercial practice and consumption).

The management of this project involves some introductory teaching and research into digital radio, along with study of soap opera, which is dealt with in Chapter Seven. Alongside this, students need tuition (and self-discovery) on digital audio software. Taking the example of Cool Edit, the key principle to communicate is that the quality of the final product rests on the quality of the recording and the acting. The ease of use provided by Cool Edit makes the manipulation stage infinitely more pleasurable but it cannot compensate for mistakes in the script or its realisation.

Key critical questions for students to consider in terms of technology are:
- Who is using digital radio?
- How must this digital soap be produced and marketed to reach this existing audience?
- How might this soap serve to extend the digital radio audience (there are parallels here with BBC4 and E4 convincing more people than sport and film enthusiasts to 'go digital' in their television consumption)?
- How does digital audio editing shift the conventions of radio?
- How is this soap defined by its status as a product of either local, community or national/networked digital radio?

Further technical opportunities are as follows:
- Broadcast the finished product on the school/college station.
- Situate the radio soap in terms of convergence – what platforms will be available for access to the programme (in particular, internet radio)?

- Produce a review of the programme that focuses more on the nature of the product as a digital-only soap.
- Develop interactive elements for the soap (could listeners shape the narrative through interacting via the programme's website or even by text?).

Doing technologies

This chapter has linked teaching about technology with teaching through technology, and as such I hope it has offered a view of Media education that resists the separation of theory from practice. Whatever label or level the course you are teaching, your students need to engage with a set of key questions about digital technologies that can best be understood through experience. These questions involve the social and historical contexts of technologies and their emergence, and the spread of existing technologies into new domains. In addition, the implications of convergence are of great importance to any study of contemporary media. Perhaps most important in terms of audience and the key conceptual framework of media learning, students need to engage with questions about access to media and whether digital forms increase this. Put simply, whether students are pursuing a course in Moving Image Production, or considering a media text within Key Stage 3 English, they need to approach technologies in terms of the difference they make to production and consumption, along these lines:

- What can people do now that they couldn't before?
- Who is using technology and who isn't?
- Who benefits, and how?
- What are the wider social implications?

Taking one example, the mobile phone as the potential 'hub' for a host of media services, the first question can be addressed in terms of portability, convergence, ease of use and access. Wider demographic research would easily lead to some interesting debates about the range of markets for different types of mobile phone. The 'benefits' question is wide ranging, from considering the parents of a female teenager who might feel more secure in the knowledge that she can phone from outside a nightclub if she can't get a taxi, through to the deals made by mobile phone companies with cinemas, for example, and from debates around convergence, downloading and piracy to possibilities for text-voting. Wider social implications take us into questions about democracy, security and surveillance, globalization, citizenship and health. Contemporary media learning has technology at its core, not as a mere practical element or as a topic area, but as the nexus of the subject's conceptual *raison d'etre*.

Key to Gauntlett's premise (in which he savages traditional Media Studies for its obsession with outdated cultural forms) is the centrality of the web to everyday life and culture (2004). But he shares with all the sensible theoretical commentators in this area the view that the interesting thing about the internet is the creation of meaning through websites and online communication forms. This provides us with a simple yet fundamental starting point – if you are teaching *about* the internet, this is no different to teaching *about* television. While you may deal with the development of television as a technology to some extent, it is more likely that you are engaged in discussion with students about programmes and how they make meaning as cultural forms, or more importantly, how viewers make meaning. The same logic must be adopted for 'Web Studies'. It is the social and cultural 'meaning-making' on the web that interests us, rather than the technology itself. This is why, in my view, the teachers that voice anxiety or intellectual doubts about the expansion of technologies as a teaching topic in Media education get it wrong – the questions we are asking our students to address in this area are at least as critical as the ones we pose when dealing with texts or debates about media in society. In fact, it is no longer possible to engage with either texts or more macro areas of study without foregrounding the 'digital meaning-making' now in abundance. Gauntlett's 'call to arms' is founded on a set of principles for further study that involve a socio-cultural 'take' on analysing the web. These principles are that there is online self-expression to consider (Gauntlett's body of work relates often to the construction of identities) along with social, community-building and the tension between the democractic potential of the web and the response to threat by big business. But how do we get into these areas with students?

Gauntlett, it seems, shares the view I am presenting here that you have to 'do it yourself':

'Unless you want to be a very detached critic who argues that all new media developments are really bad and that we're all doomed, in which case you won't really understand the web very well anyway, then you'll need to experience the agony and ecstasy of building and promoting your own website.' (2004: 13)

A recurrent theme throughout this book is my desire to offer a kind of updating to Masterman's 1980s work but at the same time to add a shift of emphasis. I think the most obvious tangent is in the area of production work and its value.

'Practical activity does not, in itself, constitute media education. In particular, the commonly expressed belief that, through practical work, students will *automatically* acquire critical abilities and begin to de-mystify the media needs to be challenged. Rather, the link between practical work and analytical activities needs to be consciously forged by the teacher. It must be worked for. It cannot be assumed.' (Masterman, 1985:26)

The reason for responding to this assertion here, rather than in the chapters on production, is that I believe digital technology has enabled something of a 'third way' between these two positions. This position moves away from either seeing practical work as a vehicle for theoretical reflection and analysis (for example a news bulletin project to put news values, editorial agendas and manufactured news for target audiences into practice) or vice versa (learning how radio producers operate and then having a go yourself). Instead, students are the people charged with 'forging the link' by developing their own theoretical models with which to investigate their own 'technological constructedness.' Working in online domains, downloading and producing music electronically, playing and designing games, experimenting with future-gazing for digital TV content guides, students are not in the traditional role of theory-receipt, but nor are they merely imitating conventions as described to them by teachers. Crucially, I think Masterman presents theory as political (critical is the term he preferred, but this is often articulated in terms of being informed and sensitive to ideology) and production as apolitical in itself (becoming purposeful only when clearly related to analysis). Offering a profoundly visible application of 'theory' to considerations of technology, Lunenfeld (2000) suggests a reclaiming of idea (or ideal) of the dialectic through a thesis – antithesis dialogue between techno-sceptics (articulating concerns about the internet, for example) and 'network idealists' (celebrating the democratic and communicative potential of the web). While the kinds of theory circulated by Hegel (1996) and Habermas (1985) (on the dialectic and the ideal of communicative consensus) may be alienating and far removed from students' technological life worlds, I do think this is a great example of us finding an opportunity for some pretty heavy critical theory in the unlikeliest of places. As such, the 'digital dialectic' provides a convincing riposte to those who lament the 'detheorizing' of Media Studies and cite the increasing attention to technology and production as an example of such.

Case Study – Children's Media Group

Following web links from research projects at the Institute of Education's Center for the Study of Children, Youth and Media, I stumbled upon the Children's Media Project's site. This project runs in New York State and involves young people in a range of activities, from health education to a 'digital café', There is nothing unique about the center and there are many similar projects in the UK. But the work produced by the participants, accessed by myself through the website, struck me as being profoundly 'critical', and yet the starting point for it was clearly access to digital technology. For example, a video stream called 'What?' by Eldine Whitling offers 'a personal montage of rapping, music reviews, and hanging out, designed to address issues of representation and identity while promoting girls access to and achievement in the field of media technology'. The striking thing about this text is that there is no evidence that a teacher worked hard to forge clear links between Eldine's use of technology and theoretical concepts. But there is little doubt that the creator herself was able to negotiate a space in which she could use new technologies to express some political ideas about gender. If we can avoid patronising students by assuming that we need to 'equip' them with models of being critical that come from a world they don't inhabit (usually our own academic life worlds), we might find that they 'get critical' in ways that might teach us something.

Further reading

Bates, S., 2003: 'You and Your Media: New Media Technologies and Audience Consumption' in *Media Magazine,* 6, London: English and Media Centre.

Bazalgette, P., 2005, *Billion Dollar Game: How three men risked it all and changed the face of television.* London: Time Warner.
Rather self-congratulatory series of grand claims, but essential for a balanced debate about reality TV, whatever your take on it.

Bennett, J., 2003, 'How to create a Simple Website' in *Media Magazine,* 3, London: English and Media Centre.

Berners-Lee, T., 1999, *Weaving the Web: The Past, Present and Future of the World Wide Web,* Orion, London.
The inventor of the web outlines his democractic vision of its potential.

Carr, D., Buckingham, D. and Burn, D., 2005, *Computer Games: Text, Narrative and Play,* London: Polity.
Essential contemporary analysis from the Institute of Education.

de Bono, E., 2000, *Six Thinking Hats,* London: Penguin.
A nice approach for making the distinction between description, opinion, analysis and creative thinking clear and visible for students.

The Children's Media Project can be found at: http://www.childrensmediaproject.org/

Fraser, P., and Oram, B., 2003, *Teaching Digital Video Production,* London: BFI.
Excellent resource for nervous teachers!

Feldman, T., 1997, *Introduction to Digital Media,* London: Routledge.

Fraser, P., 2001, *Teaching Music Video,* London: BFI.

Gauntlett, D., 2004, *Web Studies: Rewiring Media Studies for the Digital Age,* London: Arnold.
A set of theoretical perspectives on the internet, along with a challenge to Media teachers to reconfigure the subject as Web Studies.

Gee, J., 2003, *What Video Games Have to Teach Us About Learning and Literacy,* New York: Palgrave MacMillan.
Gee's account is controversial but offers a very interesting challenge to assumptions about computer games, social development, cognition and learning.

In the picture magazine, 2001, 41, Digital Media Technology themed issue.

Johnson, S., 1997, *Interface Culture: How Technology Transforms the Way We Create and Communicate,* San Francisco: Basic Books.

Joseph, A., 2004, 'Identity Crisis: How to Create Your Own Digital Identity', in *Media Magazine,* 8, London: English and Media Centre.
A practical approach to exploring virtual worlds.

Krug, S., 2000, *Don't Make Me Think! A Common Sense Approach to Web Usability,* New York: New Riders.
Excellent for supporting students with web design projects.

Lunenfeld, P., 2000, *The Digital Dialectic,* Massachusetts: MIT Press.
A range of academic perspectives on new media, technologies and new cultural forms.

Luhrs, G., 2002, 'Why Convergence Matters' in *Media Magazine,* 1, London: English and Media Centre.
Student-friendly introduction to convergence.

Luhrs, G., 2002, 'New Media Technologies: a Glossary' in *Media Magazine*, 2, London: English and Media Centre.

Luhrs, G., 2005, 'The Future Will be Blogged' in *Media Magazine*, 12, London: English and Media Centre.

Meigs, T., 2003, *Ultimate Game Design: Building Game Worlds*, Emeryville: Osborne McGraw-Hill.

Musburger, R., and Kindem, G., 2004, *Introduction to Media Production: The Path to Digital Media Production*, Oxford: Focal Press.

Nock, D., 2004, 'Confessions of a B-Movie Writer' in *Media Magazine*, 8, London: English and Media Centre.
David is an example of a media student who is also a film-maker, and his account of this experience in *Media Magazine* is well worth a read.

Priestman, C., 2001, *Web Radio*, Oxford: Focal Press.

Readman, M., 2001, *Teaching Scriptwriting, Screenplays and Storyboards for Film and TV Production*, London: BFI.

Spraggon, L., 2004, *Into Animation*, London: BFI Education.
Practical guide to animation as a practical work activity across the curriculum, including a CD Rom and video compilation.

Tapscott, D., 1998, *Growing Up Digital: The Rise of the Net Generation*, New York: McGraw Hill.
A celebration of the digital generation, which offers a refreshing optimistic riposte to the morally panicked!

Taylor, P., 1999, *Hackers: Crime in the Digital Sublime*, London: Routledge.
Interesting insight into an area students might easily get into to consider 'pros and cons' of new digital forms.

Walker, C., 2004: 'Are MP3s Killing the Music Business?, Birmingham: Unpublished undergraduate dissertation, Coventry University.

Winter, G., 2005, 'Future Media Trends and Audiences', London: presentation to *The Guardian/Media Magazine* 'Changing Media' conference.

Zimmerman, E., and Salen, K., 2003, *Rules of Play: Game Design Fundamentals*, Massachusetts: MIT Press.

Please note that, due to the content of this chapter, inevitably there will be more contemporary resources at your disposal than these at the time you are using this book.

See also the 'Top 40 Websites' section.

chapter five

Industries

. . . .

'If students are to get real understanding of how media institutions work, they need to grapple with concepts of ownership and control and the often mysterious ways in which practices develop within media organisations of all kinds.'
(Stafford, 2003: 2)

Class strategy – Eye-opener quiz

Ironically, given that this book intends to foster an approach to teaching centred on inclusive, confidence-building practice, this quiz is designed to produce poor results. In this way, it will open your students' eyes to how little we tend to know as consumers about the economics of the media we depend on in our everyday lives. I would suggest students compete in teams for a prize, or you could pose the questions in the style of 'Millionaire', and have teams take it in turns to see how much they can collect:

1. List five media industries and one leading company in each one.
2. Name two independent music labels.
3. Name three organizations that own British newspapers.
4. Who owns the BBC?
5. What is Ofcom?
6. Who owns Channel 5?
7. Who owns your regional ITV channel?
8. Who responds to viewers' complaints about adverts?
9. Which is the biggest film industry in the world?
10. Which media company do you pay the most money to?

Introduction

There are a number of different starting points for how we enable Media learning about media industries in these times. The 'classic' model is concerned with raising political awareness, in essence. Despite this book's spirit being to do with learners reflecting on their own pleasures, creative potential and situatedness as consumers, more than transmitting knowledge and ideas for regurgitation, this is an area where it would be very difficult to argue against some 'telling and finding out'. However, as always, the devil is in the detail of the process. So while we *do* want students to discover some important truths about who owns what, we need to avoid telling them how to feel about it. A deficit model of Media learning (which is fairly common) is one in which students write heartfelt essays about the evils of Murdoch while enjoying Sky and *The Sun*. We might wish students would read *The Guardian*, but that has nothing to do with what we do for a living. So I want to argue that students 'waking up' to the problems of cultural imperialism may well be a very happy outcome of our work with them, but it should never be the objective.

If this position seems to be a 'dumbed down' or depoliticized model, let me counter that by suggesting that it is never patronizing or insulting. I have never thought of Media Studies teaching as a political pursuit or any kind of emancipatory project. Rather, I am fortunate to have had the opportunity to be paid to discuss popular texts and their contexts with young people. One such context is institutional, so it has been part of my vocation to facilitate discussion about, say, the major Hollywood studios and their control of the film industry through vertical integration. But if a student arrives at the conclusion (as they often have) that the reason why people in the Black Country see *Gladiator* in their droves but either reject or don't know about *Anita and Me* is simply that the consumer experience is more enjoyable within the Hollywood blockbuster paradigm, then it doesn't mean I haven't done my job. Indeed, I would be more concerned if a student regurgitated my own views about cinema and cultural identity but did not share them.

So, let me suggest a set of principles for Media learning about institutions.

1. Students need to know the facts about who owns what and how the patterns of ownership have changed, and these must be accurate and contemporary (which is why it is dangerous to use prepared case study resources). I will offer a set of case studies in this chapter. I hope they are helpful, but you will have to update them, especially given the determining nature of digital technology when it comes to ownership.

2. Regardless of the kind of course you are teaching, students should find out about employment in media sectors, how it is changing and what it is like to work within legislative frameworks. Again, let us smash open another myth about theory and practice, by asking who is better equipped to answer an exam question on broadcasting in the UK in the era of deregulation. Is it the A Level student being taught this topic for about fifteen hours in total, or the National Diploma student producing media products every day for two years within a vocational context that requires him to work within contemporary media law? Even if he has a 'kinaesthetic' learner preference, I would guess he might be more tuned in to the specifics of the regulatory frameworks. So I would champion an approach that is more vocational, and that ought to include visiting speakers from industry, if possible.

3. Once equipped with the knowledge in a simple 'white hat' sense, students need to know their way around the debates. So, the obvious questions are to do with winners and losers.

What is at stake in battles for the licence fee? How can the tabloid press sidestep press complaints and who thinks this matters? Why is there concern over the reporting of the US presence in Afghanistan? Did Michael Moore manipulate his relations with Disney to sell his film? And will *Metro* really undermine community values by threatening the existence of the local paper? The broader issues that you can get to from this 'micro' work are to do with globalization, fragmentation of audience, symbiosis and, again, technology.

What we are doing here is trying to give students an informed position so that when they write and talk about these issues they are doing more than we all do when talking in the pub about politics. That, for me, is the acid test – is this the work of a Media student? Is it informed and accurate? This is far more important than a vague notion of whether it is 'critical', or whether or not I agree with the politics.

So we can establish a triangular relationship between up-to-date facts (who owns what, what has changed, what are the regulations?), the impact of such facts on working practices (the process, ethics and agendas of those making the media) and arguments about the social implications of the changing scene. Additionally, I would advocate maintaining a close link between the study of institutions, the creative process and the analysis of texts. Students are often most disengaged from institutions work when it is divorced from text-work, and clearly, neither deconstruction of meaning or understanding of how ownership impacts on meaning can exist independently of the other.

I would not necessarily advocate an approach (which I have taken myself) that includes a brief potted history of British politics up to New Labour, so that students understand the terms left wing and right wing. If these terms have such little currency that they need explaining, what is the point of using them? Terms we do need to discuss include democracy, access, impartiality and power, but these are relevant and heartfelt for Media learners. Michael Moore, Mark Thomas, John Harris and others all manage to communicate political ideas without alienating their audiences by deriding their lack of traditional political knowledge and the best Media teaching does the same thing. The worst, on the other hand, sets up the mass media as an object of study along simply demarcated lines of left and right, good and bad, and then condemns its audience for its lack of engagement.

Convergence

We have discussed how the convergence of technologies changes the world for media consumers. Here, we turn our attention to the convergence of traditional media industries and in doing so we unravel an irony in the organization of Media education itself ('Subject Media', as I have called it). It is said that the media industries are no longer understandable in terms of the media they produce (e.g. television, film, telecommunications and computers) because they are operating across these boundaries (what kind of company is Sony, or News International?). If so, then why are specifications for Media education labelled either Moving Image Production, Games Design or Film Studies, or divided up along separate media lines (e.g. Print, Film, TV options)? Does this make sense anymore? Perhaps your students could be the judges?

Convergence is defined by Watson and Hill (2003) in this way:

'Convergence has operated at the technical and operational level and at the level of ownership and control. Just as individual items of hard and software have been centralized into one multi-media outfit, so media production has been centralized into fewer corporate hands, most of these transnational.' (2003: 65)

Because converging technologies have expanded the market horizons of previously confined big players who can now use the internet to market and distribute media, there has been an increase in concern about the imperialist ramifications of global media. On the other hand, the same technologies make resistance to corporate domination easier, and provide new audiences for artists and producers who lack the financial means for traditional distribution modes. Converging ownership is another story, however, and it is difficult to take a balanced view when the 'natural' law of the market seems to prevail and profit dominates media provision.

On the other hand, the pace of change catches us out. At the time of my involvement with two books for Media students, the most popular case study in this area was Time-Warner/AOL and we were all busy making grand claims for this model of global cross-media convergence, suggesting this was to be the new world order. A few years on and we are looking back at the collapse of that deal, aware that it was technology, the existence of which made the merger possible, which caught these giant corporations out. In short, the combination of a stock-market crash and AOL's failure to respond to the threat of broadband culminated in the downfall of a deal that looked globally invincible.

It is still the case that the top media companies globally are cross-media entities. Viacom owns several US TV channels and is also active in publishing. Comcast spans broadband cable and TV in the US, Bertelsman owns the MBG music brand, Channel 5 in the UK and a range of publishers, and Disney run their own channels, film production and distributors, including Miramax and several American magazines and newspapers. News Corporation, worth £25 billion, owns television channels across the world, a vast range of newspapers, film companies and publishers. Sony spans music, gaming, film and television. It is still obvious, looking at this list, how the merging of online gatekeeping and entertainment is the rainbow's end for the global media conglomerate. The terrain is one of cross-media empire building, cutting across not only media forms but also hard and software. In this sense we might see Sony as the ultimate media institution.

Media ownership, politics and us

The following six quotes provide accessible, recent examples of the difference media institutions make to our lives. Following each, I list some starting points for work with students using our triangular approach:

'Perhaps the biggest success story of the past year is *al-Jazeera*, the Qatar-based TV news channel, which attracted worldwide attention for its coverage of the war in Iraq. Footage of US prisoners of war and dead British servicemen proved controversial, but the channel was a worthy antidote to the gung-ho approach of some channels. *Al-Jazeera*'s worldwide audience rose to around 54 million.' (Bell and Alden, 2003: 204)

- Facts: case study on *al-Jazeera*, in comparison to CNN.
- Impact on production: news agendas, commercial imperatives of selling news.
- Debates: war coverage, accuracy, bias, ethics, embedded reporting and the relationship between military and media practices.

'Sport and the media have been inextricably linked since broadcasters became willing to invest their own money in a particular game, event, league or cup in the hope of making a large return. As media organisations seek to promote some sports rather than others, this association has inevitably led to some sports benefiting, while others have been marginalised and have therefore struggled.' (Bates, 2005: 50)

- Facts: case studies on a range of deals struck between the institutions who run sports and broadcasters (for example the recent deal struck between Sky and English cricket and less well-known examples from sports such as tennis, squash and badminton, as well as the crucial Premiership football contract).
- Impact on production: scheduling, advertising revenue, interactive features and other attempts to enhance the viewing experience.
- Debates: deregulation, subscription and commercial imperatives, sport as a national resource, issues about grassroots sports development, fragmentation of audience, influence of media on sport.

'The BBC is in thrall to the politically correct liberal consensus of the metropolitan chattering classes that run it – and has less and less feel for the values of the real people of Britain.' (*Daily Mail* editorial, March 3 2005)

- Facts: the renewal of the BBC's charter in March 2005 and the removal of the governing body in the wake of the Hutton enquiry. (Clearly, there are more facts here to cover in preparation.)
- Impact on production: Tessa Jowell's instruction to the BBC to retain a public service approach to programming and not to 'chase ratings' and the difference this will make/has made to the content of the BBC's schedules.
- Debates: the licence fee, and the power relations between the BBC and Government. Arguments (such as the view expressed by the *Mail*) over whose interests and values the BBC currently represents.

'Traditionally centralized news-gathering and distribution is being augmented (and in some cases will be replaced) by what's happening at the edges of increasingly ubiquitous networks. People are combining powerful technological tools and innovative ideas, fundamentally altering the nature of journalism in this new century. There are new possibilities for everyone in the process: journalist, newsmaker and the active "consumer" of news who isn't satisfied with today's product – or who wants to make some news, too.' (Gillmoor, 2004: vi)

- Facts: the emergence of '*We Media*' through blogging and other online means of authoring news, and the response of news providers to this.

- Impact on production: news production as a creative process for ordinary people, and the ways in which newspapers and online news providers have changed their approaches in order to live alongside this potential revolution.

- Debates: what is news, what is a journalist, what is truth – all the classic philosophical foundations of Media education are laid bare – the nature of mediation, the 'hyper-real' nature of contemporary media reality, and debates around media access and representation (and of course, this should be learned through practice – students should become agents of 'we media').

'The media are not isolated phenomena dispassionately observing and reflecting the society upon which they report and comment. They are, rather, thoroughly integrated at a corporate level with a vast range of service and consumer industries. It is this fact which makes it of some importance that the media should be considered as a whole (rather than in isolation from one another), gives some substance to the idea that the media serve important economic and ideological roles within the processes of capitalist production in general, and makes it unsurprising that, on the whole, the values and assumptions of media texts are not greatly at variance with those of the capitalist system.' (Masterman, 1985: 85)

- Facts: what does ownership actually mean? How much do we know about who owns what? What else do they own? Case studies on clear cases of owners using media to support other interests.

- Impact on production: how is working for a media organization related to the politics and interests of its owners? Examples of media texts either being produced in certain ways or being amended, censored, or not produced at all because of a clash between content and owners' agendas.

- Debates: power and responsibility, regulation and access. What texts are at odds with the 'dominant ideology'? How do ordinary people fight back? Are texts like *Supersize Me* politically powerful products? If the most commercially successful British films are those that provide comfortable viewing for audiences at ease with the 'order of things', is that anything to do with commercial power or just a reflection of people's preferences?

'Ageism is still the media's dirty little secret. Many media companies – in common with the rest of industry – still recruit younger, relatively inexperienced (and cheaper) staff in preference to someone over 40. A survey for *MediaWeek* in April 2003 found that 94 per cent of respondents were under 44, while research by the Institute of Practitioners in Advertising found that 51 per cent of ad agency staff were between 24 and 34'. (Bell and Alden, 2003: 265)

- Facts: the demographics of media producers and administrative staff in the companies that produce media are skewed towards younger people and in many cases males.

In addition, ethnic minorities are under-represented in mainstream media production.

- Impact on production: establishing a career in the media is incredibly difficult and the hours of work and conditions of service, along with the increasing domination of freelance activity, are more conducive to some sectors of society than others. This can only credibly be learned through direct encounter with media professionals or a placement in a company.

- Debates: rather than thinking that finding out how media employment works and who gets to work in media sectors are peripheral activities for vocational students, we should realize that all of our debates around media representation, ideology and access are inextricably linked to the question of who is producing our media, and this doesn't just mean who owns it. Is it possible that the owners of media companies (who in many cases are over 44) might prefer their organizations to be staffed by eager careerists with little life experience for reasons other then their energy levels and how cheap they are to hire?

I hope this set of examples offers illustration to my triangular suggestion. At the heart of all of this work there remains a duty, though, to let students work out for themselves their responses to these debates. While I agree with Masterman's observation, I would not advocate teaching students about the capitalist predisposition of the media. This is likely to be the outcome of the activities, but we would probably be using a different language.

The late Anthony Sampson offered an accessible, entertaining journey through the 'anatomy' of the UK, and spent considerable time investigating the relationship between media ownership and political power. This is a good starting place for some observations students could usefully be encouraged to make. The following is intended for the new Media teacher who needs a grasp of the state of play (but will be obliged to check for updates at the time of reading).

'The media class has enjoyed a dizzy rise in its status and prominence relative to other professions. People at the top of nearly all the institutions I have visited have depicted the overwhelming influence of the media as the biggest change in the power structure over the last decades'. (Sampson, 2004: 240)

Press ownership

At the time of writing, there are seven companies dominating the British newspaper market. Rupert Murdoch's News International (*The Sun, The Times, The News of the World* and *The Sunday Times*) has the largest overall share of circulation, with by far the most readers consuming *The Sun* (almost 3.5 million). *The Mirror, Sunday Mirror* and *The People* are owned by Trinity Mirror, and in 2005 *The Mirror*, having recently disposed of its high-profile editor Piers Morgan over a fake photo scandal, was losing out to both *The Sun* and *The Daily Mail* for readers. *The Daily Mail* and *Mail on Sunday* are owned by Lord Rothermere (or rather his company, Daily Mail and General Trust) and both have a readership (likely to be the same people) of almost 2.5 million. *The Daily Express, Daily Star, Sunday Express* and *The Daily Star* are owned by Richard Desmond's Northern and Shell company. *The Daily Star* is their most successful paper, with 900,000 readers. Press Holdings International, owned by the Barclay Brothers, owns the two versions of *The Telegraph* with almost as many readers as *The Star*. *The Guardian* and *The Observer* are owned by the Scott Trust (a different ownership format altogether) with a small share of the market, considerably less than half a million in each case and *The Independent* and its Sunday version are owned by Sir Anthony O'Reilly's Independent News and Media.

Rather than tell students what this all means, and how it has changed in your lifetime, a web search will allow students to research this for themselves: then you can facilitate some exploration of implications for representation, access and bias.

Once the map lines of the debate are drawn out, you can offer some contemporary case studies on different approaches to the same news, examples of litigation and dismissals or resignations, and then start to make connections to the larger debates about 'the news we deserve' and power/responsibility. But I suggest starting with some simple questions about the people who own the papers. Who are they? Where have they come from? What interests do they have? To whom are they accountable? Some of the issues that may arise are: does it matter that every one of Murdoch's editors (nearly 200) across the world, supported the war with Iraq? Will this make it less likely that our Prime Minister will seek to reduce Murdoch's commercial powers, or give him more responsibility? Is it a problem that one family (the Harmsworths) have had control of one of Britain's best selling dailies for four generations, and that this is a family of Lords? Can students see how the tone and opinions of the *Daily Mail* might reflect this? (They might usefully consider how a newspaper would look if *their* family had handed it down in this way.) And is the unique ownership of *The Guardian* visible in its journalism?

Some heavyweight commentators like the aforementioned Anthony Sampson, Roy Greenslade, John Pilger and John Lloyd offer some pessimistic portrayals of the British press in these times. For these journalists, the effect of the 'tabloidisation' of the British papers (usually attributed to Rupert Murdoch, his incredible resurrection of *The Sun*, and *The Mirror*'s subsequent imitation of it in a circulation battle) has been to offer readers a regular diet of invasion of privacy, sleaze, obsessive treatment of celebrity and the berating of politicians. This kind of political reporting has led to the observation from these critics that it is no longer possible to govern Britain properly. This last assertion arises from the constant awareness the Blair government has had of its press representation, to the point where this has arguably become more important to government than long-term policy strategy, let alone political ideology.

'As the traditional institutions have become less effective counterweights, the media have come to see themselves as the main opposition to government and as correctives to the abuse of power, with a duty to expose lies and corruption. Yet their own legitimacy is uncertain. They have never been elected by anyone; and tabloid journalists are distrusted, according to opinion polls, as much as politicians. They are outside any constitutional constraints or control. And they are dependent in the end on commercial masters who are much more interested in profits than in public service, and to press them to boost circulation or ratings by dumbing down and trivialising.' (Sampson, 2004: 212)

Of course, we can never take for granted such notions of 'dumbing down' when we teach a subject that has reaped great rewards in funding terms from the practice of broadening education and widening participation. Many of our students are *Sun* readers, and why not? Contrary to popular opinion amongst Media teachers, what newspapers our students choose to read, and indeed, whether they read news at all, is of no consequence to us. We are not on some kind of mission to transform our students into younger versions of ourselves, or of ourselves as we were when we were their age. I read *The Guardian* at aged 16 and went to the cinema to see art-house films, but so what? There were ideas in circulation at the time about mainstream and alternative cultures and you could get cultural capital through textual consumption. It is all a bit different now. So what is our job, in the light of Sampson's claim (above)?

Returning to my three-way approach, we need to provide examples of newspapers publishing material that encourages readers to take an oppositional stance to the government of the day. These examples must be mapped to the research that students have carried out on owners and their agendas. Then we provide a framework for learners to engage with the concept of news production along political lines. A good example of this is the Blair/Brown dynamic. Where is the origin of this rift? Is it created by politicians briefing journalists, or by journalists seeking to disrupt the cabinet? And what of the opposition – how are their policies reported by the different papers? Finally, we introduce the debates – should newspapers act differently in relation to government? Can we trust political news in the tabloid papers? Are the broadsheets really offering higher quality journalism or is this part of a discourse of snobbery? And were tabloid papers likely to be more responsible in their reporting of political news to 'the masses' pre-Murdoch, or is this just another piece of 'good old days' rhetoric?

It is possible to tread a path through a Media course without much attention to these political questions, and I have tended myself to design courses which do so, simply because there were other options for study that students were more excited by. On the other hand, you may feel that taking this approach patronizes students and doesn't give them the opportunity to discuss important aspects of their citizenship. With this angle in mind, the Hutton enquiry would seem to represent a mandatory subject.

Hutton

Whatever your opinion of the Iraq war, the government response to the population's opposition to it, and the battle between Greg Dyke's BBC and Alistair Campbell's New Labour, a tiny consolation was that these events provided a neat, easily understandable and much-analysed case study through which we can help students get to grips with previously alien and historical notions of public service broadcasting.

Here, in dramatic and controversial fall-out, is the power-play at its most fundamental. The BBC is owned by us but funded through government. It applies for charter renewal, and in return for its side of the bargain (impartiality and range) the government justify to us its protection from commercial competition. Like *The Sun* reading issue above, be prepared for the likelihood that most of your students may desire the abolition of the licence fee, living as they do in a consumer economy in which choice is the holy grail. Your job is not to change their minds, or to celebrate the BBC, but to facilitate informed judgement.

To summarise, students need to research the allegation of 'sexing up', the Whitehall response and the outcome, as well as the controversy over Hutton's appointment as mediator. The big players who can tell this story for you with exciting polarization are Campbell and Dyke, both of whom have published their sides of the story.

The debate hinges on this statement, made by Richard Sambrook, Director of BBC News:

> 'It is our firm view that Number Ten tried to intimidate the BBC in its reporting of events leading up to the war and during the course of the war itself,' (in Sampson, 2004: 224–6)

Charter renewal

First, students need the facts and figures. The BBC receives 85 per cent of the licence fee carve-up. The other 15 per cent is split between the other terrestrial channels, and in turn, they have public service obligations. Of the commercial players, ITV is the largest, taking £1.67 million in advertizing revenue in 2004, and enjoying just under half of the market for commercial TV. In order to allow ITV to continue honouring its public service commitments, while reliant on analogue advertizing revenue, Ofcom are likely to shift to a market-driven approach to regulation (rather than insisting on a quota of such content as arts or religious broadcasts). Channel 4 receives no government funding and has always had a remit to provide challenging television to add value to the terrestrial range. After 23 years, the channel has now requested a share of the licence fee in order to survive the analogue switch-off. Critics of the editorial policy at Channel 4 have not been convinced that the channel has sufficient public service ethos to justify this. These details show that the future of public service broadcasting is threatened both culturally (by the success of subscription and download TV) and by the changing relations between state, regulator and broadcaster. All three of the terrestrial presences are facing uncertain times.

In March 2005, the BBC's charter was renewed until 2016, with the caveat that the Board of Governors was replaced by an independent board of trustees. This governmental intervention directly arises from the Hutton enquiry and the feeling of cabinet that the governors were confused in their dual role of regulator and management. Alongside this came a compulsion to avoid broadcasting 'narrowcast' programmes for high ratings and the insistence on a further review of BBC funding in 2010. These commandments were in response to arguments from other broadcasters that the BBC was 'having it both ways' by justifying the licence fee on the back of its public service ethos while outbidding other channels for US imports such as *The Simpsons* and *24*.

As I have established, it is difficult to separate any Media learning from an interest in technology, and ownership is no different. The Green Paper on the future of the BBC cannot be separated from technological developments. Its rationale for the modernization of the state's broadcaster is entirely grounded in a sense of the Reithian values (that television should inform, educate and entertain in equal, prescribed measure) no longer holding firm in the digital world. Mark Thompson, who took over from Greg Dyke, summed up this digtal 'status anxiety' in his response to the announcements:

'There is for the first time an explicit purpose for the BBC to lead the building of digital Britain. Audience expectations are rising all the time and it's hard to predict what platforms, technology and innovations will emerge between now and 2016. But the assurance that original British content from the BBC will be a guaranteed fixture of any future landscape is good news for the industry and our audiences.' (*The Guardian*, March 3, 2005)

Picking apart the contradictions and ambiguities in this statement would be a good exercise for Media learning. The hybrid nature of the BBC is crystallised here. On the one hand, technology has been the main threat to its existence, providing as it has the possibility for subscription channels, downloaded TV and the content guide (see Chapter Four for more on how this facility might threaten current definitions of channels and scheduling). On the other hand, the BBC's website is hugely successful and has embraced both digital TV and radio. The contradiction in Thompson's claim above is this: if audience expectations are the driving force, as opposed to Reithian prescription, then might we choose a diet of American television, as we have largely done with film?

The remainder of this chapter offers a range of industry case studies and suggested class strategies that demonstrate a varied, collaborative approach to finding out how media professionals operate in their respective contemporary and converging sectors.

Google

The phenomenal success of the Google search engine is an important case study for Media students, as it shows how the definition of a media organization has shifted in these technological times. Is Google a company? Is it a media provider? This is a statement from its personnel department:

'Looking for an adventure? Google's approach is to foster creativity and cooperation in the pursuit of a common goal: creating the world's best search service. In doing so, we have developed strong revenue streams enabling us to attain profitability in a competitive marketplace. While developing services to be used by millions of people daily, you'll enjoy challenging projects and a unique work environment.' (google.com)

Google makes a claim to internet democracy, emerging as it has from the potential to draw upon user activity and transform this into a coherent tool for organizing the internet. If people did not visit sites, Google could not identify them. It makes money from attracting advertizers, while at the same time advertizing itself. The brand name itself is becoming a verb. If you consider Google users as a media audience, and Google as a new form of text, than the relationship between Google as a company and traditional forms of media organization is a really interesting case study. As Google pilots its news selection and ordering tool, the boundaries between the search tool and the text are further obscured. Google has operated on a unique business model in which advertizers receive a linked presence in return for payment. One clear reason why I would define Google as a company is this: traditionally business analysts look for competition between brands as a definer of such things. Clearly, Google is perceived as a threat by Microsoft, who are about to launch a counter-attack in the form of attention to search engines (previously not part of their empire). Google is, at the time of writing, valued at $24 billion; a small company compared to Microsoft, but a significant player by average standards. Google's acquisition of blogger.com is another area of interest, as a 'free spirit' becomes a metacompany. Students might benefit from collaboration with the Business Studies subject area, if they are to get to grips with how new media technologies are not only changing how media companies operate but how business works in broader terms.

Class strategy – Collaborative research

There is little point in a whole group of students researching the same information, but to avoid the problem of one student doing it all, strategic role allocation is important.

In groups of four, students might research Google's response to blogging by dividing the work up as follows:

1. Status of Google as a media company – its history and success.
2. Current status of blogging as an alternative to traditional news services.
3. Google news and its status as an alternative to traditional news provision.
4. Google's acquisition of blog.com – strategic reasons and implications.

If you have several groups of four, then an interim activity might involve students 'jigsawing' (see Chapter Six) to refine their material in comparison to students from other groups. The end result is collaborative, broader and more accurate research, even if along the way there are some who benefit from the work ethic of others.

Having used technology, research and collaboration to get this far, there is no reason why you cannot ask students to pool research evidence, discuss terms and agree on perspectives, and then ask for an individual response in the form of an essay or report on Google and its response to blogging. After all, current assessment practices will tend to privilege those who can evidence their Media learning in this way. Alternatively, a website, video documentary or PowerPoint presentation would perhaps be more interesting ways of sharing material.

At the time of writing, the blogger site mentioned in the case study has changed little since Google bought it. This may, then, be a classic case of 'if you can't beat 'em. . .' as Google decide to profit from a potential threat. Or there may be plans for a more hegemonic absorption of blogging into the online mainstream (if you think of Google as mainstream), similar to the music industry's attempts to reduce music downloading to a service they offer for a price. At the time of reading, you may know the answers.

Nintendo

The enormous computer games market (dominated by America and Japan) is interesting because it is targeted by a relatively small industry of major companies (such as Nintendo, originally a playing card manufacturer) and small designers. The key players tend to move around from company to company and there is considerable freelance activity. The battle for the market can be seen as a fight between consoles which is talked about in the same way as many of the games are (e.g. Sony PS3 versus Nintendo Revolution). Students will be familiar with computer games and consoles from other parts of their Media course (as far as we can separate them, of course), but in this case study the focus shifts to the companies and the ways in which they promote their products.

Class strategy – Case study

We take the term 'case study' for granted, but is there a consensus on what this means for Media learning? The term has medical or psychological overtones – the study of a particular case in order to more generally understand a condition. In education generally, we tend to understand the approach as the presentation of a particular micro example of a macro area of study. The idea is that this teaching strategy transfers a great deal of the responsibility for learning from the teacher on to the student, whose role shifts to active construction.

In this example, the case study is Nintendo's strategy for competing with Sony's Playstation 3 and Microsoft's X-Box Live with its own Revolution console. The focus should be on how the company's overall strategy was formed, and it may be useful for this reason to involve staff and students from Business Studies.

The key questions are:

- Who owns Nintendo, and what kind of company is it?
- How is it different to Microsoft and Sony?
- Before the launch of the new consoles, what was Nintendo's position in the market?
- Through consumer research, what conclusions can students draw about Nintendo's brand identity with its target audience, in relation to its competitors?
- What features do each of the consoles have as unique selling points?
- How do Nintendo market their product in relation to their competitors?
- How successful is Nintendo's strategy?

> My suggestion for the presentation of this information may seem radical, but it offers an opportunity for students to demonstrate their abilities to work with this business analysis criteria in a more creative, media-friendly way. Groups of students should draft ideas for a computer game (or depending on their course they might program it) called 'Console Launch'. The game puts the user in a narrative in which they have to market a new console against competitors. These ideas would be accompanied by an account of the research and responses to the questions above. The assessment of the work hinges on the ability to capture the reality of the market battle arising from the research in the creative ideas for the game.

To consider Nintendo as a case study further, see Newman (2004), who draws together existing research and cultural theory, to address a range of critical questions. An interesting recent development that Newman considers is the marketing of 'old school' computer games:

> 'Retrogaming describes the growing interest in "vintage" or "classic" videogaming. The fascination with 1970s, 1980s and even early 1990s "vintage" videogaming is often expressed in terms of its "purity". This sentiment is echoed in Nintendo's 2002/3 Gameboy Advance marketing, which, in the UK at least, positions the platform as dedicated to "pure gaming".' (2004: 165)

Indymedia

Indymedia UK is a website founded on a 'DIY' ethos. The organization operates without hierarchy, is anti-discriminatory, has no political affiliations, but offers this gambit:

> 'Inherent in the mainstream corporate media is a strong bias towards capitalism's power structures, and it is an important tool in propagating these structures around the globe. While the mainstream media conceal their manifold biases and alignments, we clearly state our position. *Indymedia* does not attempt to take an objective and impartial standpoint. *Indymedia UK* clearly states its subjectivity'. (www.indymedia.org.uk)

Is there such a thing as unbiased media? Perhaps not, but then again there are occasions when both sides of an argument see bias against them in the same media material. Certainly it is interesting for students to encounter a website such as this, which does not attempt impartiality. And I include it here for no other reason than balance – it is important that students are aware of the permanence of resistance movements in media.

Indymedia is an open publishing forum, where anybody is free to author and publish reports on issues concerned with oppositional politics and struggles for freedom. At the time of writing these include anti-racism, ecology, education, animal liberation, social struggle and gender. The site is part of a worldwide collective.

Class strategy – Whole group reward

Sometimes a simple contract, focused on a single activity, can be very effective. In this case, the onus is on a tangible reward, which might be a social activity, waiving of a rule on one occasion or a staff forfeit of some kind, which might help students engage with an activity that resonates less than others with their life worlds to date.

The task is for the whole group to work collaboratively to produce a report on one of the *Indymedia* topic areas. The objective is for the piece to be published on the site, and for it to yield at least one response. The teacher has a key role to play in helping students to work in the appropriate register for a site of this nature, but other than that, this is a self-supported exercise.

Taking this approach will excite students as they will need to check the site regularly throughout the process. After posting the material they will be visiting the site to see if their report has appeared and elicited any response. You might 'up the stakes' by saying that the first student to spot the first response and email you the link wins a further prize.

MP4

Media students need to be aware of the importance of the Japanese market to media institutions seeking to profit from technological developments. The latest technological development to offer potential riches, but also to pour petrol onto existing legal flames, is MP4, which compresses video files, as MP3 did for music. As we have become accustomed to downloading material for free (do our students see this as a right now?), media industries are battling to offer opportunities for users to carry on their practices but without engaging in piracy. This is potentially a battle, between the industry and the customer or the user, over a new form of copyright – digital rights. As a hundred million people download free content, we are taking advantage of compression technologies for music (MP3 and AAC/MP4 audio format) and film (ITU-T.264) which have reduced audio and video file sizes to one tenth of their original size, so that a feature film can take less than half an hour to download, and a song takes only minutes. A broadband user in Japan will only need 20 minutes to download an uncompressed DVD. Broadband has created such a rise in peer to peer file-sharing that traditional media industries have been unable to organize profitable digital distribution and have thus fallen behind a parallel market, currently led by Kazaa. The likelihood is that you will have regular users of this facility in the classroom, so it is really over to them at this point.

Class strategy – Live downloading

I can think of no more effective method for introducing students to the facts, industry impact and arising debates of MP3 and MP4 than having students download music on a laptop connected to a projector.

Using the example of Kazaa, students would observe a typical downloading session, logging the time each activity takes, and considering issues for the industry in three groups, each with a different angle:

- Legalities and threats to profit – what dangers for the music industry are evident?
- Audience coverage – how well is Kazaa reaching out to the broad music audience?
- Futures – what will seem outdated in two years' time?

After the downloading is complete, each group drafts two interview questions for the user, based on their angle. The answers are recorded in notes and discussed. The information that is generated from the process can be set alongside perspectives from industry, media theory and consumers from a variety of sources, depending on the outcome you intend from this area of study.

Media industries have responded legally rather than creatively, in the first instance. They are striving to reduce the illegal copying of content, for the obvious reason that it constitutes a threat to the economic basis for creating future material (though this argument is overblown, since these companies are so huge). The music industry claim that downloading and peer to peer sharing costs the big players 10 billion dollars a year.

Starting with the providers (the famous example is Napster) the industry then turned to the users, issuing hundreds of lawsuits to individual file sharers. However, it seems unlikely that any amount of prosecution will stop the digital distribution of media, and so industries are moving away from criminalizing the audience and instead, considering ways of transforming their activity into commercial consumption. Media industries see digital media distribution as a promising source of revenue. Apple's iTunes music store is a test-case, offering great incentives for others to follow, but there are still problems for the industry in that there are inconsistent regulations for copyright from country to country. But it seems the future will see the introduction of new Digital Rights Management (DRM) technologies, which will control access, regulation and payment for content. iTunes uses such technology to allow users to play music on three computers, perform unlimited synching on iPods and burn unlimited CDs of individual songs and ten CDs of an unchanged playlist, and podcast over the internet.

Class strategy – Students teach the lesson

There is not much to this strategy, but it is a 'must' with content such as this. All you do is identify a few students who are enthusiastic users of MP3 or

MP4 and give them a clear brief for designing a lesson that introduces the class to this area of media consumption. Approach this exactly as you would with a trainee teacher or new member of your team.

Provide them with learning objectives, and describe good teaching practice in terms of active learning, clear transitions and differentiation. Then leave them to it. Trust them and you will be rewarded.

UK Film Council and piracy

Most students will have consumed pirated DVDs, just as they are enthusiastic music downloaders. Many of us feel ambivalent about the claims of the major music corporations that piracy is threatening the future of the music industry. But it is harder to be sceptical about the UK Film Council's campaigning, given the precarious nature of the UK industry, towards which students tend to take a sympathetic stance.

According to the Council (*Film Theft in the UK*, 2004), only Austria and Germany have a higher degree of DVD piracy. The industry's recommendations include a strategy for responding to internet distribution opportunities, and for working with other media and communications industries.

Class strategy – Self-supported study

I have worked in one Media department where self-supported study became the nucleus of the whole approach to learning and teaching, and in another where it would not have been so successful. It tends to be most productive when the whole institution takes it on board, with an appointed manager to work with course teams and to provide space and time in the curriculum for it. There may be a tendency to confuse it with independent internet research. Self-supported study, though, involves the provision of high-quality learning materials that harness the potential of the internet but provide a 'walled garden' of differentiated learning aims.

A starting point is this – from your own virtual learning space for Media Studies (on the school or college intranet area), link to the UK Film Council's website, and to the PDF download of *Film Theft in the UK*. Then produce three 'click on' tasks, designed to offer choice by ability or extension (and you can intervene more or less in these decisions, of course). These might be:

- a simple comprehension task demanding that students understand the UK Film Council's findings, their concerns and their recommendations
- a more specific creative task asking students to design an alternative publicity campaign for the council to attract attention and make the audience consider the issue before downloading – this would be a

> campaign based more on protecting British film-makers, as opposed to the campaign that highlights the criminal activities of the pirates
> - a higher level activity in which students produce a proposal for an internet distribution strategy for the UK film industry.

The local press

Questions in Media exams about the local newspaper industry tend to present a threat to be considered, thus offering a view of the 'local rag' as a curiously outdated medium in these global, high-tech days. This represents a specific view of the world, rather than common sense, and as such you should challenge this notion from the outset. It is not clear exactly what threat to the local paper is presented by the internet, rolling news or the free distribution of *Metro*, but this might be a good starting point for students' research.

They do need to be aware of local competition, ownership and circulation. And there is a marked difference here between this institutional study and more strictly textual work with news values and modes of address. Here we are thinking about the local paper as a product, and the services it offers to its customers, who continue to consume it, despite a plethora of alternatives that may be cheaper and less traditional. Like most media industries, the picture is one of concentrated ownership, so that a handful of companies control over three quarters of the regional press. This is an unsurprising figure, but students may be more shocked to be informed that more adults read a regional paper than a national one (despite a downward trend in newspaper circulation overall, regionals have maintained this lead). Students' easiest way into the questions they need to ask about the local press is through access to a local journalist. The nature of employment in this case encapsulates many of the more abstract issues about regional identity and democracy.

Class strategy – Interviewing a Media professional

This is another activity that only works if the preparation is in place, and the teacher's role in knowing the desired outcomes and making these clear is paramount.

Equally, you will be the link to the (in this case) local journalist so you can send them the scheme of work in advance and discuss the common shortfalls of students' work in this area. The most significant outcome students need here is data. By this, I mean facts, anecdotes and points of view from somebody working within the institutional framework that they need to analyse.

With a group of twenty students, step one is to divide them into five groups, each working in a different area of the scheme of work. These groups become effectively committees within the wider group. The five areas of study might be:

- ownership
- community values
- legislation
- editorial control
- threats.

Each student is asked to produce five questions, and then each group chooses two from the 25 on the table. This is an important process, as it will create a clear agenda for the interview and the desired outcomes.

The next step is to agree on who will ask questions, in what order and with what recording mechanism and then to rehearse so as to avoid badly phrased questions or answers going unrecorded on the day.

Clearly, there is extra work to be done if you take this approach, and many teachers feel daunted by the prospect of forging links with industry professionals. But you will find that many local journalists are happy to help, as you will be demonstrating an interest in the work they do. And your students' preparation to discuss the broader issues around news provision and regionality will be enhanced greatly by starting from the perspective of the employee as opposed to the textbook.

Blogs

Earlier in this chapter we considered ways in which the rise of blogging might be seen to at once threaten and at the same time transform, traditional models of news production and consumption. The following *Observer* article ('Turn on, tune in, blog out' by Readers' Editor Stephen Pritchard, 13 March, 2005) offers an industry perspective students might easily consider alongside the music industry's attempts to colonize downloading for their own ends. In this case, the 'fifth estate' is of interest – the attempts by newspapers to 'join in' and ultimately, if successful (I presume), impose their traditional ethical codes and editorial agendas, just as the music industry seek to eventually control the economy of MP3.

Comment

Turn on, tune in, blog out

Stephen Pritchard
Sunday March 13, 2005
The Observer

A week is a long time in politics, and for a Sunday paper it's also a long time before publication: time spent in discussion, debate and argument; in making decisions and then changing our minds; in writing and rewriting. Until now you have largely been kept out of that process and confined to writing letters to the editor or contacting me. But now you can learn more about how the paper is put together before it drops on your doorstep.

The Observer Blog, our new daily internet conversation with readers, is a weblog launched with the intention that you should know more about us, while we, in turn, learn a little more about you. It's barely a fortnight old, and so it's early days yet, but it is already bearing fruit.

Between 10,000 and 15,000 unique users logged on in the first 48 hours and it quickly became apparent that items about day-to-day business in the office – ranging from how last week we hired a Dalek for a photoshoot (not as easy as you might think) to weighty discussions in the editor's conference – were generally pretty popular. 'You make the editorial process transparent and capture the informal, behind-the-scenes personality and voice of your paper, the one that normally doesn't get heard,' wrote one reader.

Others were less flattering. 'You're trying too hard to be casual.' A valid point, but the blog is intended to have a less formal voice than that of Britain's oldest Sunday newspaper, reflecting the nature of what is already out there on the net.

Some established bloggers were unhappy about corporate media moving into their territory – the unstructured 'fifth estate', an area of the internet that challenges the outpourings of the established press, taking it on (and sometimes beating it) at its own game in a new journalistic free-for-all. We wouldn't have known about Bill Clinton and Monica Lewinsky, for instance, without the US Drudge Report, and as Blog editor Rafael Behr noted here two weeks ago, four news reporters lost their jobs after bloggers exposed as forgeries documents produced in a CBS story claiming to prove George W Bush dodged the Vietnam draft.

'We are impressed by the quality and breadth of writing and reporting that is available on blogs and elsewhere on the net,' says Rafael. 'We recognise serious competition when we see it. But we are unusual in that we are blogging not so much about issues but about what we do. We are lifting up the bonnet and saying 'this is how the engine works'.

'It is difficult to get a sense of what really interests people, what engages them, but weblogs follow people's daily lives and offer us a clue. If readers have their own blogs, then we want to read them; it helps understand what goes on in their heads, and produces an instant community, governed by its own rules and protocols. It's a sophisticated way of engaging with internet.'

But blogging is not always concerned with the minutiae of people's lives. It's often a platform for amateur journalistic risk – risk that the traditional press won't always entertain. Revelatory articles are published in The Observer within the conventions and codes of established journalism, but a blog is uncharted territory for us. It carries certain dangers, not least because it has to be open to all contributions in the true spirit of blogging.

Publication on the net under our masthead carries with it the same responsibilities as publication in print: subject to the laws of libel and contempt.

Cases against bloggers are starting to come to court in the US, where some are claiming the immunity granted to established journalists under the First Amendment. Last week, a California judge ruled that online publishers could be forced to reveal their sources.

Critics say that since web reporting is not bound by the same code of ethics as print media it should not enjoy the same privileges. UK journalists have a degree of protection regarding sources, yet in extremes these safeguards can be set aside. Courts are far more likely to find against an amateur internet blogger working outside any ethical code than a journalist on a reputable newspaper.

Consequently, we will be treading carefully, deleting libellous, insulting, nonsensical and offensive comments and plain unalloyed plugs, posted by people with no regard for the subject of the blog they are commenting on.

'Blogs need housekeeping,' says Rafael. 'An open door is not an invitation to vandals.' You have been warned.

· The blog is at www.observer.co.uk/blog.

Ofcom

Ofcom came into effect in 2003, and the most interesting angle for your students will now be: How effective has this body been in comparison to what was there before? The 'history lesson' needs to tell students that five regulatory bodies (ITC, Oftel, Radio Authority, Radiocommunications Agency and the BSC) were replaced by one (in other words, here is some regulatory convergence, in effect). Ofcom's website is a useful starting point for the industry view, and this will help students get to grips with some of the counter-arguments, also. These have most repeatedly been articulated in relation to competition (Ofcom are a 'light touch' regulator operating entirely in a market forces discourse), the BBC (especially as it moves from self-regulation through governance to independent scrutiny in the wake of the charter renewal) and convergence again (the existence of Ofcom is testimony to this new era as previously each separate industry had its regulator).

Once students are familiar with what Ofcom is there to do, and some of the debates around its status, they can easily access a more complex range of specific case studies via

'Ofcom-watch', an organization with the following mission statement:

> 'Ofcom-watch is an informal group blog commenting on the processes and
> practices of the Office of Communications (Ofcom) Ofcom-watch is an equal
> opportunities blog with no overarching agenda. All political leanings and
> viewpoints are welcome. So our mission is also yours if you choose to accept it.
> Accordingly, Ofcom-watch is open to all. Ofcom-watch aims to provide an
> independent, informal, non-partisan, well written, easily readable, occasionally
> humorous online resource. Ofcom-watch also aims, over time, to form a
> discursive current of opinion that results in new perspectives and progressive
> thinking in regard to media and communications regulation in the United
> Kingdom. Ofcom-watch hopes to be seen by the Office of Communications
> (Ofcom) as a positive online resource – bolstering the regulator's own (and the
> legislative) demands for external accountability while embracing the essence of
> democratic grassroots/community media activism.' (www.ofcomwatch.co.uk –
> accessed 18 March 2005)

Once again, a blogging facility offers us an example of expanding media access and the
potential of new technologies to keep 'in check' the major commercial players. This example
reminds us of Foucault's technologies of surveillance – the regulator is regulated, the watcher
is watched. In turn, this reminds us that the most 'vocational' learning (that is, about
industries, companies and the world of work and commerce) can be the most profoundly
theoretical.

Class strategy – Multiple-choice test design

While I would not advocate multiple-choice testing as a summative
assessment technique, focusing on this particular learning style once in a
while can reap benefits (ultimately, exams are memory tests, whether we like
it or not, so it could be argued that never to test memory in this way is
irresponsible). But a more interesting and productive approach is to ask
students to design the questions and the bank of possible answers.

Provide five groups each with an aspect of Ofcom's operations and ask them
each to draft three levelled questions. The first question should be
straightforward and factual, the second more of a problem-solving question,
for which the respondent must make a choice based on their understanding of
how Ofcom works as opposed to a true/false distinction, and the third question
must be related to debates surrounding Ofcom (although the answer may be
factual – e.g. name the blog website set up to scrutinise the actions of Ofcom).

Each group must therefore produce three questions and nine answers, of which
three will be correct. Ideally, use software (Hot Potatoes is one example) to
produce an online test, which other students can then trial for the group.

If our job is to help citizens become media literate (though I would argue they already are by the time we start teaching them), then we need to remember that our own assumptions about 'bits' of courses, who teaches them and how, need to be challenged for this to be possible. There can be a tendency for Media teachers to assume that placing textual analysis at the centre of their work is useful for generating discussion about media meaning in context, and that practical work is a creative element of textual work. In this model, teaching about technologies and institutions can be marginalized and treated as a mandatory but rather 'dry' aspect of our work. This perception obscures these relations and fails to recognize that active, creative learning about media institutions is at the heart of both textual interpretation and creative production. If technologies are providing opportunities for media consumers to become producers of content, and the proliferation of such organic media content continues apace, then our current models for conceptualizing 'the media' and for 'textual analysis', with all of their attendant assumptions about where texts come from and how they are interpreted may be blown apart.

Further reading

Each edition of *Media Magazine* and *In the Picture* includes excellent resources for students and teachers respectively in this area. As repeated throughout this chapter, industry resources have a very short shelf-life, so I would suggest you generate materials in each case the week before you teach. There follows a range of sources that are available at the time of writing.

Alden, C., 2005, *The Media Directory 2005,* London: Guardian Books.
You will need several copies of the latest edition of this resource.

Balvanes, M., Donald, J., and Donald, S., 2001, *The Global Media Atlas,* London: BFI.
Excellent visual introduction to global ownership and consumption patterns.

Bates, S., 2005, 'Squashed Out – Money, the Media and Minority Sport' in *Media Magazine,* 11, London: English and Media Centre.
Interesting account for students of the relationship between the survival of sports and their media coverage.

Bazalgette, P., 2005, *Billion Dollar Game: How three men risked it all and changed the face of television,* London: Time Warner.

Caldwell, J., and Everett, A., 2003, *New Media; Practices of Digitextuality,* London: Routledge.
Argues for a reconceptualization of what we understand as 'the mass media'.

Clark, V., 2005, *Media Briefing: The Global Picture and Teaching Notes,* London: BFI.
Excellent introductory resource for Media students with teachers' notes.

Curran, J., 2002, *Media and Power,* London: Routledge.
Concerned with the 'big questions' at the heart of learning about media industries.

Dyja, E., (ed.), 2005, *BFI Film and Television Handbook*, London: BFI.
Annual publication.

English and Media Centre, 2003, *Production Practices*, London: EMC.
Resource for industry simulations, offering practical ways in to understanding vocational practice.

Film Education, 2004, *Film Industry teaching pack*, London: Film Education.

Gillmoor, D., 2004, *We, The Media*, California: O'Reilly.
A statement/overview on the rise of online journalism and its democratic potential.

In the Picture, 2003, 47, *Institution*. Keighley: itp Publications.
Themed issue.

Holland, P., 2000, *The Television Handbook*, London: Routledge.
Overview of contemporary features of the UK television industry.

Lacey, N., 2004, *Media Institutions and Audiences*, London: MacMilllan.
Very useful overview for teachers and students alike.

Langham, J., 1997, *Lights, Camera, Action – Careers in Film, Television and Video*, London: BFI.
Useful student guide to the vocational opportunities available to them.

McKay, J., 2000, *The Magazines Handbook*, London: Routledge.
Introduction to the workings of companies in this competitive market.

McNair, B., 2003, *News and Journalism in the UK*, London: Routledge.

Newman, J., 2004. *Videogames*, London: Routledge.
Useful introduction to a range of research perspectives in this relatively new area for cultural analysis.

Robinson, P., 2002, *The CNN Effect*, London: Routledge.
Explores the relationship between the state and media.

Sampson, A., 2004, *Who Owns this Place?* London: John Murray.
A lively, contemporary anatomy of UK power-brokers, with excellent sections on media power, media influence on politics and the Hutton enquiry.

Skillset, 2005, *Future Trends* research (available to download from Skillset website). London: Skillset.
Useful research findings from the national training provider.

Stafford, R., 2003, 'Ofcom is Up and Running' in *In the Picture*, 47, Keighley: itp Publications.

Thussu, D., 2000, *International Communication*, London: Hodder.
Offers a range of international case studies to explore the information revolution and its impact on media industries.

Taylor, N., 2005, *Search Me: The Surprising Success of Google,* London: Cyan.

UK Film Council, 2004, *Film Theft in the UK,* London: Film Council. Useful industry report on the threat of piracy.

Viney, R., 2001, *Teaching Contemporary British Broadcasting,* London: BFI.

See also the 'Top 40 websites' section.

chapter six

Media Literacy

Introduction

Textual analysis has forever been the bedrock of Media education of all kinds. GCSE and A Level courses have traditionally set this up as the dominant mode of study with the text very much placed at the centre of learning. Perhaps we are at a time now when, due to the ease with which digital technology can be harnessed for creative ends, Media education is shifting from a reactive to an active set of practices. People in general are much more involved in creating texts of their own, whether these are video pieces contrived for Media courses, or blogs authored to offer a critical voice for democratic ends. As participation in creative processes becomes an expectation, or even a way of life, one could assume that the representative, mediated or even biased nature of mass media texts might be more clearly visible.

Burn and Parker (2003) advocate 'multimodality', an approach rooted in social semiotics:

'The sign-maker always has a social interest, or motivation, to communicate. It may be driven by the need to represent something in the world, whether this be an event, a belief, or the sign-maker themselves. Or it may be driven by the need to establish relations with other people. In practice, whatever the emphasis, it will always perform these two basic functions. However, our communications are dependent upon not only the semiotic resources available, whether these be paintbrushes, words or binary code, but also upon the social and cultural contexts in which we communicate. Analyses of the semiotic structures of texts produced for and by children and young people must, therefore, try to relate the analyses to these contexts, to determine what interests motivate the communications under scrutiny.' (2003: 5)

Len Masterman, in a recent edition of *In the Picture*, reminds us of the far-reaching political importance of the kinds of interpretive work that we might be in danger of labelling 'old school':

'Once again it is war, with the attendant horrors, pain and misery which it inflicts upon innocent men, women and children which heightens awareness of the paramount importance of media literacy. As George Bush and Tony Blair were casting around for publicly credible reasons to justify their invasion of Iraq, both of their governments were engaged in a vigorous propaganda war against their own publics' scepticism about the necessity for war. It was a process bolstered – as it also was on the Iraqi side – by misinformation, distortion, lies and the vilification, stereotyping and demonisation of the "other", the enemy. It is a familiar process whose contribution to the total sum of human misery is incalculable. Could the need in all societies for a critical mass of knowledgeable and sceptical citizens who can understand, see through and oppose this process be clearer?' (2004: 4)

I offer this extract at the start of this chapter because it is so strikingly contrary to the discourse of derision which articulates a view of Media Studies as a vacuous, 'dumbed down' series of everyday discussions about soap opera and reality TV. In keeping with this call for media literacy as an aspect of citizenship, the BFI in particular have called for a cross-curricular approach to moving image analysis (as opposed to a general media awareness, obviously due to the specific remit of the BFI) in schools, developing a strategy for 'cine-literacy' with government approval. Media education groups world-wide, most notably some proactive communities in Canada, have forwarded strategies for promoting media awareness within a wider agenda for citizenship, and in this country links between Media education and citizenship are proliferating.

But we should have no time for the setting up of any oppositions of 'serious' media awareness which is to do with war and politics against 'media literacy lite', which is to do with popular TV genres. I am sure that these divisions (which are really class based) serve to perpetuate what we used to call 'false consciousness'. We need to be tuned in to the audience communities students operate within and between and understand that the ability to actively interpret media texts in relation to our own cultural situations is important in relation to any text, whether it be a 'distorting' Fox News item about the 'war on terror' or an episode of *I'm a Celebrity*. . . . The endgame for us as Media educators should be the negotiation of meaning and identities through creative endeavour, not an unveiling of 'truth' hiding behind propaganda.

David Buckingham's recent overview suggests a fairly radical remodelling of our approach to media meaning, departing somewhat from the predominance of print analysis and the influence of approaches from English teaching:

'Literacy involves both reading and writing; and so media literacy must necessarily entail both the interpretation and the production of media. Media teaching has historically been dominated by "critical analysis" and indeed by a relatively narrow form of textual analysis, which is primarily designed to expose the "hidden ideologies" of media texts. By contrast, media production has been regarded with considerable unease and suspicion. The model of media learning I am (suggesting) attempts to provide a more dynamic, reflexive approach which combines critical analysis and creative production'. (2003: 49–50)

So again we return to a realization that it is folly to divorce critical autonomy from creative experimentation. Only by 'doing' will we get to grips with 'thinking'. Therefore, while this chapter will annexe textual work for the purpose of the book's coherence, it must be recognized that the strategies included here must, to be successful, be entwined with the production methods offered in other chapters.

Class strategy – Jigsawing

A common, and obvious, problem in film language analysis in the classroom is that the images move quickly and the ability to watch, decode and analyse within a conceptual framework at the same time is very hard to acquire. And yet we sometimes take for granted that students will do this, showing them clips and expecting feedback within the same lesson on camera, editing, sound and *mise-en-scène*. This method breaks the process down and maximises collaboration, saving time and ensuring the task is more enjoyable.

Give each student a number 1–3. Each will have a different element to analyse. Number 1 students will study camera (angle and movement), 2s will take on editing (pace, nature of transitions) and 3s will decode sound (dialogue, FX, ambience).

Show the clip twice just for comprehension (you cannot analyse film unless you are already situated by the narrative – you need to understand what is happening in time and space).

I believe students are being poorly treated in this era if you are not projecting film sequences onto a large screen in a blacked-out room, but this is a resource issue for you to consider. Analysing fast-moving, complex combinations of time, space, light, movement and sound is hard enough in a cinema, let alone on a monitor that has seen better days.

Provide a template for note-taking, and ask students to make notes during four more screenings, just on their element (I am assuming this activity is undertaken after a series of introductory lessons and some reading on the elements of film language I include here).

After the screenings, group the students together by number so they can share ideas and each end up with a comprehensive list of examples. The emphasis must be on the 'why?' (i.e. why this type of edit, why this sound effect, why this camera angle?) in terms of choices made in production (deconstruction at a basic level).

When all students have a full list, group them so that each group has at least one of each number (i.e. a 1, a 2 and a 3).This is the 'jigsaw' effect which results in everyone having, directly or indirectly, shared their ideas with everyone else.

When students return to their original places they will each have every example of every element. You can then ask directed questions in a perfectly safe environment, because every example you ask for will be the result of lots of group discussions, as opposed to a more disconcerting 'what is in my head' approach to public questioning.

This strategy is referred to throughout this book. It works well because it gets students working with one another safely, and you can design the original groups strategically, depending on your motives (for example, mixed ability, gender, differentiated).

For homework, students should use their notes from these jigsaw discussions to produce a 500-word analysis of the *mise-en-scène* in the extract. This gives you the opportunity (through marking the work or peer assessment) to monitor the individual learning on this complex and central aspect of Media learning.

Media literacy is a term now in common parlance (and to an extent it has subsequently replaced 'textual analysis') and has been most visibly granted mainstream status in the form of attention from Ofcom, who include the promotion of it as a central aspect of their work:

'In an increasingly converged communications world, people face greater media choice. Changes in technology mean that parents may have to take more responsibility for what they and their children see and hear on screen and online. Media literacy will provide some of the tools they need to make full use of the opportunities offered, to manage their expectations and to protect themselves and their families from the risks involved. Through confident use of communications technologies people will gain a better understanding of the world around them and be better able to engage with it.' (Ofcom, 2005)

In November 2004, Ofcom hosted a research forum on media literacy. The outcome was a connecting of media literacy with emotional and political literacies, due largely to the input of the Bournemouth University Media School. The resulting bulletin describes a conception of media literacy through which popular entertainment is seen as a vehicle for emotional learning, the media in general are seen as potential agents of democracy, and creative practices are a dimension for the enhancement of media literacy (Ofcom, 2005: 4).

What is up for grabs in this manifesto from the regulator (and I shall leave you to form a view on this) is the question of whether media literacy is taught or developed and then 'used' to engage with media in new ways. If this is the case, then we really can place media literacy alongside traditional views of literacy and ultimately, develop strategies for its development, just as policy-makers have with the National Literacy Strategy. And just as writing is an essential aspect of language acquisition, so media production (which is, after all, writing) cannot be merely a tangent to the acquisition of media language.

Class strategy – Game show

A staple feature of Media education, no matter what the course or specification, is recognition of conventions. At a basic level, the learning can stop at mere recognition (texts in this style will have these conventions, for the self-fulfilling reason that they are popular when produced in this way). An intermediary stage is the discussion of alternatives, and consideration of texts that experiment with, expand or ignore convention (I am deliberately avoiding reference to genre here, as it is useful to introduce the notion of convention first before considering the value of genre as a categorizing device). More advanced learning will be to do with the nature of convention, the socio-cultural contexts of pleasure and recognition and the big questions about whether media texts merely represent societal norms which are already there or whether they play a role in constructing these.

When OCR made the study of games shows mandatory at AS level, some Media teachers were concerned that this gesture played into the hands of those who attack the subject. The counter-argument is that if the subject is to have the courage of its convictions, students must study the most popular of popular culture (as well as texts that the majority would deem to be of higher 'quality'). So for every moment of *Citizen Kane* appreciation, there should be a consideration of the popularity of reality TV, for example.

The game show genre, like soaps and sitcoms, enjoys long-standing popularity at the same time as widespread derision from those who scapegoat television for its contribution to our devolution into 'junk TV' addicts. Interestingly, when I surveyed Media teachers' own media consumption for my research degree, they often described their listening to *The Archers* as 'devotion' but their consumption of TV soaps as 'addiction'!

In order to get to grips with the pleasures offered by the TV game show, I suggest asking students to put Fiske's (1987) theory of ritual into practice. Fiske identifies ritual at the heart of game show pleasure, in so much as the text offers at once social cohesion (the order of things, rich and poor, occupations, ordinary people as different to celebrities) and escapism (the possibility of achieving riches and emancipation from the everyday through appearance in a televised contest). Audiences vicariously experience identification with winners and losers in a highly conservative arena in which we believe in the equality of ordinary folk in a rule-governed structural arrangement.

How can students creatively engage with these ideas in a collaborative situation? Put simply, the acid test for any artificially created media text will be its proximity to authentic media product. So students in mixed-ability groups need to produce a template for a game show that can be tested out on fellow students who will decide which format is most likely to engage the audience.

Each game show template must include:

- a clear, semiotic distinction between celebrity presenters and ordinary contestants
- clear, easily understandable rules
- the opportunity for audience identification
- the opportunity for humiliation and for great reward in equal measure
- a structure which mirrors society as it is
- a theme that will guarantee derision from the middle-classes.

This approach takes the bigger ideas about textual pleasure and then works back down to the imitation of convention. In each group, the more able students can 'translate' some of these socio-cultural ideas into another register for their colleagues. The end result should be some high-level media literacy, achieved through active, practical, collaborative activity, as opposed to watching game shows and learning from the teacher how to theorize them.

'Isms' of the real

Engaging with ideas about realizm is an important element of media literacy, and in keeping with the flavour of this book, I suggest starting with already held notions of texts' proximity to reality and then building on this work with theoretical ideas about verisimilitude, reality TV, social realism and documentary approaches.

Research has shown that children are in general pretty well-equipped to understand the constructed nature of television, for example, at aged nine. My daughter can do this at the age of six, but I guess this is one of the few ways in which having a Media teacher as a Dad is an advantage in life! The interesting classroom work is to do with unpicking the criteria we all use to judge the realizm of texts, and then investigating the cultural origins of these notions. Then we can work out how media producers are tapping into these notions, or trying to shift them.

I like to start with a continuum, where students plot film and television texts on a line, in between 'least real' and 'most real.' Usually we end up with *Lord of the Rings* at one end and *Big Brother* at the other, but never without great debate, and from this dissensus we can get into the 'honesty factor'. *Lord of the Rings* claims nothing but fantasy, yet creates a believable text-world with an internal logic, continuity and great mythological detail. In this sense, it is 'sealed' and everything makes sense. *Big Brother*, on the other hand, claims reality, yet all viewers are constantly aware of the heavy hand of the producers, who turn the contestants into characters for our pleasure, through the mediating techniques of the edit, the voice-over and the manipulation of the extra-textual world in the shape of the tabloid press in particular.

This discussion takes us into interesting territory – realizm is in our minds, not on the screen.

Class strategy – Deconstructing the classroom

Media Studies, as a form of cultural studies (and I include production-based learning in this) is largely to do with deconstruction. Which is not to say necessarily that Derrida should loom large at any point, but rather to highlight the necessity of exposing the constructed nature of the everyday.

For example, when introducing semiotics as a way in to codes of realizm, it is helpful to take the classroom itself as the object of study. Ask students to storyboard a four-shot sequence that will make it abundantly clear, through the shorthand of visual language, that viewers are observing a scene set in a classroom. When this is done, ask students to account for selection (of visual information) and construction (of time and space through editing). What cultural knowledge were they reliant on? Then move toward a critical discussion about the reasons for classrooms being as they are: what are the power dynamics and assumptions about human interaction expressed in the construction of the room, the furniture, the position of the 'players' and the ambience? In other words, what is the *mise-en-scène*?

The point is this – when media producers need to speed-reference a moment in narrative that is not especially important, they use a form of semiotics that is absolutely reliant on reinforced notions of the everyday – a stereotyping of time and space. Realizing this, and being able to 'stop' the process of signification for long enough to recognize it, is the first step to media literacy. This impulse cannot be assumed, it must be developed.

Image analysis

Working with students to develop media literacy skills, a sensible approach is to start with still images and progress to moving pictures. A basic semiotic approach starts with students' perceptions of the conventions of visual language. For example, why might a male teacher wear a tie? What kind of symbol is this? What does the Nike 'swoosh' connote? Why is the word 'chair' used to represent the object it does, as opposed to the word 'zoo'? Which signs or symbols have natural or logical connections to that which they represent, and which do not (or in the language of structuralism, which are iconic and which are arbitrary)? (I have used an ordinance survey map, birthday cards for Mum and for Dad and students' names and family photos, volunteered by them, to start the ball rolling in this area.) The shared theoretical language at an early stage should include 'signification', 'denotation', 'connotation', types of signs ('icon', 'index', 'arbitrary') and, crucially, 'anchorage' (the attempt to 'pin down' meaning through text, for example a caption or the combined effect of a photo and a headline). Students then need to exercise this kind of application in a range of contexts, until they are comfortable with inter-textual references.

But the problem with this approach can be that there is a stage at which we are saying something we don't really mean – that is, that signs simply have meanings. So you need to be skilful in handling the tension between wanting to share an analytical framework that allows students to theorize everyday textual meaning, while maintaining an acceptance that meaning is plural (or polysemic).

Class strategy – Gender swap

Assuming in this case that your students are in the 14–19 age range, I hope you will agree that this is not an easy age at which to be deconstructing your own identity. Most teenagers are busy forming an identity to assert at every opportunity, through a range of semiotic codes and cultural forms of expression. With this in mind, the act of deconstruction can be safer (if less reflective at first) if students adopt the identity of 'the other' for the duration of the exercise.

After a series of sessions covering still image analysis, focus on a particular magazine cover which is clearly aimed at a gender. Provide institutional detail (publisher, target audience, place in market, relationship to other products with the same audience, sales and so on), and then focus on the front cover for textual analysis.

Using the language of semiotics, ask students to analyse the cover text and images in three ways:

1. Signification to the target reader.
   Relating to Winship's notion (1997) of the complicit understanding between model and reader of a shared world, of aspiration and of the presentation of self, here students are asking: How is the gender targeted encouraged to (mis)recognize itself?
2. Signification of the gender in question to the other.
   What messages about being male or female are being provided here that may reinforce or challenge ideas of 'the other' in circulation amongst the other gender? Put more simply, if a man picks up his partner's *Cosmopolitan*, what notions of the female life world are in play?
3. Signification of the other gender to the readership.
   What myths about men are reinforced by the cover of a woman's magazine, and vice versa?

The purpose of the 'gender swap' is to depersonalise the experience and to make the job a little harder. In addition, it is important to insist on the use of semiotic terminology, so that when students are annotating, they are working with a framework for high-level analysis. For example, a male student might identify for discussion the chiselled, muscular torso of the black and white model on a cover of *Men's Health* and indicate that this iconic sign is also indexical, as it suggests to the readership that this body is achievable. In addition, this index reinforces commonly held gender notions and anxieties that we might refer to as 'male narcissism' and signals to women that men value strength and agility primarily as a means through which to attract the opposite sex and to compete with other men. These discussion points emerge more lucidly, I have found, when students are outside of their own frame of reference for thinking about gender, and when they have to strive to make the theoretical process work for them, to make their points.

Polysemy

In semiotic terms, the extent to which meaning is fixed is referred to as the degree of motivation, so an image with little ambiguity and heavy anchorage will have high motivation, and an ambiguous image (perhaps from abstract art) will have little motivation. Students need to grapple with the idea that highly motivated signs may appear so within a dominant mode of seeing, but that there are always already a plurality of interpretations of any sign. For example, an image of Tony Blair, captioned: 'Tony Blair, Prime Minister' will at first appear to have a clear, unitary, fixed meaning. However, one's response to the image will depend entirely on opinion, experience, political situation and so on. The focus, after a short induction to the idea that semiotics is a form of 'science' that must be learned, is on the active nature of decoding, and the ways in which we are ourselves 'written' in discourse. If we merely get students to the point where they can recognize types of signs and explain what things 'mean', we have in effect reduced their media literacy. And this is why textual analysis can never be productive if it is 'cold' and divorced from creative work and an appreciation of institutional practices: the nature of reading is in some ways defined by the relationship between producer and audience, and the proximity of the latter to the discourses articulated by the former.

Class strategy – Interactive whiteboard annotation (Real Media)

Here is another potentially provocative statement about resources: students cannot really be expected to analyse images well if you do not present them well. I think we have to say the days are gone when we can work with shaky freeze frames and black and white photocopies of still images. The technology exists, and is affordable to all institutions, to allow you to project images onto an interactive whiteboard, and use smart pens for students to annotate them to present their responses.

In the class strategy on magazine cover analysis, students should pair up with a member of the other (adopted) gender to compare notes, and then you can give each pair a different focal point for presentation (one of the three critical questions, and within that a particular aspect of semiotics or of magazine conventions). This way each pair can contribute a unique response. This is achieved by each pair using the technology to circle/point to label their chosen example on the smartboard. This facility is not merely a gimmick. Rather, it gives students a cognitive advantage, and gets them more involved in every lesson.

Moving images

To step up from still image to moving image analysis, the grammar of the edit is a logical starting point. I have enjoyed working with Eisenstein's dialectical montage with Media students of all ages and levels, simply because his philosophy is so accessible and incredibly far-reaching in terms of its potential to shift the way we think about visual communication. At its most basic, Eisenstein's work suggests that shot A plus shot C can only be understood through B (the edit, the connection). The famous Odessa Steps sequence from *Battleship Potemkin* offers a historical example to illustrate the director's theory/practice contribution to film history (and here is an interesting question in terms of labels: are directors like Eisenstein, and also Godard and Truffaut, who made films but also theoretical writings, vocational or academic?). I would not necessarily provide students with Eisenstein's own writing, unless you have more time to work on political and historical context. Instead, most introductory Film Studies books offer accessible summaries of his radical editing approach. Alongside this, action film sequences, television adverts and documentary clips all serve as good examples of the power of the edit, as at least a form of punctuation, but more significantly, through the manipulation of time and space, as an invisible metalanguage framing our pleasures.

Computer games

A recurrent theme in this book is technology and the question of whether the conceptual model for Media learning established partly by Len Masterman in 1985 can hold firm and accommodate new kinds of textual experiences mobilised by digital innovations; or whether we need new approaches, a fundamental rethink of textual analysis to engage with new literacy practices. Studying computer games as texts is a relatively recent opportunity for Media students, and it seems to me that this area is at the heart of this debate.

There is an emerging body of knowledge with which to theorize this form of textual experience, most notably from the Institute of Education's research (see Burn *et al.*, (2003), Toland (2004), Newman (2004) and Wolf and Perron (2003)). A range of interpretations is offered by these contributors, from the traditional conceptual approach to a rethinking of the notion of audience. And as technology such as the 'Eye Toy' for Playstation arrives (which allows the gamer to appear on screen and thus visibly exist in the text-world of the game via a camera placed on top of the monitor), some argue that computer games will offer a form of 'internal' and physical textual pleasure that will make comparisons with film and television consumption obsolete. At this point, surely studying narrative through the same theoretical prism as we would for action films will make little sense? On the other hand, we might argue that conceptual starting points are entirely flexible anyway, so we still need to study audience in order to articulate how we feel about these shifting relations.

> 'Video games remediate cinema; that is, they demonstrate the propensity of emerging media forms to pattern themselves on the characteristic behaviours and tendencies of their predecessors. That video games are starting to resemble movies more than they do "real life" suggests that games, as a cultural form, are produced and consumed in phenomenological accord with pre-existing technologies of representation. At the same time, video games plainly rework the formulas of cinema – and spectatorship – in ways that demand addressing. . .the crucial relationship in many games is not between the avatar and the environment but between the human player and the image of him – or herself encountered onscreen.' (Rehak, in Wolf and Perron, 2003: 104)

If we are to maintain our old models to theorize computer games as they currently are, and taking *Medal of Honor* as our example, we can adopt the MIGRAIN acronym (Bruce, 2002) for this purpose, just as for any other form of text, as follows:

- Media language: looking at the construction of verisimilitude through *mise-en-scène*, the *Medal of Honor* series offers intertextual references to *Saving Private Ryan* and seeks to establish a recognition by the gamer of a learned sense of the 'look' of the Second World War from the Allies' perspective.

- Institution: Computer games are part of a hugely competitive and lucrative market, and the companies that distribute them are convergent entities Games designers operate in the midst of turf-wars such as the Microsoft, Nintendo and Sony fight for control of this market. Designers have their own styles, and most games have a great deal of intertextual franchise elements for students to analyse.

- Genre: This is a refreshing area when compared to traditional Media learning, since there are no 'tried and tested' resources packs on this genre or that. As a result, discussions are more organic and negotiation of genre labelling can happen 'live'. The relationship between genre as subject matter (e.g. football games) and format for the player (e.g. single player) is an interesting, transformative area for study. Whether online gaming is a genre or a technological development might also be considered.

- Representation: As I have said, I think all Media learning is really about representation, and the other concepts are merely roads to this destination. Key questions are to do with the viewer/reader/player identities – who is good and bad, how are nations, genders, occupations, societies, species, real personalities represented, which dominant discourses are circulated, and crucially, if I am in the game, am I represented, or do I take on another represented identity? What power do I have to negotiate this role? Am I inside or outside of the text and its representational devices?

Students at Long Road Sixth Form College studying by playing games.

- Audience: Students cannot get into this kind of work without researching their peers as audience members. Who is playing what games and in what context (online, solitary, with friends)? What pleasures are obtained? What connections with other media pleasures are evident? Is the audience really a kind of 'learning community' (see Gee, 2003)? What does student research offer in response to the popular assumptions about gaming and the attendant moral panics?

- Ideology: This is the area that demands the most caution. If we tell students that *Medal of Honor* represents a horribly crude, simplified, American mis-remembering of the Second World War and, as such, is firmly entrenched in a Bush era dominant ideology of cultural imperialism masquerading as the 'spreading' of democracy, we might be pretty justified. But this is a particular view informed by an English historical perspective and as such, it is not ideologically neutral. The more interesting work is to do with game players' perceptions of their identity within the game and the degrees to which this is abstract and 'just gaming' in relation to the historical specificity of the drama.

- Narrative: As the construction of game stories is reliant on the player progressing through the programme by trial and error and by learning, we are presented with a fundamentally new, interactive form of narrative (certainly Todorov will not suffice here!). The equivalent might be watching the first twenty minutes of a film ten times before moving on, but this analogy won't hold due to the active nature of viewing in this case. So is game narrative linear? How are binary oppositions used to inform the player's learning? The irony is, I suppose, that while the narrative structure of a computer game text is as complex and negotiable as one can imagine, the thematics and characterization are incredibly reductive and simple in many cases.

To sum up the complexity of this old/new tension, consider this from Burn, Carr and Schott (2003):

> 'The way that Lara Croft acts when one person plays her might vary a great deal from the ways that she moves or acts when another person is at the controls. This is why theories drawn from older media (film or literature, for example) can't fully describe digital games. Games also complicate old notions about the relationship between authors and readers, because players determine how the "hero" behaves. By compiling and distributing software modifications and cheats, gamers also disrupt the distinctions between the text's producers and its consumers.' (2003: 10)

And this contribution from Grodal (in Wolf and Perron, 2003):

> 'The repetitive and interactive nature of video games leads to changes in the function of central devices in the emotional experience of "narratives", namely curiosity, surprise and suspense. In a film, the curiosity that is cued by secrets of the narrative world is a passive one, and mainly linked to first-time viewing. The viewer will activate a passive curiosity that supports the viewer's attention. In a video game, however, curiosity takes the form of explorative coping. The game only develops if the player performs a series of explorative actions.' (2003: 148–9)

Medal of Honor : can traditional ways of doing textual analysis adapt to such interactive modes?

Class strategies – Guided screening/note-taking

Media learning can be bankrupt and demoralising for both teacher and students if too many assumptions are made about basic study skills (such as note-taking) and more advanced strategies (selecting useful material from a video extract).

Textual analysis of moving images is difficult enough in a classroom with the distraction of your peers and your diminishing energy levels (even the most enthusiastic Media learner will become passive when shown a film on a Friday afternoon).

Experience has told me that students should never be merely 'shown' a moving image text or simply asked to 'make notes'. Explaining the objectives of a screening and providing a prompt sheet, rather than asking learners to make notes on their own volition, serves to remind them that there is a task in hand, and frames their response appropriately. For a TV news broadcast, I would suggest tailoring the prompt sheet to the demands of the specific unit, but generally, you may wish to include the following headings (with the micro linked to the macro):

Micro
- Intro sequence
- Music
- Order of stories
- Presenter performance and dress
- Studio *mise-en-scène*
- Supporting footage (live)
- Supporting footage (incidental).

Macro
- Mode of address
- Agency/representation
- News agenda.

The strength of this approach is that it disciplines students' viewing and note-taking by visually representing the mental process they need to adopt and become familiar with – that is, the recognition of textual elements at a micro level and the ability to frame these in broader responses about the socio-cultural context. Through such an old-fashioned medium as a worksheet (which in essence, this is) you can make tangible a framework for media literacy.

In summary, students need to explore the tension that has arisen in the pursuit of applying narrative theory to computer games, a schism increasingly described as a distinction between ludology and narratology (Newman, 2004). Whereas the narratologist will seek to analyse the game by breaking down the element of its narrative, the ludological approach is to problematise the notion of narrative by seeing how the playful audience experience defies such a description:

> 'While in cut scenes, the distance between story time, discourse time and viewing time is reinstated in much the manner of narrative, the player's ability to act – or rather to play – implodes these relationships.' (Newman, 2004: 103)

So far, visual images have dominated this section, as they do in much of Media education. Now we will turn our attention to radio and new media, in their convergent state. Although the 'conceptual toolkit' for the study of texts in a literacy context should be flexible enough to accommodate anything from an Ian McEwan novel to web-streamed radio, realistically we need to approach the latter with care if we are not to reduce its impact by understating its transformative qualities.

Web radio

This rapidly expanding area can be explored in two ways. Students can focus on analysis of radio from a traditional perspective (codes and conventions, representation and listener decoding) and consider how its transmission over the internet makes a difference to the making of meaning. Or they might approach this from a 'Web Studies perspective', analysing the conventions of the websites that host broadcasts. The latter might seem to return us to a predominately visual paradigm, but we must remember that one contributory (yet underrepresented) factor in the proliferation of web content is its relative ease of access for people with disabilities. Visually impaired people are making great use of web radio, and the advantages for this group of consumers (they are not an audience, as an audience is defined by choice of media use as opposed to access options) are revelatory for students, who may otherwise assume that radio is simply an 'easier' medium than television. If part of our media literacy agenda is to do with social inclusion and democracy, it is beneficial for students to consider media consumption from under-represented groups. Clearly, this is best achieved through research, and while there are sensitive ethical issues to consider, and access opportunities will vary greatly from region to region, a carefully constructed project that allows students to analyse radio conventions from the situation of visually impaired consumers will offer great opportunities for further discussion of representation, access and public service in other areas of the specification. The key critical questions in this context, to be asked of any radio text are:

- How are sound signs used to make meaning (remembering that meaning is actively produced by audiences and as such is polysemic)?
- What is the mode of address?
- What are the traditional conventions, how are they culturally grounded and how do they make meaning?
- Does the text have intertextual relations with non-radio texts?
- Are there generic features?

- What narrative devices are at work? How are they different to visual communication (although another approach is to focus only on radio and not feel the need to understand it in relation to other forms of media that may have arrived later)?
- Does the internet distribution of the text make any difference to the meaning for the audience?
- What is the nature of access to the creative process? Who is behind the text? Are the audience also producers?

Class strategy – Data analysis

One might expect to find a reference to this type of learning in a chapter on research projects. It is placed here to assert again that textual analysis, or media literacy development, should not be divorced from other areas of Media learning (such as audience research, creative work and institutional learning). In this example, I am assuming that a group of students have conducted some research with visually impaired radio consumers and have brought both quantitative (who listens to what) and qualitative (pleasures, interpretations of textual meanings) data back to the classroom. An important point to make here is that it is not necessarily of any importance that the audience group researched have a disability. By always focusing on disabled people's access issues, rather than simply treating them as a group of consumers to be researched, we can be guilty of perpetuating the inequality of representation we would want to reverse.

The process of data analysis will be as follows (assuming the whole group will collaborate to produce a group research outcome):

1. Agree on methodology for analysis. Will this involve transcription? How will data be measured? Who will take responsibility for which elements of data analysis? What will be the time scale?
2. What will be the limitations to state from the outset? What cannot be claimed in terms of representative data? How micro is the information?
3. What theoretical perspectives will the data be related to, and how? For example, if the focus is on a particular aspect of media representation, how will representation be defined and whose definition will be adopted?
4. What were the research questions and how are they related to textual analysis/media literacy?
5. Is there a potential for this data to transform approaches to textual analysis rather than 'slot into' existing models?

While these may seem complex, with careful explanation and tutorial support these research groups can move easily into an advanced realm of media literacy in which they can articulate the relations between text, textual analysis and audience response.

As the interplay between textual analysis, literacy and the conceptual framework for Media learning is ever-present, the chapters that follow will offer a range of strategies that could easily be housed in this chapter. I hope that this section has summarised an approach that works with, and indeed celebrates, the tension between tradition and transformation. Overall, we are operating within the conceptual paradigm in place since Media Studies morphed out of English, but we are at a transition point that we should embrace, and we need to ask our students for the answers.

As I said earlier, media literacy is an active process of deconstruction. In some ways it is an attitude, or a state of mind, rather than a learned skill or set of competences. It is a temporal function, in the sense that it demands we 'stop' the rapid process of signification for long enough to think about the constructed nature of the meanings at stake. The theoretical framework for this 'taking apart' of media texts is a catalyst for this shift in reading practices (literacy). Reading texts through the use of semiotics and multimodality to recognize and analyse intertextual and interformal codes; applying genre theory where it is helpful; considering texts in the context of the effects debate; experimenting with traditional narrative models to see whether they work for (post)modern texts and interrogating the discursive operations at work in media meaning – these amount in the end to a reflexive ability to understand the nature of the self. How am I produced as a subject in the modern world, and what is the relationship between this constructed state and my reading of, and playing in, media, my rootedness in a culture that is always already 'languaged'? (see Jencks, 2005: 203)

Sometimes we can dress up the simplest of operations in the most absurd academic language, and compensate for the everyday nature of our subject matter (compared to literature, say) with an overly theorized view of Media learning. I include myself in this (indeed I am probably more guilty than most).

Our work, then, can amount to little more than the transference of complex essay writing techniques and the acquisition of a bourgeois, elaborated code if we do not pay attention to the primary objective: media student, deconstruct thyself.

Further reading

Bignell, J., 1997, *Media Semiotics: an introduction,* Manchester: MUP.

Buckingham, D., 2003, *Media Education: Literacy, Learning and Contemporary Culture,* London: Polity.
Chapter 3 is devoted to media literacies.

Bruce, C., 2002, 'Analyse This!' in *Media Magazine,* 2, London: English and Media Centre.

Burn, A., Carr, D., Oram, B., Horrell, K., and Schott, G., 2003, 'Why Study Digital Games?' in *Media Magazine,* 5 and 6, London: English and Media Centre.

Burn, A., and Parker, D., 2003, *Analysing Media Texts,* London: Continuum.

Fiske, J., 1987, *Television Culture,* London: Methuen.
Seminal, much referenced collection of theoretical perspectives on small screen texts.

Gee, J., 2003, *What Video Games have to teach us about Learning and Literacy*, New York: Palgrave MacMillan.
Essential reading.

Izod, J., 1984, *Reading the Screen*, London: Longman.
Excellent resource for moving image analysis.

Jencks, C., 2005, *Culture,* London: Routledge.
Very helpful slim volume introduction to Cultural Studies.

Masterman, L., 2004, 'Visions of Media Education; The Road from Dystopia' in *In the Picture*, 48. Keighley: itp Publications.
A passionate reminder to us all of the importance of media literacy in a world of spin and demonising of the media.

McDougall, J., 2003, 'Games in the Classroom – Whatever Next?' in *Media Magazine*, 6, London: English and Media Magazine.

Newman, J., 2004, *Videogames*, London: Routledge.

Ofcom, 2005, 'Media Literacy Bulletin', 1 and 2. London: Ofcom.

Selby, K., and Cowdery, R., 1995, *How to Study Television*, London: MacMillan.

Stafford, R., and Branston, G., 2004, *The Media Student's Book.* London: Routledge
In my opinion the best textbook for students on textual analysis.

Toland, P., 2004, 'What are you Playing At?' in *Media Magazine*, 7, London: English and Media Centre.
Covers representation in computer games in a Cultural Studies context.

Winship, J., 1997, *Inside Women's Magazines*, London: Pandora
Important theoretical perspective on the ways in which gender texts produce complicity and recognition.

Wolf, J., and Perron, B., 2003, *The Video Game Theory Reader*, London: Routledge.

See also the 'Top 40 Websites' section.

chapter seven

Doing the Big Concepts

Introduction

This chapter offers a more detailed approach to working with the key concepts of representation, narrative and genre with Media students on all courses. This is possible because, for better or worse, all Media Studies specifications demand the ability to work with this kind of 'conceptual committee'. This approach differs in sequence to some others, as I want to argue that genre must be problematised as a concept in the classroom, existing as it does (to some extent) as an accident of the former two concepts. Equally, representation (and discourse) is at the heart of this book's strategies, so I suggest that if conceptual learning is to be productive (and reflecting on this with students throughout is mandatory), then the question of how media realities operate should be the starting point, with questions of narrative and convention following from this foundation.

> 'Technological and social change has affected Media Studies at every level of the subject. It is not yet clear whether the existing models of analysing and creating media products are continually adapting to new developments or whether these changes have transformed the whole field of study.' (QCA, 2005: 65)

At the time of writing, every Media specification with 14–19-year-old school/college students as its 'core business' features a compulsion to be conversant in these concepts. We might discuss this as an approach, when compared to other ways of thinking about Media learning, and certainly we should not assume either that texts are at the centre of study or that they can best be analysed through such concepts. In addition, production work, through explanation of process and evaluation of outcome, is usually written about by students in conceptual terms, addressing questions such as:

- Which genre did I choose and why?
- What conventions did I employ and how?
- Did I use a linear narrative?
- Who and what was I representing and how?

A problem with this tradition might be the proliferation of set responses or 'right answers' about how texts, in particular genres, make meaning, which goes against the grain of the kind of Media learning that acknowledges the negotiated, fluid and situated and 'languaged' nature of audience responses to texts. My key suggestion is this: building a conceptual approach around audience and representation, and facilitating a reflexive approach to these areas. In other words, focusing on active reading of representation, reappropriation of meaning and identity and questioning assumptions about media representation will enable students to gain the required knowledge of how these concepts work, but avoid passive and mundane acceptance of academic language. If students are going to engage with genre in their creative activities, then consideration of how their work plays with conventions maintains this spirit. Equally, work that seems merely to imitate is better understood as an application of conventions, as all new activity within a paradigm is ultimately dialectical and constitutes a shift (see Buckingham, 2003: 134). At the same time, if students are looking at texts from an analytical perspective, then the focus should always be on how audiences interpret representations in different ways, and how representations reflect claims to power and truth that may be more or less successful.

Class strategy – Self-deconstruction

A nice way in to reflective study is to introduce deconstruction as an approach with a focus on self-analysis. There is a double-approach here: first students analyse, then they create, both arising from the same principle.

Individual students are given three adverts – print, television and radio. They are asked to plot themselves on a 1–5 scale against each one. 5 is 'highly persuaded' and 1 is 'of no consequence'. It is worth spending some time agreeing that advertising does not work on the basis of pleasure. Many adverts work by really annoying us, but they get our attention (think of Michael Winner!). So a student will give a mark of 1 if they are unlikely to recall the product. Next, students are given time to draw/construct a visual representation of their own tastes and consumption patterns in terms of what their money is spent on in an average week, and what they make use of in textual terms. This should be left open to encourage more creative responses. The adverts must feature on these outcomes, so the viewer can see a representation of each text's proximity to the student's pleasures, choices and tastes.

Next, individuals are given the task of representing themselves in a 30-second advert for them as a citizen. There is no particular agenda to this – the student is merely advertising herself as a human being. They can choose a straightforward narrative approach (summarizing the unique selling points) or a set of more symbolic, abstract representational devices. This outcome might be produced in the form of a script/storyboard, or an actual mini-production.

> These tasks give you something to use throughout the study of representation and narrative – they are very 'close to home' examples of how meaning is made through shorthand use of convention, cultural code and targeting. You can build existing theoretical approaches to texts and groups of texts on these foundations.

Representation

When media students analyse ways in which texts and their readers make sense of representations, they are usually thinking about the world of the text in relation to competing notions of what the world is 'really like'. This is evaluative and deeply problematic, of course, if it relies on an assumption that we can know the world outside of our own perception. The ideology of a text can be considered, in the sense that it is possible to say, usually, that the text relies on some assumptions and will work only if its readers share some of these. More importantly, most versions of this conceptual study get to the point (usually fairly late in the proceedings) where students consider the possibility of oppositional or negotiated responses to texts. Who might be excluded? Might there be other ways of reading this? Might it be more complex than we first thought? My central suggestion is that you start with this discussion.

Most specifications require students to study representation in two ways. The most obvious and common is for them to use a range of concepts when studying any single text, and in this context, how the text represents people and things would be one consideration amongst a range of others (and as such, it might be given fairly brief attention). The other common approach is for particular genres or time periods to be given attention for their significance in representational terms. For example, students might analyse situation comedy for its comedic representation of common experience, soap opera for its portrayal of gender and social class, computer games for the ways in which conflict and competition are depicted (and *experienced*, in this example), gangster films for their take on the 'American dream', or magazines for their presentation of gender. In this second context, a more 'macro' approach is taken and students make intertextual and historical connections, with the help of some received theory/research from writers who have become expert in a particular genre of time period.

In both approaches, it is impossible to separate representation from questions of narrative, genre (perhaps) and audience, so again, exam questions or coursework requirements tend to be broad in scope. As a result, it is possible for students (and teachers) to place more or less emphasis on representation. A student writing about documentary might spend more time on the history of the genre, its development in conventions from Grierson to *Wife Swap* and its function institutionally, and then place this in a debate around 'quality', access and democracy. And another student might focus much more on the claim to realism made by documentary and, through scrutiny of editing and televisual language in general, question the nature of the reality and its representation in particular cases. A student working on British Cinema might produce promotional materials for their own UK film, and either 'major' on co-funding and commerce (how successful might this film be for an international audience) or on how their text represents British people in the contemporary historical context (the 'history of the present').

To illustrate a range of examples for working with media representation I consider here Paul Abbot's television drama *Shameless* for its representations of class, gender and family in comparison with British soap opera (which we will return to when we focus on genre). Alongside this, I describe a study of two computer games in terms of the effect that participation in narrative has on representation.

Class strategy – Collaborative summarizing

This is a strategy that can be used for any detailed piece of written text (or indeed video or other form) that you want students to read and summarize on their own terms. It is a simple approach to collaborative work that can be used regularly to save time and develop skills in selection and presentation of information.

In this example, the work in question is the chapter on 'Studying Comedy' in *The Television Genre Book* (Creeber (ed.), 2001). This extract is 10 pages long, so it can be divided up for a class of 20 in the following way. Each group of four students takes one of the following areas to read and summarize:

- humour theory
- sketch comedy
- family sitcoms
- workplace sitcoms
- narrative architecture/storytelling grammar.

They then 'jigsaw' (see Chapter Six) and present their summaries (in three sentences only) and one chosen quotation to students from the other groups. They are not allowed merely to read out three sentences from the text – their contributions must be summative. The outcome, in the space of one lesson, is a clear summary of the theoretical ideas in the chapter, in students' own language, alongside five key quotes from the material.

There are three advantages to this organization of reading and synthesis:

1. You can differentiate by organizing the task strategically and tailoring the material to different groups of learners.
2. You can save time and money (covering more in less time, and using 'class sets' of smaller extracts).
3. Over time, students will come to an understanding of how to 'pan' a summary to cover the whole of the material. If this works, then eventually when you ask them to read and summarize they will arrange the task in this way for themselves.

The comedy drama *Shameless* (described on *The South Bank Show* by its creator Paul Abbott as '*Little House on the Prairie* on acid') is broadcast by Channel 4 and features a family living on a fictional estate in Manchester. Frank Gallagher, an unemployable alcoholic, and his many offspring survive through hard work and some criminal activity. Students need to get to grips with the complex range of representational devices at work in this text. Whether or not the family and their environment are represented in any one stable way is difficult to say, is a reason for choosing this text to work with.

Shameless – a rich text for analysis of representation

'You know Frank's totally derelict. The fact that you don't want to kill him is a really serious piece of processing on the audience's part.' (Abbott, speaking on *The South Bank Show*, 2005)

Representation is best understood as a flow of energy arising from a text's status as a site of conflict. Understood in this way, media texts construct narratives through which competing discourses (ways of understanding 'truth') battle for supremacy. A classic realist text sets up one discourse as dominant (usually through the actions of the main character with whom we empathize), whereas more complex texts offer a variety of positions to take (in which case the 'sayable' is less delimited, in Foucault's (1988) terms). Students might look at a range of texts with this in mind, not to work out how and what each one represents, but to compare the degree of motivation at work in representation. *Shameless* seems to present the world most clearly through the eyes of Frank's eldest, Fiona, who acts as mother to the family in response to Frank's fecklessness. Fiona is an angelic character, despite her constant smoking and profanities. Her partner Steve ('posh lad') turns out to be a master car-thief. He is the character with the most cultural capital (and the only middle-class representation), yet he is the most corrupt and dishonest, in the end. Representations of law and order, religion and sexuality are equally polysemic. In any one episode, there is no fixed point of moral or social judgement for the audience to take. For this reason, it is really productive to start with a text as complex as this one and then look at more 'black and white' alternatives later. I have used a an extract from *South Park*, in which white America is lampooned for its racial paranoia, and then showed a clip from *Training Day*, in which a white rookie cop is taken to a 'ghetto' by his worldly black partner. The *mise-en-scène* (which spells out danger, drug deals, guns and prostitution) is constructed through the eyes of the white character (this is the 'white gaze', to extend Mulvey's theory). This scene is not unusual – we get the view of black neighbourhoods we are used to from mainstream Hollywood cinema, to the extent that we do not question it on first viewing. But screened in the context of the *South Park* clip, it becomes an example of the ridiculous phobic landscape of white middle-class America. This intertextual strategy serves to show students that texts exist in relation to other texts more significantly than in relation to any fixed sense of reality. The ghetto we see in *Training Day* matches our expectation of such a place in the 'real world' and yet this (mis)recognition is based on other films and television sequences rather than lived experience of such urban locations. Students need to acknowledge these textual operations before proceeding to analyse such concepts as realizm.

Class strategy – Group presentations

One of the assessment methods used by all teachers, group presentations work best when some serious consideration is given to fitness for purpose. You should encourage students in your group to avoid:

- reading from paper (there is no value added by the format if this is the case)
- freeloading from one another (not a collaborative learning experience)
- taking too long or not presenting for long enough (preparing for a specific length of time is a skill to be developed)
- all presenting from the same perspective on the same topic (it gets very dull and they do not learn from one another, so a great deal of time is wasted).

An attempt at a more strategic approach follows, taking the example of *Shameless* and representation.

- Take one episode and select five key scenes (or negotiate these with the class).
- Each group takes one scene.
- Provide a very clear framework for the presentation for each group, providing a different angle for each: representation of the family unit; representation of gender; representation of social class (in relation to the

subject matter of the episode – not in isolation from anything else); representation of 'ordinary people' – the extended community; representation of occupation in this community).

- Each group is additionally required to find an article from a newspaper which presents a stereotype of 'problem families', and the *Shameless* clip must be discussed in relation to this alternative representation.
- The presentation must be exactly 10 minutes long, including screening of the clip, and it must feature a handout and visual presentation (OHT, PowerPoint or other). While it is not essential that all students speak for the same amount of time (in my experience this can reduce the presentation in quality), a record of tasks carried out by each must be provided as a kind of 'credits list'.
- If one student is absent without having phoned in, the presentation is failed.

The advantages of this approach are that the discipline of the presentations is increased, so that students can learn from each other (they will have detailed notes on five scenes rather than a repetition of the same material), and some of the common pitfalls of this approach are prevented. The teacher's job is to pull out the areas for scaffolding with higher level questions – students are only expected to present an introduction to the theoretical issues arising from the text.

A range of angles for representational study include: popularity (reasons for enduring success); negative representation and social consequences (for example, objectification of women in music video, the tabloid press or 'lad mags'); questions of realizm; debates around truth (for example, the selection and construction of news) and access (the absence of representation, for example of people with disability or the representation/absence of ethnic minorities). What many of these versions tend to avoid is a scrutiny of some (in my view) outdated assumptions about mediation. A prevalent model is still at work in Media teaching that is not too far away from the 'classic' Shannon and Weaver (1949) sender-message-receiver conception of communication. More interesting Media learning arises from placing questions about the *nature* of meaning at the heart of the work. So in the case of *Shameless*, how are viewers culturally situated in their responses? How does intertextual meaning make a difference? To what extent are traditional representations of working-class Northern communities played within this text (we might look at *Saturday Night and Sunday Morning, Coronation Street, Boys from the Blackstuff* and *Brassed Off* to consider representational changes over time)? We should avoid attempting to 'stop' the chain of signification for too long, lest we might present media texts in an artificial state of isolation from one another.

Comparing a text like *Shameless* with a seemingly more straightforward soap opera such as *Coronation Street* is most fruitful when the more complex text is dealt with first. We want to avoid a reductive approach that ignores the range of possible readings of characters and situations in the narrative. Also, you have a choice (one that will be more or less pinned down by the requirements of the specification in question). Do you take students through the received body of work on, say, representation of the family in the British soap opera, and then apply this to particular episodes, storylines and extra-textual dimensions (such as tabloid press treatment of actor/character duality)? Or do you help students create something new, by looking at an area such as disability and considering the presence/absence of such representation in such a popular text? Taking the former approach, there is a body of theory available, including the work of Geraghty (1991) and Buckingham (1987). In addition, I have used extensively Linda Grant's (1996) argument that *Coronation Street* and other soaps (early *Brookside*, in particular) act as social documents of their times, inheriting and transforming the legacy of the 'kitchen sink' films of the 1950s and 1960s. Students might test this hypothesis (they should never just accept it) by watching films like *Saturday Night and Sunday Morning* and comparing the degrees of motivation in each case, or in Bakhtin's (1981) terms, the extent to which each text is monoglot (one discourse comes to dominate) or heteroglot (there are a variety of possible responses available and there is no clear hierarchy of viewpoint at work). Students can easily get into this kind of work, despite the fact that East-European formalism is considered 'high theory', because these are straightforward analytical questions. In *Saturday Night and Sunday Morning*, Arthur Seaton's voice is in our ears throughout. The film is anchored by his philosophy: 'Never let the bastards grind you down' (which refers to post-war social class and the nature of his exploitation) and 'Take a tip from the fishes, they never bite until the bait's good enough. Mind you, they all get caught in the end' (on marriage). Arthur's celebration of hedonism, his rejection of consumer culture (most notably his annoyance at his father's television viewing and his sceptical response to new houses) and most importantly, his understanding of his alienation in the factory, provide a preferred reading, or at least, the text is hierarchically organized so that we understand other character's perspectives (such as those of the women Arthur sleeps with) only in relation to his view of the world.

An episode of *Eastenders* cannot be organized in the same way, as its configuration of space and time is more varied. As a result, the viewer (who is often in a social context rather than alone) can form alliances and prejudices in a much more idiosyncratic way. Students might also throw into equation the suggestion that soap opera has historically been understood as a form of melodrama with a female orientation. Does a film like *Saturday Night* offer a more logocentric sense of meaning founded on a notion of a present, identifiable take on the world, compared to the more fluid dynamics of the soap opera? Note that here we are not considering how the text represents people, but how the text represents. We are reflecting on the concept and its dynamics, as opposed to applying theory as though it were a science. As always, the best way to take this further is for students to design (and preferably film/edit and screen) a soap opera sequence that will offer a plurality of audience responses.

To return to the more rudimentary questions of soap opera representation, here are some 'ways in' to this kind of study:

- How is the representation (of a particular group) mediated through the specific televisual language of this kind of text?

- To what extent does the verisimilitude achieved by the illusion of ongoing real time seal a sense of greater proximity to real life than in other texts (for example, the situation comedy with its condensed and self-contained 30 minutes)?

- In what ways are soap operas topical and sometimes controversial in their treatments of current affairs/social issues? Related to this, what is the responsibility of a soap opera producer? Is it to reflect society 'as it is' or 'as it should be'?

- What is the balance of realizm and drama in particular soaps? This balance is very important to the remit of a soap opera – it must cling to a very specific verisimilitude (as in the opening credits of *Coronation Street*) which may be outdated, or at least nostalgic and romantic, at the same time as competing for ratings with other soaps through the development of exciting, ongoing and climaxing storylines. Students might trace changes in a particular soap at times of 'crisis' in ratings terms to see how this operates.

- A case study on the representation of family life will be productive. On October 17th 2002, *The Daily Mail* published 'Scarred by Soaps' (by Steve Doughty, Social Affairs correspondent), in response to research carried out by the National Family and Parenting Institute. The article explained that the findings of this research were that children are encouraged by soaps to believe that family breakdown is the norm and that soaps fail to promote moral values. On the same day, John Carvel (Social Affairs editor) summarized the same research in *The Guardian*, but concentrated mostly on the research's evidence that parents regularly discuss soap opera storylines with their children. If this is the case, then the texts act as a resource for a (perhaps) healthy level of discussion about the family unit that may be more difficult to mobilize in isolation from this media catalyst. Students might (to keep things active) research this debate through their own work with viewers, and then experiment with the creation of storylines that might offer a range of more or less positive (or at least different) representations of the modern family.

- Analysis of the intertextual and/or extratextual meanings circulating around soaps are essential if students are to understand the specific nature of representation at work in these programmes. Tabloid newspapers (since Murdoch's intervention) have routinely confused actor/character and drama/reality at the time when popular storylines are broadcast. These articles might be analysed in terms of second-hand representation. In addition, soap trailers are becoming increasingly sophisticated (especially in genre study terms, all the British soaps have played with *film noir* and thriller conventions in their promotional work) and there are a range of magazines offering a range of additional meanings for the audience.

- In terms of popularity, students might consider whether the reason for the longevity of the pleasure offered by these texts is to do with representation, or not. In other words, are forms of vicarious pleasure offered by the (mis)recognition of the everyday in these programmes, or are they 'just' good drama? And ultimately the 'social document versus junk TV' debate hinges on theories of popular culture. Is the representation of the domestic sphere the reason for middle-class distaste and closet viewing ('I don't set out to watch it, but it is always on in our house'), and equally for devotion from the 'masses', or is the audience acting in a more discerning, 'pick and mix' way with these texts?

Returning to media literacy and creativity as the two-pronged approach suggested throughout this book, I should say that this kind of work should never be divorced from the construction and deconstruction of specific textual moments. Students cannot sensibly approach the kinds of debates and research approaches above without relating notions of realizm and representation back to choices made about camera, sound, *mise-en-scène* and performance. Technical and symbolic codes are always at work in representational meanings. A simple substitution exercise will highlight important semiotic principles. What happens if one character wears different clothes? What if the design of the set was changed so that one family's house got a designer makeover? These interesting, entertaining and very 'low level' questions lead to rich discussion about stereotyping and myth. It is not a million miles from here to Roland Barthes.

Class strategy – Anonymous statement banking

This approach can be used for any debate or hypothesis. It is a nice way of representing a debate visually without worrying about the dynamics of side-taking or the anxieties some students feel in the public forum.

In this example, the debate is 'Soap opera, disability and responsibility'. ('Disability' could be replaced with ethnicity, sexuality, the nuclear family, asylum or any other area of public dissensus.)

The teacher provides six pieces of flipchart paper, positioned around the room. Each one has a headline statement so that a range of hypotheses are represented:

- Soaps are a reflection on how society is.
- Disabled people are under-represented in soap operas.
- Soaps are just entertainment and the audience must not be put off by sensitive subjects.
- Soaps should challenge stereotypes.
- Soaps are not social documents because they do not accurately represent social difference (including disability).
- Analysing soap opera in this way is over the top – they are irrelevant to social democracy.

Set up the exercise carefully, then get students to move around the room, adding their own statements in a dialectical fashion. This means they must add to a 'chain reaction' in each case, so the debate moves forward. By the end of a fixed time period, the statements on each sheet can be categorized in small groups into the various competing discourses in circulation.

This is a good way to make the lived, energized nature of a debate make sense (as opposed to a more fixed, reductive explanation of each side).

The focus on disability is an example of Media education at its most important. At the BFI Media Teacher's Conference in 2003, Andrea Stanton reported to delegates on the 'Invisible Children' conference that year, with the following statement:

> 'There was general agreement that to continue to portray disabled people as invisible or one-dimensional reinforces the discrimination and isolation disabled people experience in all aspects of life. This can include becoming targets for bullying and physical attack. It was felt that children are particularly affected by the images to which they have access. Unfortunately, most children and young people rarely meet disabled children in their schools and form their views of them mainly through the media. The inclusion of disabled people in producing and creating images and portrayal of disabled people as "real people" is crucial.'

A production task in which students are charged with collaborating with disabled people (if they are not themselves disabled) can bring to life these issues and lead to some worthwhile and transforming experiences. The focus should be on the production of narratives in which characters are disabled but where this is *not* what the story is about. It is not only the relative absence of minorities from media representations that students need to consider, but also the focus, when they are represented, of their 'status' in narratives. Put another way (and using a different example), imagine a world in which Bruce Willis' character in *Die Hard* was gay, and the audience got to know this because his male partner was in danger, but this was of no consequence to the story otherwise. That would *really* be equality.

Working with computer games in the classroom forces us to address once again the question of whether the traditional conceptual approach still holds water in the wake of digital technology, or whether we need to adapt our modes of thinking about such concepts as representation to the hyper-reality of our contemporary condition.

As part of a research project in March 2005, I observed Wayne O'Brien teaching computer games and representation with a group of AS Media students at Halesowen College. (I was interested, from a phenomenological perspective, in what happens when 'toys' from their life worlds are brought into the context of the classroom, but we are concerned here with this work as an example of 'doing representation'.) In all the lessons I observed, students were playing Playstation 2 games, with the console connected to a monitor. Ideally, this would be a data projector (and indeed the other lessons this group had were in a different room, with this facility). When I have discussed this approach with teachers, they have often expressed concern about either purchasing a console with the department budget, or about asking students to bring in their own. I agree with the latter concern, but the former is ridiculous. Could you teach film without any DVDs? Once computer games took their (rightful) place in the media curriculum, any concern about 'having them in the classroom' was taken away. The games have the same textual status as film, video and print materials. The consoles are in an equal relationship to DVD players.

Class strategy – Playing games

Wayne used the 'spectacle' of students playing games (in this case *Medal of Honor* and *The Sims*) in four ways over three lessons that I witnessed. These different approaches demonstrate an approach to teaching that I think bridges the old/new paradigm issue I have described.

In one lesson, the experience of gaming was the area for study. Volunteers, in turn, played Eye Toy games, cleaning windows and boxing using the specific spatial facility created by this technology (you move your hands in the air to navigate menus, as a camera on top of the screen reads your manoeuvres). The rest of the students observed the game playing, as Wayne prompted their analysis with questions about the gaming experience, types of learning and by setting up discussion about the future: will the type of gaming predicted in *Existenz* be with us sooner rather than later; and will film seem like an old medium shortly, due to its lack of an interactive, ludic dimension?

The following week, *Medal of Honor* was treated in an 'old fashioned' way as a text for analysis. At some points, the cut scenes were played as a video sequence for analysis (students were considering ways in which the player is motivated by the missions, ways in which the enemy – the Nazis – is constructed, and the American ideology represented by such a narrative). At other times, students took turns to play various chapters. Again, while this was happening, other students were engaged in directed textual analysis, and I noticed that the novelty of gaming in the classroom was soon replaced by a traditional 'watch and make notes' approach. The key difference was that Wayne was able to question each player and relate their responses (in the Vygotskian tradition of theoretical scaffolding (1962)) to his conceptual focus. In particular, students were thinking about teamwork in the game in the context of military practices and ways in which conflict between nations is constructed as a battle between teams (in contrast to the popular derision aimed at gamers as solitary, socially ineffective individuals). I would argue that a far more reflective approach to learning was evident in this structure, due to the interplay between teacher (as 'carrier' of theory), students as players and students as analysts.

In the final lesson I observed, Wayne set up a 'carousel' of activities. Students, in turn played *The Sims*, with a set of contextual questions to consider. These were focused on comparing the experience with *Medal Of Honor* in terms of agenda, motivation, learning and understanding of competing/winning. Other students were continuing a practical activity, designing promotional images for an anti-war game (some of their ideas were: a Red Cross mission; delivering a letter to an Iraqi general that would stop the war; and a game in which the player moves between sides so that she experiences the effects of her previous actions. This last idea was very sophisticated – the students suggested that this would be a game you couldn't win. This allowed Wayne to extend the discussion in terms of the importance to the gaming experience of narrative closure and ultimately, victory. The third task set was a straightforward question-and-answer analysis of *The Sims* in terms of target audience, representation of competition and player motivation/learning.

This variety of activities were at once transformative and traditional. The strength of the approach was not to do with the novelty value of having a Playstation 2 in the classroom, but in the traditional teacher-craft of facilitating pace, transition, variety, theoretical framing and reflective enquiry.

Narrative

As we have already considered, interactive technologies are threatening the kinds of approaches to narrative that Masterman described in 1985. We are renegotiating our ways of analysing text-reader relations in the context of media experiences where the line between activity and passivity is exposed as fragile (it always was thus, but now we can see it):

'There are layers to narratives, to be sure, and they inevitably revolve around a mixture of the present and the future, between what's happening now and the tantalising question of where it's all headed. But narratives are built out of events, not tasks. They happen to you. In the game world, you are forced to define and execute the tasks; if your definitions get blurry or are poorly organised, you'll have trouble playing. You can still enjoy a book without explicitly concentrating on where the narrative will take you two chapters out, but in game worlds you need that long term planning as much as you need present tense focus.' (Johnson, 2005: 55)

The best way to introduce narrative as a concept is to ask each student to talk for one minute about what they did the night before. Inevitably, you can deconstruct their linear sequencing, selection of material and, far more importantly, omission of minor detail. For comic effect, you might ask: 'What, so you never went to the toilet?' to illustrate this point, providing your rapport is robust enough.

I want to suggest an approach to narrative theory that does not use Propp or Todorov (which in this sense, might be unique!): not because there is anything wrong with an approach that uses these old models to demonstrate the fixed, narrow and predictable nature of storytelling in the West, but because I think it presents a model of narrative flow as fixed and 'applicable' and I do not agree that we read texts in this way, necessarily. Teachers and students, I think, tend to be comfortable with such theory because you can apply it and be right or wrong about it, but having marked exam scripts and production commentaries in their thousands I have started to wonder about the more interesting discussions of narrative that we might get to if so much time were not spent painstakingly describing disequilibrium in *Paddy and Max* or working out who the donor is in *City of God*.

Narrative is rarely (if ever) studied in its own right on Media courses at Levels 2 and 3, so narrative theory as such is less important than a working approach to texts and production work that can be used to articulate an understanding of space, time and active reading at work in the following of a story. Essentially, in fiction texts we are talking about plot and story, and in non-fiction, order, selection and convention. In a film, a character getting on to a train, reading a paper and then departing from the carriage can be 'told' in 20 seconds without an outraged audience complaining at the preposterously rapid nature of the journey. Equally, we take for granted the relative 'importance' of the first news item and the 'natural' location of sports news at the end. In many ways, narrative can be understood in terms of cognition or as language acquisition. If we make sense of our lives through representing them in narrative form, then are media narratives socially and psychologically beneficial? Next to me on my desk I have a handwritten list of the order of content and class strategies for this chapter. Further down my computer screen from where the cursor is I have inserted reminders to myself to write about these things. In the process, this is forgotten and I stumble back to this ordering later on and try to cut and paste the text into some kind of logical flow. Narrative informs all these processes (and their attendant anxieties in this case).

Once again, rather than starting with older narrative theories and ending up with postmodern approaches as a kind of quasi-extension activity, I suggest going straight for the more complex, less straightforward work with students. The 'element' of postmodernity that is of interest here is the ambiguities that exist around space and time. Some readily available examples include films like *Pulp Fiction*, *The Usual Suspects* and *Memento*; in television, a comparison of *Big Brother*'s 'live' and edited versions, *24* and *The Royle Family* (for different reasons, to illustrate the exception to the rule), rolling news in a variety of media and any number of computer games in which space and time are more interactively constructed. As Nick Lacey describes it:

> 'Postmodernism places the reader in a self-conscious position as the (re)creator of the texts she or he is experiencing. Similarly, the central concern of postmodern media texts is less to do with the traditional objective of 'knowing' (epistemology) and more to do with being (ontology). The reader is not simply using information to create the text, he or she is interacting with the text in "reference spotting" almost as if it were a quiz'. (2000a: 99)

I think all media reading has always been as Lacey describes it, and postmodernism is not so much an approach to textual production as a way of understanding reading in new ways. In other words, knowing has only ever been a subsidiary of being. In classroom practice, then, how can we translate this set of philosophical considerations into accessible Media learning?

We can get straight into this by talking with students about how plot and story work. In simple terms, we can say that the reader constructs the signified story from the plot as signifier. Through the study of editing (which would be my preferred starting point for dealing with narrative on any course) students soon realize that what is *not* there is of more importance than what *is* (as we found with representation, of course). Received theory in this area leads up to consideration of 'classical narrative', but as with Propp and Todorov, I am not sure of the function of such an approach. I prefer to complicate, rather than simplify students' perceptions of how meaning gets made in media texts. The reductive nature of classic models (for instance, the classical narrative is normally equated with Hollywood's dominance of cinema since the advent of sound) can be that their 'application' presents a rather narrow view of how the reader operates. This then jars with other moments in Media learning where we ask students to consider the reader as the key negotiator of meaning. Certainly, students need very early on to create sequences, most easily in video, and to talk about what they left out and why, and (returning to Eisenstein and, if you like, D.W. Griffith) how the combinations of their images (the sum) makes more meaning than the parts in isolation. If we are looking at film, then linking the micro features of a particular narrative (for example shot/reverse shot, cross-cutting, examples of continuity, ellipsis, dialectical montage and referential moments that rely on inter or extra-textual understanding) with the macro narrative approach, is the obvious next step. The central concept, I think, is diegesis (the world of the text). What happens outside of diegesis is where the active reading can be located.

In Susan Levan's analysis of *Fargo*, she describes the directors' approach in this way:

'The term postmodern is often used to describe the work of the Coen Brothers. . .their telling of stories which comment on the nature of stories and of storytelling. . .' (2000: p18)

I think Levan's analysis points out a significant error made by critics who distance the Coens from other directors, as though other films are not 'stories about stories' when really the 'postmodern embrace' is just a new way of thinking about texts, rather than new kinds of texts. We should be working with our students to think about all media meaning as 'postmodern', if what we mean by this is an approach to texts that is most interested in the conditions of their possibility, of their textual nature, as opposed to what they 'mean'. As stated earlier, there is little in Media specifications to demand a consideration of narrative as a concept (this is different for genre, for instance) and for this reason, you will most likely be helping your students to apply narrative models. I think this is a problem, because all the key concepts are best understood through being challenged and made complex. That said, the key questions for students to consider about the construction of any text might be:

- Is it linear?
- What meaning is made outside the diegesis?
- What micro examples best illustrate the overall narrative approach?
- How does the narrative serve conflict between discourses?

To deal with the micro elements, I suggest two approaches. First, the elements of media literacy should not be divorced from narrative at any time. So if students are working with technical codes in their own work and in their analyses, they can consider how these add up to a narrative style or approach overall (although equally they must articulate the complexity of texts which shift between approaches). Alongside this 'meat and drink', an example of 'handed down' theory I do advocate is Roland Barthes' narrative codes. A summary of these, in the form of questions for students, looks like this:

1. How does the text use images and meanings which tap into already held oppositions and responses to symbols?

2. What enigmas are set up and what simple, understandable actions are evident (and what is the balance of action and enigma?)

3. What cultural meanings are created by *mise-en-scène*, performance and setting?

4. What inter/extra-textual references help make meaning?

This is not a faithful paraphrasing of Barthes' original theory. Instead, it reformulates his ideas in (I hope) simple questions that lead to longer, more negotiated answers than some other narrative models offer. I think the work we do with students on narrative as a formal mechanism has strengths and weaknesses. It helps us (and students) feel secure that there are some 'right answers' about how stories are told, but it risks simplifying the very interesting and ever fluid interpretive work that audiences do with stories. There is a dilemma at the heart of this – if we want to teach students about binary oppositions and their function in media meaning, we don't have the time for the ultra-sophisticated Derridean approaches we might want to take to this. For this reason, can we avoid reinforcing and perhaps overplaying the very polarizing tendency in discourse we are really seeking to challenge? I think we can, if we adopt a questioning approach, especially to the students' own narrative creativity. Turning back to Barthes, I would encourage students to consider those questions about their production activities during production, rather than before they start (in which case you end up with a rather artificial attempt to 'evidence' conceptual understanding through making a film) or after they have finished (in which case you can end up with some less than heartfelt claims, as in: 'my video has lots of images and is postmodern').

The degree of closure offered by a text is another measurement students will make, and clearly, this is best done through comparative work. Going back to our example from the representation section, *Shameless* is partly closed each time as each episode has a central self-contained narrative alongside others that continue over the duration of the series. This flow is perhaps disrupted (in terms of the rhythm of a TV serial) by the option to watch the next episode immediately on E4 instead of waiting a week for the next scheduled broadcast on Channel 4. Consider my strange habits for a moment. Why is it that I always want to do this, but prefer to wait to watch the next episode at the 'right time'? Is it because I am using the series to punctuate my life and if so, what does this do to the narrative? Is 'my' narrative the same as another viewer who does take the instant E4 option? And in the future, when (according to some) we will all use downloads to produce bespoke schedules and there will be little in the way of collective media experience, will narrative shift paradigm? The important point here is that we move very quickly into asking questions about narrative, as opposed to applying models to provide stable answers. The nucleus of these considerations, I think, are two questions which are always useful: what assumptions are made by the narrative, and who is more and less included by such an approach? Pretty soon, these discussions take us back to the consideration of media discourse. In other words, when students are thinking about cause and effect, space and time, plot and story, cultural codes, intertextual references, diegisis and conflict between characters, they are never far away from deconstructing their own understanding of the world through discourse. The strength of the 'postmodern' approach, for me, is that it emphasizes and indeed celebrates the difficulty of this reflective work.

Chris Mottershead, in a conference workshop on Teaching Narrative, offered this rationale:

'Narratives do not just have a beginning and an end in the sense of starting and finishing. Rather they offer a movement from a situation to another situation. The initial situation presents some kind of problem or disturbance to the world of the fiction. The events which follow are about the solution of the problem which is when the narrative ends with a change from the initial situation overcoming whatever was wrong and offering some new future. It is in their choice of both problem and solution that narrative fictions offer accounts of "how life is", of "what makes a happy ending", of how "a hero" should behave and provide explanations which seem to make sense.' (2001: 5)

Mottershead here brings to our attention a big point about narrative that I think takes us away (helpfully) from the 'nothing changes' adherence to Propp and Todorov. It is a commonly held view that while subject matter and ideology change to reflect socio-cultural preoccupation, the structure of narrative remains intact (in other words it is just the type of disequilibrium and the nature of the villains that change). However, if we consider the revamped *Dr Who* series, here is a text that relies on an 'old fashioned' set of concerns (not to mention images and effects) to make sense. The notion that we have two separate elements to a story – its content and its structure, and that we can say that popular texts tend to update the former, but it is only postmodern texts that play around with the latter, is unsatisfactory.

Another model which has pros and cons is offered by Medhurst (1994) who pinpoints seven narrative patterns that are used as story currency in Western culture. (Let us not forget, by the way, that we will have many students who can tell us about narrative forms from other cultures.) According to Medhurst, pleasure is repetition and in this sense we could get pretty easily to a version of Nietzsche's 'eternal recurrence' through a study of media narrative. That is, if we accept Medhurst's premise (or Nietzsche's, for that matter). The seven narrative types, prevalent from Greek mythology through to the obligatory Shakespeare and into soaps and sitcoms, range from Romeo and Juliet (dramatic irony) to The Spider and the Fly (the web of deceit) and Cinderella (rags to riches). I think this is a really useful model, if treated as a hypothesis for students to test out through research and analysis. If treated as a model which is absolute, then this is an example of critically bankrupt Media learning.

It is important to spend some time on non-fiction narrative. Popular areas for study are news, in both broadcast and paper form (selection and construction of news are activities of narrative construction no less than novel writing, we can propose to students), games (see other sections of this and other chapters for discussions of how narrative works in game design and playing, but the question of whether games are fiction or not is also open to student reflection) pop video, documentary and reality TV. I have also done some work with students on football coverage, considering the narrative construction of a live match with particular attention to ellipsis and the plot/story dynamic. What narrative energy is created by presenter and pundits, commentator, editor, interviewer and the characters (players, managers and more often than not, referees)? Most importantly, what inter and extra-textual knowledge and referential understanding is required to be included by the text?

Class strategy – Writing to learn reflective writing

Often, students end up writing to demonstrate: to be shown for judgement of various kinds. This changes writing. We neglect the function of writing as discovery, as part of learning. Writing in this sense is creative and open to a variety of outcomes. This approach uses writing as a way of opening up narrative analysis to a greater range of considerations.

Ask students to consider this passage from Lyotard:

'Realism can be defined only by its intention of avoiding the question of reality implied in the question of art. Eclecticism is the degree zero of contemporary general culture; you listen to reggae, you watch a western, you eat McDonalds at midday and local cuisine at night, you wear Paris perfume in Tokyo and dress retro in Hong Kong, knowledge is the stuff of TV game shows. . .The lack of reality in reality.' (1992: 18–19)

This may need some explanation but it is pretty obvious stuff. Lyotard's major claim is the death of the 'grand narrative' – claims made in history and philosophy to absolute ways of understanding the order of things. The quote explains itself really: it is most accessible if considered as an alternative to a previous territorially and culturally local human condition. Yet in turn, the author here might be accused of setting up his own set of assumptions about eclecticism (the death of origins, fixed meanings and absolutes as a grand narrative of his own).

Students can write a narrative of their cultural choices, expressed through consumption, in order to test Lyotard's hypothesis. There must be no format for this, no word length, but you should negotiate a deadline and the means of presentation. When the writing is complete, students need to reflect on their own work in terms of its patterning, presence and absence (editing), linearity (or not) and degree of closure.

How well this works will depend on your expectations. The intention is to use writing in a reflective, creative and idea-forming way to test notions about reality. This is the opposite (or at least it is other to) writing to prove understanding in finite terms. As such, within a study of narrative, it is a means rather than an end. Reflection on process is everything.

Again, to get into issues about narration, starting with more complex texts makes it more interesting when we return to seemingly more straightforward ones. On the one hand, a programme like *McIntyre Undercover* (in which the narration outside the diegesis is anchored to the pleasure of witnessing the danger the undercover reporter immerses himself in) might seem complicated in terms of how the meaning is worked out when compared to a film like *Taxi Driver*, which features main character narration. But I would argue that while the discourse might be more predictable (McIntyre is good but he has to pretend to be bad to do the good work), *Taxi Driver* situates us uncomfortably. The film's approach puts us in Travis' mind and we only get to see others through his eyes. It is very hard, therefore, to distance ourselves from someone who is ultimately a psychotic killer. So Scorsese uses a highly conventional storytelling approach for an unusual and challenging representational effect. *McIntyre* is more structurally complex (in terms of time and space and the undercover dynamics) but much more simple in narrative terms, if we are interested in the good/evil binary. This alerts us, I think, to the danger of assuming that complex structure means more complex interpretation. Another example is *Seven*, a really useful film for discussing structure and representation. It is my view that part of the narrative effect of this film is to make the only satisfactory outcome (for the viewer) the completion of the final murder and the subsequent tragedy for the hero of the film. This is the effect of the 'will to linearity' that we get from exposure to the conventional narrative format. In order for the film's slick, clever narrative to ultimately serve us with the pleasure it offers, our morality must be tested, subconsciously at least.

Narratives reside in daily lived experience: we represent our own lives as narratives. When I present the events of the day to my partner in three hours time, I will make sense of my day (and the notion of a day is itself a narrative construction) through what I leave out more than what I include. How I represent things will never be neutral, but more importantly, how she interprets the detail will be (for her) how the events were.

Genre

In this section, I will begin with attention to the concept of genre, and ways of helping students test and challenge its value. This will be followed by case study examples that look at action films, British soap opera, situation comedy, Bollywood and documentary/reality TV. These examples are all moving images, and I apologize for excluding others from this particular area. On the other hand, I hope the approach to genre will be adaptable to any other text-type, in any media.

Class strategy – Collaborative reading

Earlier in this chapter, I described collaborative note-taking. Collaborative reading is similar, except that here I am assuming higher level skills in summarizing and presenting back, hence there is less need for a 'reading frame' and students are not reading the same text in groups: they are collaborating to cover a broader range of material.

Looking at the concept of genre rather than a specific example, students, in groups of four, take one each of these texts:

- Phillips, N., 'Genre' in Nelmes, J., (ed.), 1996, *An Introduction to Film Studies*, London: Routledge, 127–137.
  Key idea: bricolage.
- Raynor, P., Wall, P., and Kruger, S., 2001, *Media Studies: The Essential Introduction*, London: Routledge, 54–62.
  Key idea: pros and cons of genre as a critical tool.
- Strinati, D., 1995, *An Introduction to Theories of Popular Culture*, London: Routledge, Pages 77–78.
  Key idea: standardization and pleasure.
- Neale, S., and Turner, G., 'What is Genre?' in Creeber, G., (ed.), 2001, *The Television Genre Book*, London: BFI, 1–7.
  Key idea: genre mutations.

You can differentiate this activity for a range of purposes. Strinati and Phillips are more challenging in language. Each student needs an opportunity to meet with other students from other groups reading the same option, before returning to their own group with a summary.

The seminar that follows will have two functions: you can get students to cover four texts in a shorter space of time, and you can set up the discussion so they consider the relationship between different pieces of writing and ideas around the concept. You are making clear, before you start the 'micro' work, the important premise that genre study is 'up for grabs'.

As the above strategy suggests, the most productive study of genre does not start with definitions of the contract between producer and audience (see Hartley, 1999), nor with a set of examples of classic genres and their more 'fluid' counterparts. Instead, we should begin by challenging the status ascribed to the concept. How did the notion of category evolve or shift into genre? Whose interests do generic ideas serve? The most useful writer for this is undoubtedly Altman (1999) who sets up a series of assumptions made around genre for critique. These include the notion that genres are defined by producers and are easily recognizable by audiences; that texts 'belong' clearly to a particular genre in each case; that genres develop in predictable ways; that texts in a genre share key characteristics; that genres are ideological; that they are not specifically located in history; and, crucially, that genre critics are distanced from the practice of genre, or its workings. This last point is vital, as the arrogance of theory is never more visible than when it claims detachment from its objects (or as Foucault has it, power is that which is not manifested as such). Students need to consider the concept of genre from the vantage point of their own relationship with theory and practice, not from the illusory premise of merely 'looking on'.

Genres have traditionally been treated as an 'other' to art texts (Stafford, 2002a). The range of perspectives at work when dealing with texts in this way might be student as producer, as consumer/fan, as critic and as analyst. The interplay between these is an interesting area for discussion. Students can get into genre from a critical perspective by drawing up an arbitrary list of categorizing features of radio programmes. This might include radio programmes presented by people with long hair, programmes which are listened to more in the car than in the home and radio programmes which last longer than 40 minutes (they can come up with more interesting examples). The function of this is to start to ask questions about the 'order of things' in categorical terms. Might ways in which we label and divide objects, texts and people be constructed in ways that serve particular interests, rather than in logical, natural patterns? The answer is, of course, a matter of opinion. The important thing, if Media learning is to be 'empowering', is not to forget to ask this critical question, which for Altman is over whether we read genre as noun or adjective. Mark Reid's approach to teaching genre (2001) takes this further (or at least grounds it in the work of 'doing genre' more clearly). He offers tomato puree as an example, suggesting we ask students a philosophical question – what would happen to this item if it were shelved in another part of the shop? Would the 'thing itself' be any different?

'How something is categorised is determined by who does it, for whom, where, and when. The same is true for films.' (Reid, 2001: 1)

And, indeed, for all media texts (or products). So the more interesting, and ultimately useful approach for us to take with students when considering genre is not 'how does genre work?' but 'why does genre happen?' In terms of literacy, language teachers have advocated an approach that equips students with the ability to operate within the idioms of dominant linguistic genres (now discussed as 'functional literacy') and the most progressive work is that which does so at the same time as analysing how these dominant modes of communication have become so (and indeed in whose interests). Yet some Media teaching, despite the claims the subject makes to itself to be a radical cousin of English (McDougall, 2004a), is more conservative in its simplistic and unquestioning transmission of received histories about dominant genre practices. Buckingham (2003) points out an irony when observing that the more familiar the students already are with a genre (such as soap opera) the more likely they are to demonstrate critical reflection while working with the conventions, whereas introducing students to new generic forms is less likely to yield criticality, as more time is spent on familiarizing themselves (or being taught about) the genre practices in question. An approach which acknowledges this, while putting in play Reid's use of Altman's interventions, would be one in which students create texts based on familiar genres, while considering the reasons not only for the success of the genre but the conditions for the genre's possibility: that is, the interests served by its labelling.

To 'anchor' this to an assessment point, taking the OCR A2 Media Issues and Debates exam as an example, in responding to questions about the Concept of Genre (in Film) the most successful students are those who get into this area of uncertainty. Those who write very fluently about how genres function without addressing the practices of genre in this way are restricted to lower levels in the marking. On the other hand, other specifications do not place such demands, and National Diploma and AVCE courses more often require an industry-driven understanding of genre, especially in terms of marketing products to the generic spectator, but I would argue that working with genre for commercial ends is still likely to be more skilfully done if the theory behind the practice is familiar. (To take the industry/vocational angle further, this is surely no different to the scientific theory that underlies good engineering practice.)

Class strategy – Genre busting

This strategy is explicitly set up to avoid the 'traditional' approach of presenting genre as a concept defined by conventions and popularity, and then working on case study examples (for example Science Fiction, discussed in historical terms, from *Frankenstein* through to *The Matrix* trilogy). This alternative strategy asks the question: 'How can we categorize texts?' and does so locating students as the agents of power/knowledge.

- Ask students individually to list as many types of popular music as they can and for each type provide at least two examples of bands/artists. Keep them to a strict 15 minute time limit and then pair them up.
- Each pair compares notes and upgrades their individual lists, again to a time limit.
- Form groups of four from the pairs and go through the same process, again within time constraints. Amplify disagreement – this is the learning process.
- Give each group a number and jigsaw the groups – same process (see Chapter Six).
- At the 'plenary' point, attempt to represent on the smartboard in diagrammatic form the range of different types of popular music. It will be impossible. What does this tell us?

What is revealed by this exercise is the more you know about things (whether it is nuclear physics or drum and bass music), the more complex and debatable labelling will become. At this point, you can set up exercises with students to address these questions about any kind of media text:

- What are the different ways in which we can categorize them?
- Are there labels in circulation already which are known as genres?
- Are there differences in the ways in which different people label texts within genres (this is probably what was happening in the pop music example)? What are the reasons for these different responses?
- Can we find some texts that don't work in generic terms (that we can't agree on)? If so, this should be our starting point for thinking about how useful genre is as a tool.

According to Neale (1980), genre theory is to do with a circulation of expectation in circulation between industries, media texts and audiences. This leads to (or is an effect of, perhaps) 'regulated variety'. Hartley (1999) describes a contract between producer and audience which 'disciplines' choices and reduces desires. All genre theorists agree on the 'slippery' or 'fluid' nature of labelling texts in this way. There is consensus among this community that the exception to the rule is the 'pure' genre text. In other words, most texts span more than one genre, or can be claimed by several, or seem to present a degree of reworking, or play with conventions in some way. So a grasp of genre theory actually leads students away from the notion that genre is an easy, blunt tool with which to produce texts along conventional lines. For Neale, genre is a state of combinations, more or less randomly distributed, and genre texts are those which form particular patterns of combinations, or at least are seen that way by audiences or critics.

The good news for the Media teacher is that there is a plethora of books, websites and teaching resources available to help you work on particular genres with students. By far the most useful is the English and Media Centre's 'Genre Through Practical Work' (2004). Produced for English Key Stage 3 or GCSE Media students, this is a simple plan for an activity (to construct, storyboard and film a two-minute video sequence of a rendezvous in a particular genre) which draws on existing knowledge of popular TV genres with minimal teacher input. What I really like about the exercise is that it asks students to be creative first, without any concern to introduce the concept of genre before they start filming, and at the debrief stage students are asked to reflect on the degree to which their work is typical of the text-type they were trying to produce. Through a simple, low-maintenance exercise the practical, creative tone for the study of a concept is set. This, for me, is so much more educational than students producing a genre piece after a lengthy study of the concept and its dominant textual manifestations.

In the Picture's study pack on Science Fiction begins with an interesting consideration of genre in a Cultural Studies context:

> 'Genre, referring to paintings or to forms of literature, has a history going back to the Ancient Greek philosopher Aristotle, but it wasn't until the nineteenth century and the development of new technologies, such as the cinema and mass production printing as well as basic education, that popular culture began to be talked about as belonging to genres. When the whole population and not just the educated elite could experience and appreciate narratives the need for classification changed. This switch from high culture genres to popular culture genres is interesting in that genre went from being a term associated with intellectual discussion to a term of abuse which was then used to dismiss much popular fiction and most cinema as "mere genre entertainment".' (Stafford, 1997: 1)

This brings us nicely to the five examples I use as case studies, all of which are firmly situated in these debates over textual status.

Action films

Work on this type of film gets off to a good start if students decide on a range of criteria for judgeing individual texts. For example, they might differentiate between action and effects as a criteria as opposed to plot, or they might locate films as more or less sophisticated in terms of deeper meanings. This is good practice because straight away you are into discussions about how different people evaluate texts for different purposes. One group might see action films as 'popcorn movies' that do not require intellectual engagement. Indeed, students often say they watch films that 'don't make you think' for pleasure and escapism. Fans of this kind of film might, on the other hand, make complex and discerning decisions about texts. This perspective is informed by Mark Kermode's sensible arguments about horror films, that the people who best understand the generic dynamics and relations between screen violence and reality are the people who watch the most horror films (and thus they are the least 'vulnerable' of all of us and thus in the least need of protection through censorship). Students should also be aware that, with the publication of BFI classics and other academic work on individual action films, the genre is enjoying a little canonisation, and certainly a renegotiation of its status in critical terms.

Jose Arroyo (2001) has a very interesting view on the action film, analysing the visual spectacles and ultra-sophisticated arrangements of time and space at work in the genre as works of art. Arroyo argues that the Frankfurt School tradition of critique (popular I think with some Media teachers still) misses the point that revealing the ways in which texts reaffirm capitalist culture as sinister pleasure, with hidden power discourses embedded in the sugar, only deals with one element of the text's operations.

Arroyo suggests that a film like *Mission Impossible* is so thrilling in aesthetic terms that the ideology is if anything, secondary and relatively uninteresting for the audience (and after all, the middle-classes are allowed to ignore ideology when wandering around the Uffizi):

'*Mission Impossible* is so thrilling that even hermeneutics are left behind for a while. On the ride, the viewer is too busy rushing through its aesthetics to think of anything but its erotics. *Mission Impossible* is a delight because, in pleasing the eye and kicking the viscera, it continually asks the audience to wonder. How did they do that? And that the film does this, and *how* it does this, is at least as important as *why*'. (2001)

Working from the 'how can we judge' exercise to Arroyo's ideas, we start with (again) a complex questioning of how the genre gets the press it does. The obvious link from this is some small-scale audience research to get some discursive data about consumption and pleasure. By the time you introduce conventions and micro analytical work, students are familiar with the range of competing views of the meanings of the genre. As a result, you can avoid generalizations about ideology and the audience, and consider how viewers might enjoy the pleasures afforded by the action and spectacle without 'buying in' to the view of the world represented as dominant in some of the most popular films.

Some teachers prefer a historical genre approach, placing contemporary action films in a tradition in order to explore reasons for the longevity of this text type. I have tended to spend more time on analysis of the specific technical and symbolic elements that typify (perhaps, but this is my interpretation) famous examples. The combination of sound and image is particularly rich for analysis. Dialogue spoken during moments of intense action can be definitive in audience recall and pleasure ('Hasta la vista, baby'), alongside music (which should not be described by students as 'dramatic' – their job is to explain, in detail, why the combination of rhythm, pitch and tone, when placed alongside images in an anchoring relation, is dramatic). In my view, an essential, detailed account of the technical practices at work in action films can be found in Lacey and Stafford's two-part account for *In the Picture* magazine (2002). Returning to Eisenstein, students should focus on editing and consider montage effects and the role of editing in creating spectacle. In this context, you might show students the early Lumière Brothers films and ask them to make some connections in the light of Arroyo's theory. The notion here is that audiences at the dawn of cinema were interested only in spectacle, with narrative as a secondary feature of cinema. What has changed, up to today?

Masculinities

Clearly, there is a lot of work to do around representation and gender, and the question of masculinities. This can be the most challenging, as students can be pretty homophobic, and the more interesting work, from Dyer in particular, comments on the homoerotic nature of action cinema:

> 'Come to think of it, for the male viewer action movies have a lot in common with being fellated. Whatever the reason, men cherish the illusion that their masculinity is not compromised by being fellated. Yet it's the other person, male or female, who's doing the work, really being active. So it is with action movies. In imagination, men can be Arnie or Keanu; in the seat, it's Arnie or Keanu pleasuring them. Now that's what I call speed.' (1994: 10).

I will leave you to decide whether to get into this with your students! But certainly, there must be some reflection on the construction of gender identity through response to action films. Depending on the group, course and the scope of ambition, this might be limited to some interesting audience research on female responses to action films, or it might develop into a Lacanian analysis of male physique and the imaginary. To avoid these questions is to the detriment of the analysis, as this statement from Tasker (2005) suggests:

> 'The proliferation of images of the built male body represents for critics the kind of deconstructive performativity associated with postmodernism, while for others they articulate, in their "promotion of power and the fear of weakness", traditional images which are also "deeply reactionary" (Foster, 1988, p61). Within the action cinema, the advent of the body builder as star poses quite complex questions for the development of narrative, largely to do with the need to incorporate moments of physical display.' (1993: 73–4).

Class strategy – Consequences essay

This collaborative strategy serves to get a job done that is otherwise not much fun.

After a period of time studying the action film genre (though again, this approach is transferable to any topic area with a range of theory), arrange the class in a horseshoe shape and give them an exam essay title, such as: Discuss the reasons for the popularity of the action film.

Ask each student to write the title and the first two sentences of the essay. Then ask them to pass their paper clockwise, and write the next two sentences on the new essay in front of them.

Repeat this until each student has their own paper back, making sure that (in relation to the size of the group) you move them on to a new part of the essay (from intro to first reason to second reason to third reason to summary conclusion) at the appropriate intervals.

Each student will end up with a collaborative answer, covering more points than they would otherwise have had at their disposal. In addition, the discipline of needing to ensure continuity with each new answer will mean that they will actually produce more in the way of range than they would need to for a straightforward individual response. And it is usually an enjoyable, if at times frustrating exercise, when compared to the usual 'timed essay' approach.

British soap opera

Whether this topic is housed on your course in genre study, textual analysis, broadcasting, audience or media debates, and whether it is more or less integrated with, or only studied through, production work, I strongly suggest that the learning is structured around a consideration of popular culture debates. This is because, in my view, production practices and questions of convention, realism and melodrama cannot be understood in isolation from the competing discourses around the popularity of the genre. So, rather than starting with analysis of episodes and key scenes in terms of conventions, I suggest setting out from a simple discourse analysis of the plethora of 'pro' and 'anti' responses in a range of contexts – the press, academic texts and promotional material.

If you are organized enough, you can always record TV and radio material dealing with soap operas. I used a Radio 5 phone-in, broadcast in the aftermath of research into soaps' treatment of family life and I gave students a simple chart on which to plot the callers' statements in various categories (soaps as documents of society, soaps as sensationalist junk and more negotiated positions in between). The discussion we had as a result was about the location of each discourse and the role of soap opera as a scapegoat or catalyst for a range of other identity issues. We discussed gender, the closet male viewer and the myth of the 'addict' in this context. Again, as with all of the topics discussed in this book, when we got to the 'nuts and bolts' of genre convention, illusion of real time, continuity, tease devices and cliffhangers, action and enigma, two-shots and over-the-shoulder shots, establishing shots and tableaux, social issue coverage, meeting places, outdated depiction of community, interweaving storylines, partial closure, balance of realizm and melodrama, music as motif, intertextual time and location, anchorage, semiotics of set design, costume and *mise-en-scène*, and the complex range of representational devices at work, we were already well-informed on the wider debates around the status of these texts.

Another regular, rich resource is the TV programme *about* soaps, which can be deconstructed in terms of the ways in which they manage the relationship between text world and production world, or verisimilitude and documentary. Again, a discourse analysis in terms of the assumptions relied on by the producers takes you into a more interesting discussion about the genre than simply listing production details. On the other hand, it is important to introduce students to some of the specific context of soap production, by asking them to research budgets, the writing-by-committee process and marketing strategies. At the time of writing, *EastEnders* is still reeling from losing its flagship status, and this cannot be fully understood in isolation from charter renewal issues, taking us to another synoptic opportunity. In the section on representation (see page 123), I deal with Linda Grant's social document thesis, and as soap is a genre associated closely with representation of 'ordinary life', this is the reason why a more complex analysis of the relationship of text to students' life worlds is crucial for a mature understanding of this genre and its contested existence. This can only be satisfactorily achieved through production work, so I would argue that any study of soap opera must include the creation of at least a scene from an episode. Whether this creation challenges conventions or imitates the current orthodoxy is up to you, but I agree with Buckingham that many teachers make invalid assumptions about imitation:

> 'A brief glance at even the most outwardly "imitative" student productions would suggest that there is nearly always an element of negotiation, parody or critique. Furthermore, in using existing media forms or genres, students do not automatically take on the values those genres are seen to contain. On the contrary, they are actively and self-consciously reworking their prior knowledge of the media, often by means of parody or pastiche – a process which might be better understood as a form of intertextuality or dialogic communication, rather than mere slavish imitation.' (2003: 134–5).

Class Strategy – One, two and three-minute essays

A way of refining students' summary skills in preparation for exam questions on genre learning, this strategy helps to focus students on the discipline of covering a range of different concerns within an essay.

You can work this exercise any number of times in a lesson. The simple approach is this – give students a one-minute essay (Why do people like soaps?), followed by a two-minute essay (Why are soaps often criticized?) and then a three-minute essay (What makes soap such a recognizable genre?)

You can continue this until you get to forty minutes altogether (an average exam time for a single question). The point to establish is that actually they have written one essay, answering the first question, but they have explicitly fulfilled the 'unwritten' requirement of exam answers – to integrate all sorts of other things into the answer, and relate them to the question (which on this occasion you have done for them).

If Media students are not always the most natural essay writers in exam conditions, then exercises like these that make transparent the 'hidden curriculum' of assessment (i.e. that you don't actually just answer a question) can only help level out the playing field a bit.

Situation comedy

As I keep reiterating, strategic use of 'theory' works for any Media student. Regardless of level or the nature of the course/unit of study, if the theory is right, the student will benefit from considering media in this way. Here is an example:

'The sitcom character, because he (and the gender is significant) cannot learn from his experiences – or if he can learn, cannot put his lesson into practice and lacks the will to escape or improve, is therefore shamed and unmanly, and in Sartre's terms, lives in "bad faith" (the opposite of the existential hero).' (Hirschorn, 2003: 17)

In a way, this reminds me of a comment made by an eminent TV executive who did a Media Studies degree and was surprised when it kicked off with a lecture on Hegel. It is a matter of 'use value'. Sometimes we over-compensate for the 'everyday' nature of the subject with absurdly intellectual approaches or redundant theoretical models that have little currency in contemporary media practices. You may think I do this myself at times with my insistence on working with Foucault, Derrida and Baudrillard. But if a 'thinker' has written something which has direct relevance to media texts, audience responses and pleasure (as I think Hirschorn rightly spots in Sartre), then it helps students make the leap from viewing to analysis more easily. Understood in this way, theory is a kind of distracting device.

There are three angles to take on this topic, all with representation as the key concept. One approach is to compare British and American sitcoms (where different configurations of social class are likely to be evident), another is to look at the genre in Britain historically (and trace social changes, prejudices, myth and taboo in this way) and a third option is to analyse the reasons for the popularity of the genre and debates around its status (similar to soaps in this respect). I suggest that rather than starting with more 'traditional' contemporary examples like *My Family* and *One Foot in the Grave* and then moving on later to the complex alternatives, you start with *The Office* and *Phoenix Nights* and work back. How do these texts rely on an understanding of the genres they parody (the documentary as well as the sitcom is up for grabs) to form their 'otherness' for comedic effect?

Narrative is of great importance to any study of sitcom. Circular, partially self-contained stories are centred fundamentally on the comfort provided by the absence of change. Some unease prevails when sitcoms move to the end of their lives, and to get to this point writers introduce life changes that will make closure inevitable. Students I taught compared *Men*

Behaving Badly to *Friends*, looking at episodes with the same narrative theme – unexpected pregnancy and male reaction. In addition to a comparison of gender representation (laughing *with* women *at* men), students analysed the narrative in relation to the typical sitcom structure. What we could see was that these episodes were taking the audience to an unfamiliar territory (the inevitability of growing up, moving on and taking responsibility) and this allowed us to consider the ways in which characters in sitcoms are really 'frozen in time' in terms of the life cycle. Representations of gender, occupations, ethnicity, social class, location and consumption (for example, *Spaced* pays great attention to popular culture tastes) all function only in relation to this temporal stillness – things don't change. Interesting work for students to do (again, most effectively through producing their own example) includes considering the moments at which sitcoms meet other generic forms (for example *Green Wing* and its 'play' with hospital drama), and the ways in which the form and structure can adapt to societal change. You may wish to get more or less into an historical account of this, along the 'social document' road, depending on the outcomes you need.

James Baker's *Teaching TV Sitcom* (2003) is a useful resource. Baker's suggestions focus on conventions – typical locations, themes and characters, target audience, typical storylines and, less straightforwardly, why these are funny. He suggests a scheme of work which considers 'buddy' sitcoms, female sitcoms and case studies on sitcoms which were exported to the US (*Men Behaving Badly*, which failed and *Absolutely Fabulous*, which was a success). Baker explores the ways in which characters are trapped, ultimately by themselves:

'The majority of sitcom characters are frustrated by the situations they find themselves in and which they cannot escape. The situation can be physical or emotional, and although they often strive to change their situation, they are inevitably doomed to return to a similar starting point'. (2003)

Asking students to consider how their own lives might be represented in sitcom form gets us into this easily. In order to provide this adaptation, an individual needs to exaggerate certain characteristics that might be considered typical of a certain social group or disposition, and then amplify the 'typicality' of their situation through stereotyping and myth. So this might involve stereotypes of teenagers, of college life and then more specific combinations of gender and regionality codes.

It is vital that your attention doesn't wander away from the fact that readings of sitcoms are polysemic. The fact that comedy is notoriously difficult to analyse is important here. It actually isn't any harder to make sense of, it is just that we have mistakenly made assumptions about other media forms and the ways audiences respond that we can't make with comedy simply because when people don't laugh you can't ignore it!

Consider this. I recently acquired a full DVD box set of *The Fall and Rise of Reginald Perrin*, which I used to watch as a child in the 1970s. When I watch this text now I realize it revolves around a deficit model of gender traits, which I would distance myself from personally (I think). The humour in this for me is partly nostalgic and partly decadent. If sitcoms ride on a myth of common experience, where does this place the kind of pleasure I get from the character CJ in 2006? It is a simple point, but I suggest there is a new form of sitcom pleasure now, founded on nostalgia for the time in which texts were produced. But this nostalgia isn't for a comforting return to the 'real world' of the 1970s, but for the televisual reality of those times.

Bollywood

Statistically, there are something like a thousand films a year coming out of Bombay's industry, distributed worldwide to nearly 15,000 cinemas and exhibited to nearly 100 million viewers a week. But while certainly significant as a 'type' of film, Bollywood is no more a genre than Hollywood or British film. There are a number of variables here that I need to set out in order to avoid making assumptions. Like MP3 and the music industry, this is an area where I have always been lucky enough to have students to provide the content, as they know much more about the topic than I do. Another privilege I have enjoyed has been the highly reflective nature of these presentations. Bollywood consumption is, according to these students, highly postmodern in the sense that the films are taken incredibly seriously and yet not at all seriously at the same time. My job then, has been to place their knowledge in a theoretical framework and provide a range of ways in to a more critical approach. If you do not have Bollywood enthusiasts, then more teacher input will be necessary. As already stated, Bollywood is not a genre. But how it relates to (Western) genre theory is interesting and it will cast a critical light on other genre study.

Bollywood is a massive industry (students are often surprised by the data), but it is not Indian Cinema. So a working definition needs to be established, and the most accurate one is simply that Bollywood films originate from Bombay. They are often described as 'Indian popular cinema' which of course reinforces the derisory use of 'popular' as distinct from 'serious'. The 'ollywood' relates more to industry practices and global successes than it does to textual elements, as the content and style of Bollywood films is usually very different to Western cinema, as is the audience response. Tyrell (1988) offers a sound introduction:

> 'Bollywood – the affectionate name for Bombay's Hindi cinema – is the biggest film industry in the world. In India, Hindi-dubbed Hollywood releases can't touch it (even the occasional Hollywood hit takes but a tenth of Bollywood's average box office) but it is also an international export with audiences in Africa, the Middle East, Russia, South East Asia, China, Europe and the United States. These viewers are not always Indian – Bollywood offers an alternative popular cinema for nations with a religious or political aversion to Hollywood (as in the Middle East) as well as crossing over from an Indian audience to a mainstream one (as in East Africa) on its merits as entertainment.' (1988: 20)

So, at the very least, students need to avoid making mistakes by understanding that it is Mumbai's film industry that they are studying, that this industry is more successful, financially, than Hollywood (to compare the cultural imperialist effects of both is a very interesting, but different question), and crucially, that while the success of Bollywood products is often described as oppositional to Hollywood conventions (bound up with theories about Classical Narrative Cinema touched on earlier), the films in question clearly share elements with popular American cinema. So notions of 'alternative' media come into question with this topic area. Once again, Bollywood is not a genre, but we might come to understand genre theory (and whether we believe in it or not) through scrutiny of the ways in which popular Indian cinema plays with genre conventions.

If we are defining Bollywood as an industry, how does it fit into genre study? Analysing the pleasures provided by films such as *Bombay, Dil Se* and *Sholay* reveals that genre theory in its traditional Western form doesn't really work. On the one hand, a film like *Sholay* is a reworking of the Western genre but it isn't satisfactory just to assess it as 'parody' because of the collision of cultural codes at work. Equally, most Bollywood films contain so many different genre elements (musical, action, thriller, romance and comedy, at least) that they take the concept of hybridity so far it no longer has credibility. This range of elements had led to these films being called 'Massala movies' (the range of ingredients) but the question students need to consider is whether Bollywood 'shows up' genre as an inadequate device that only works in a simplifying manner, or whether it is just that it does work for Western films but not for popular Indian cinema, in which case it is not flawed, but is deeply culturally specific. Either way, studying Bollywood from this perspective will lead to a much more informed, considered and less 'naturally' situated use of the concept of genre.

Class strategy – Who Wants to be a Millionaire?

Doing Bollywood from a standing start means that many students will probably have more factual information to learn and remember than in other areas of the subject where to some extent they already know their stuff. For these uninitiated students, using a structure like *Millionaire* can be a lively way of testing memory (this is, after all, what the TV show does).

Individual students act as contestants in turn (or they can be in pairs or even groups) and you take them through a series of factual questions which get progressively harder as the 'money' gets bigger.

These might start with: 'Which of these is not a Bollywood film?' with a rather obvious answer, range to names of particular films' directors or box-office figures for particular examples, and lead on to more testing questions about theoretical ideas (such as the names of writers you may have quoted).

Whether you play for real reward or just for fun will be up to you and your students, of course.

Taking one specific Bollywood film can be useful for students, as long as you help them avoid assumptions. You can illustrate this danger by asking them to identify a 'typical' Hollywood film and then ten others that are nothing like it. One example is *Kabhi Khushi Khabie Gham* (Johar, 2002). Highly moral (a reinforcement of family tradition, ultimately), this film features spectacular sets, two celebrities in leading roles (students need to research the Bollywood star system and be aware of the range of magazines, websites and other media texts that support audiences' interest), and is subtitled in English. Ideally, any scheme of work on Bollywood should include the viewing of a film like this in a Bollywood cinema. I have always taught in cities where these are easily accessible, but I appreciate for some of you this may be a mission. However, it is worth it for the rich discussions about spectatorship it can yield. The behaviour of audiences in Bombay is certainly very different to that of English multiplex visitors, and it is common for audiences to dance during films. Finding out to what extent this form of spectatorship is preserved in Birmingham or Leicester is an interesting research activity (although those of us who teach the initiated need to make clear that we are learning *from* them, or there is great danger of patronizing assumption).

Documentary/reality TV

Another example that serves to 'problematise' the concept of genre more than apply it, documentary and its relative 'reality TV' are not fixed in genre theory. Again, this makes it all the more useful to study in this context. One approach might be to place reality TV in the context of debates over quality and choice in the digital era. There are more documentaries available on the schedules than ever before, but many critics would not accept that this makes our current television more informative (in the Reithian sense). Why is this? What are the debates in the deregulated era? Were there really 'good old days' of public service broadcasting, or was this 'golden age' merely an era of middle-class prescription and acceptance by the masses?

> 'In the digital era, the world's most accessible medium has become even more so, and it's had a democratising influence on programme content, the viewing experience and on our ability to access information. So rather than there ever having been a golden age of television, it's my contention that it is the television of today that offers a gilt-edged opportunity to viewers and broadcasters alike.' (Arey 2005)

Developing this view, Peter Bazalgette, of Endemol (the creators of the *Big Brother* format) argues that the current proliferation of ordinary people on television is democratic public service broadcasting in action and furthermore, that it offers liberation from both state control and a patronizing, middle-class approach:

> '*Big Brother* arrived just at the point when, with multi-channels, content began to be driven more by popular taste than the dictates of a cultural elite. TV was no longer different or special, as it had been with only one or two networks. From the start, *Big Brother* was different, too. With its nudity, sex and bald (sic) language it was an extreme provocation to television regulators and governments. Across the world it became the catalyst for fierce censorship debates, clashes between Church and state and constitutional crises. No single television idea had ever had such an effect before.' (2005: 270)

Others argue that it is merely cheap, intellectually bankrupt entertainment serving to distract us from more enriching matters. Students must decide for themselves, of course, but an approach based on contesting assumptions made by documentary about reality, representation and authenticity will inform them better. Consider this suggestion:

'Winston argues (1995) that much traditional documentary has as its subject "victims". For all its postmodernist style, this is essentially true of *Big Brother*. This series appeared to produce, as did the multitude of TV docusoaps, those alter egos, victims and celebrities'. (Withall, 2000: 40)

Close textual analysis of a range of 'traditional' documentaries alongside new reality TV shows should revolve around how each text, through 'old' and 'new' conventions, constructs for itself and its audience a 'claim to truth'. How does voice-over, selection of material, use of experts, hidden camera footage and most importantly of all, the editing together of all these and the subsequent rhythm of the text (who speaks when, after who and before what) construct a particular version of reality, and whose interests does this serve? And why is it that audiences seem curiously more trusting of this kind of media text than a range of others? Working with audiences is useful for this last question, of course. In keeping with the approach this book has advocated throughout, and at the risk of repetition, let me state that a sophisticated understanding of how documentary constructs these 'truth claims' in complex ways can only be acquired if you make a documentary, or design a reality TV show yourself.

Whether or not the key concepts of Media Studies dealt with in this chapter are here to stay will be determined by you and your students, over time. Certainly, there is an entrenched legacy and an industry in producing resources to support this way of studying. My view, which I hope I have consistently applied in the examples above, is that the concepts are only as useful as the testing of them, and as such they should be treated as hypotheses for students to work with. Can we label media texts on genre lines? Do media texts share common approaches to narrative, or does the audience make sense of things in more complex ways? Can we ever say for sure that a text represents the world in a particular way or is the meaning of any representation more polysemic and hard to pin down? In these ways, and especially through practical work and audience research, we can help students experiment with these models, and we can learn from their results.

Further reading

Altman, R., 1982, *Genre: The Musical*, London: Routledge.

Altman, R., 1999, *Film/Genre*, London: BFI.

Arroyo, J., 2001, 'Mission Sublime' in Arroyo, J. (ed.), *Action/Spectacle*, London: BFI. Offers a view of action films as artefacts of aesthetic sublimity.

Baker, J., 2003, *Teaching TV Sitcom*, London: BFI.

Bazalgette, P., 2005, *Billion Dollar Game: How three men risked it all and changed the face of television*, London: Time Warner.

Buckingham, D., 1987, *Public Secrets: EastEnders and its Audience*, London: BFI.

Buckingham, D., 2003, *Media Education: Literacy, Learning and Contemporary Culture*, London: Polity.

Creeber, G. (ed.), 2001, *The Television Genre Book*, London: BFI.
Includes detailed sections on the concept of genre itself, soap opera, comedy, drama, quiz shows, advertising, children's television, news and documentary.

Dyer, R., 1994, 'Action!' In *Sight & Sound*, October, London: BFI.
Fascinating analysis of action film viewers and codes of masculinity.

Geraghty, C., 1991, 'Representation and popular culture', in J. Curran and M. Gurevitch (eds.,) *Mass Media and Society*, London: Edward Arnold.

Geraghty, C., 1991, *Women and Soap Opera: A Study of Prime-Time Soaps*, Cambridge: Polity Press.

Hartley, J., 1999, *The Uses of Television*, London: Routledge.

Hirschorn, A., 2003, 'Sitcoms and Absurdism', in *In the Picture*, 46. Keighley: itp Publications.

In the Picture, 1997, Science Fiction Study Pack, Keighley: itp Publications.

Johnson, S., 2005, *Everything Bad is Good for You*, London: Penguin.
Includes useful comparison of narrative experiences.

Kabir, N., 2001, *Bollywood: The Indian Cinema Story*, London: C4 books.

Lacey, N., 2000, *Narrative and Genre*, London: MacMillan.

Lacey, N., 2000, *Image and Representation*, London: MacMillan

Lacey, N., and Stafford, R., 2002, 'Cut or Move the camera? Framing the Action', in *In the Picture*, 45, Keighley: itp Publications.
Excellent, technically comprehensive guide to analysing action sequences.

Levan, S., 2000, *York Film Notes: Fargo*, London: York Press.
This whole series is excellent for examples of micro/macro analysis of film texts.

Lyotard, J., 1984, *The Postmodern Condition*, Manchester: MUP.
Essential reading, in order to avoid problematic misreadings of the term.

Lyotard, J., 1992, *The Postmodern Explained to Children*, London: Turnaround.
Essential contribution to debates around modernity, shifts in time and space and a philosophy of difference.

Medhurst, A., 1994, *The Magnificent Seven Rides Again*, London: The Observer.
Article offering a model of narrative featuring seen classic stories.

Mottershead, C., 2001, *How to Teach Narrative*, London: BFI Media Studies Conference Workshop.

Neale, S., 1980, *Genre*, London: BFI.

Neale, S., and Turner, G., 2001, *What is Genre?*, in Creeber, G. (ed.) *The Television Genre Book*, London: BFI.

Newman, J., 2004, *Videogames*, London: Routledge.

Phillips, N., 1996, 'Genre' in Nelmes, J., (ed.), *An Introduction to Film Studies*, London: Routledge.

QCA, 2005, 'Media Matters: a review of Media Studies in schools and colleges', London: QCA.

Raynor, P., Wall, P., and Kruger, S., 2001, *Media Studies: The Essential Introduction*, London: Routledge.

Stafford, R., 2002a, 'Formats and Genres across Media' in *In the Picture*, 44, Keighley: itp Publications.

Strinati, D., 1995, *An Introduction to Theories of Popular Culture*, London: Routledge.
Excellent for a broader Cultural Studies context. Especially useful for students interested in postmodernism.

Tasker, Y., (ed.), 2005, *Action and Adventure Cinema*, London: Routledge.

Tyrell, H., 1988, *Bollywood in Britain* in *Sight & Sound*, August 1998. London: BFI.

Withall, K., 2000, 'Exploring Documentary Truth?' in *In the Picture*, 40, Keighley: itp Publications.
Raises a series of questions about reality TV's relationship to the history of the documentary tradition.

See also the 'Top 40 Websites' section.

chapter eight

Media Realities – Audiences and Debates

Introduction

This chapter addresses the areas of Media Studies that explicitly demand an opinion (or as it tends to be described in awarding body criteria, 'personal engagement'). All Media learning is multidisciplinary in the sense that texts cannot be analysed or produced in isolation from questions about audience and a variety of ways of understanding the socio-cultural status of the mass media. However, these are the bits of Media courses that tend to be assessed through coursework essays or exams and through student response to a question on a particular topic within the domain of a generally more sociological approach (or we might prefer a Cultural Studies label).

I hope that by now, if you have approached this book in a linear fashion or at least dipped into a few earlier chapters, we can take it as read that the best way for students to learn about gender magazines is to make one, using digital photography, desk-top publishing and photo-editing software. British cinema is best understood if you create a British film, while setting up a weblog to reflect on local politics in your area gives you a pretty good understanding of how new technologies might affect news and politics, now and in the future. But at the time of writing we are still dealing with Media Studies specifications that require students to show themselves to examiners through the medium of the exam paper, so that is what we will address in this chapter.

Media power

A few rationales for this kind of learning are:

> 'With appropriate pedagogies and classroom work, the concept of audience has the potential to develop understandings of the cultural power of media institutions in ways that won't reduce down to ''brainwashing'' or ''ideology'' the variety of relations we enter into with texts.' (Branston, 1991: 9)

and

> 'All technological extensions of ourselves must be numb and subliminal, else we could not endure the leverage exerted upon ourselves by such extension.

Although the medium is the message, the controls go beyond programming. The restraints are directed to the "content", which is always another medium. The content of the press is literary statement, as the content of the book is speech and the content of the movie is the novel. To those who have never studied media, this fact is quite as baffling as literacy is to natives who say "Why do you write? Can't you remember?!!"' (McLuhan, 1994:305.)

and

'On average we spend over fifteen years of our waking lives just watching television. Films, videos and the time spent reading newspapers and magazines, listening to music and surfing the net, means that we spend one third of our lives immersed in the media. Our abilities to speak, think, form relationships with others, even our dreams and our own sense of identity are now shaped by the media. So studying the media is studying ourselves as social creatures.' (Sardar and Van Loon, 2000, 8)

These three statements illustrate the same idea in different ways. Branston encourages us to equip our students with awareness of the complexities of audience behaviour. McLuhan provides the most explicit sociological approach, suggesting that media, as 'extensions of man' change culture profoundly. Sardar and Van Loon offer a popular justification of Media learning as inevitable and necessary, as it forms our reality (in this way, it could be argued that Media Studies is the new Theology).

My distinguishing these approaches from more straightforward topic areas, discussed in Chapter Seven, hinges on the need for an understanding of different opinions. So whereas a student can answer a question about a film genre by presenting a description of the genre's conventions, its history, specific textual examples and an account of its popularity, the same student responding to a question about film censorship would need to balance out the conflicting discourses in this area, and think much more about the nature of film spectatorship and claims about social effects.

Here are some examples, based on current specifications, of questions that call for such a socio-cultural understanding:

• Does the magazine industry contribute to gender difference, or just reflect it?

• Why does Britain need a film industry?

• Should the Press have more or less restrictions, and what is meant by a free press in a democracy?

• How has deregulation and subscription impacted on broadcasting and does Public Service Broadcasting have a future?

• Why has Hollywood dominated cinema?

• What is the relationship between the media and politics?

• How useful are various theories of media audiences?

- How credible is the 'effects model' of audience behaviour (often studied through the example of film censorship)?

- How is news 'manufactured' through selection, construction and production?

- Debates over the effects of advertising in contemporary society.

- Analysis of debates around particular types of media text and their cultural status (e.g. reality TV and soap opera).

I want, at the risk of repetition, to reiterate my strongly held belief that we should rid ourselves of any notions that certain kinds of students can handle 'theory' and others are less prepared for this kind of work. This is absurd. First, it assumes an understanding of theory (derived from a discourse of 'academia') that falsely separates it in a binary opposition from practice (and the craziness of this is hammered home to me every time a vocational student explains to me how digital coding works). Second, it sets up an insulting deficit model of 'vocational' learning which completely ignores the time factor. As Media learning is currently arranged, a National Diploma Moving Image student will spend roughly fifteen hours a week studying films and television. An A Level student might (at some points in the course only) get three, if they are lucky. How can the former fail to become more scholarly than the latter? So please take it in good faith that the approaches and topics suggested in this chapter are for *all* Media students, for when they need to engage with theories that inform debates. While it will be harder to find explicit references to such debates in assessment criteria for vocational courses, in the higher grade/level descriptors we tend to judge students on their ability to deal with the contexts in which audience response is played out, and these higher order reflections will often take students into the kinds of questions listed above. Equally, while GCSE students (and some AS) may seem to be more focused on *how* the media work rather than *why* they work in this way, or put another way they will be preoccupied by the micro (texts) as opposed to the macro (the media), a differentiated approach to Media learning will provide opportunities for those who are in a position to tackle some of these broader questions.

Having said all that, these types of study do tend to be a bigger deal most clearly for A2 students, and in my experience students are at most risk of under-performing in this area of their course because the leap from textual analysis and creative production to this type of cultural investigation is so profound. As the title of the chapter signposts, students need to deal with media realities, discussing the relationship between the world, lived experience and media representation not only in a descriptive sense (how does the media present the world?) but through a philosophical lens (what is the nature of reality understood, as separate from media imagery?). Alongside this, they need a sophisticated grasp of current thinking about audiences (if they get this wrong, a simplistic account of audience is more damaging to their cause than getting some facts wrong in an account of institution, for example). And they need to handle debates well, which is a learned skill – the fine line between personal engagement and unsubstantiated opinion tests out third-year undergraduates, so we need to work hard on this with our Level 3 charges.

When we talk about this kind of Media learning, there is a tension which divides the subject community to some extent. While some see exam papers that test students' ability to write essays about the media in society as the last bastion of an essential theoretical approach (which will be bound up with notions of critical autonomy and media literacy on a broader scale than mere textual analysis), others worry that this model of 'doing media' is outdated. Regardless of the opinion you hold, this kind of work is likely to remain in the forefront for Media students for a while, and there is a lot at stake for them. No matter how practical you make your course, regardless of how much technology you enable students to use, and how radical and transgressive your pedagogy, students will have to write essays, either for coursework or exams, and demonstrate understanding in that medium, of these more sociological, critical questions. So the remainder of this chapter will offer five detailed examples of 'doing debates', accompanied again by a set of class strategies. These 'study sites' (and their range of elements) are:

- The Magazine Industry and Gender: how do publishers create a sense of belonging based on gender codes and to what extent do students think these presentations of 'us and them' have negative social implications? And another view – that the postmodern reader plays with gender identity and as such achieves 'metacognition' of the constructed nature of gender.

- Audience Effects and Censorship: in two parts. First, a discussion of moral panics and less extreme manifestations of concern about children's television viewing and second, an analysis of the 'protection' thesis at the heart of justifications of film censorship. In both cases, a wider range of theories about popular culture are considered.

- British Film and National Identity: does Britain need a film industry, distinct from its status as an annex of Hollywood? And if so, is this for commercial/economic reasons or is it to do with culture – the need for us to tell stories about our changing understanding of Britishness?

- News, War and Politics: taking the reporting on 9/11, the war in Iraq and the 2005 general election as case studies; an analysis of the selection and construction of news, and the relationship between corporate-political news agendas; party campaigning and the use of the 'PR guru'; and the emergence of blogging as a tool for participation.

- Reality TV: investigating competing discourses at work in reality TV programmes and doing work with audiences to explore the status of reality TV and to develop student responses to the key debates around realizm, exploitation, truth and 'quality'.

Inevitably, there is overlap here with earlier chapters, as many of the texts and conceptual approaches discussed in other parts of this book share some common ground with these topics. I describe some institutional areas for study related to the Hutton enquiry in Chapter Five, and 'blogging' features frequently. The section on representation in Chapter Seven uses British cinema as an example, and reality TV texts are prominent in our discussion of media literacy. These are not particularly original areas to focus on. They are the 'meat and drink' of most media debates/contexts coursework. And of course, there are a plethora of resources available to support these areas, and most student textbooks offer discussions on these areas. So I am hardly making a radical intervention here.

On the other hand, I am more interested in *how* students learn in these areas, and this is about more than content and provision of materials – it is about a way of seeing and a way of doing language, a language game you need to play in order to articulate (which is different from understanding) some 'deeper' questions about your identity in a mediated world.

The magazine industry and gender

This topic can be addressed as an aspect of a broader study of magazines or print publishing for others, or as an example within work on gender representation for any Media course. The approach suggested here begins with a consideration of women's magazines, drawing on some classic examples and a readily available body of work on these texts, then introduces the relatively new market of 'lad mags' for comparison, and then, crucially, moves students away from the nature/nurture, positive or negative binary-structured approach to this debate, towards a more postmodern conception of audience behaviour.

Class strategy – Discourse mapping

Taking the example of *Men's Health*, this approach enables students to combine simple content analysis with more complex evaluation of the kinds of identity-play at work in the pages of this magazine (and at work in the readings from the audience).

Assuming students are at this point familiar with the term 'discourse', and how they are using it to study media meanings, you might agree on these recurrent discourses being mobilised in the pages of *Men's Health*:

- quick-fix problem solving
- male narcissism (and anxiety)
- new male sensitivity
- male superiority/manipulation.

Taking three editions of the magazine, students (in small groups) map out articles and features in relation to these discourses, distinguishing between those that fit obviously and neatly into one (for example, a feature on steps to take to avoid prostate cancer or advice for various aspects of male grooming), elements which appear to take a range of positions, meaning they could fit into more than one discourse (for example, a feature on sex in which advice for 'driving her wild' is combined with the sense of a 'trade off' – if you do these things, in return she will. . .) . . . and others which appear to defy these categorizations.

From such an activity, students will come to more complex and subtle conclusions about how the magazine represents gender than if they either stick in a matter of fact way to content analysis or go straight for broad questions of ideology without paying attention to the detail.

> Once content is mapped to discourses, the audience research and personal engagement can proceed from this – asking more critical questions about positive and negative social implications of these proliferating discourses, alongside investigation into reading practices, especially the notion of the 'pick and mix' reader.

Discussing the notion that publishers and editorial teams create a sense of 'belonging' on the part of their readers is a good starting point, but in order to avoid a reductive reinforcing of stereotypes, we need to keep our thinking sharp enough to remember that readers do not really believe in this community. For that reason, I think it is a common bad practice to ask students to use A3 paper and cut and paste to produce classroom displays about '*Loaded* man' or '*Cosmo* woman'. Better if we start with a view that '*Cosmo* woman' is an editorial construction and then start to deconstruct her. Some semiotic work can get students started here, focusing on cover design to address the simple question of how the reader is 'drawn in' through the language of signs and symbols. Students can then be given two very different theoretical perspectives to apply to their semiotic findings. Winship (1997) offers a feminist application of 'male gaze' theory to women's magazine covers, arguing that 'the gaze between cover model and women readers marks the complicity between women seeing themselves in the image which the masculine culture has defined.' I have put this idea alongside Althusser's (1971) notion of 'interpellation' (the social/ideological practice of misrecognizing yourself). If students put the two together, a feminist-Marxist reading of magazine covers is straightforward – Winship's complicity is being prepared, for gratification, to recognize the ideal version of oneself, despite the anxiety this will cause. For feminists, the male culture reinforces its power by defining women in this way and encouraging this anxiety. The alternative is to challenge it, but students will know from their experience that this is difficult. For Marxists, this is a form of 'false consciousness'. Put simply, the post-feminist backlash has served to 'redistract women' – rather than continuing to lobby for equal pay and positive representation in media, they are reading *Hello* and commenting on the waistlines of their sisters.

To get to this point of debate, though, as well as cover design deconstruction, students need a more developed understanding of the constructed audience. The easiest way to obtain this is by contacting publishers for advertising packs. These will define, for potential advertisers, the reader – where she shops, what she likes, how she understands herself.

Class strategy – Knowledge or belief?

To introduce students to the ways in which readers are constructed (and more or less complicit in this game), ask them to provide a range of popular magazines aimed at one gender in each case. After a period of time reading them, ask them in groups to answer these questions about the preferences of readers of one magazine, (without reference to the magazine in question):

- What breakfast cereal?
- What car/mode of transport?
- What accommodation?
- What drink?
- Which TV shows?
- What music?
- What vegetable?
- What sport to watch and what sport to play?
- Ideal partner?
- What holiday?
- Vote for who?
- What bar/pub?

This works even better if you ask students to provide three of their own criteria as well. A good way to follow this up is through a hot-seating exercise. After that, students are asked to discuss which of the statements about the audience/readership are based on empirical evidence (knowledge) and which are assumptions (beliefs), and most importantly, where the latter category comes from.

Class strategy – Hot seating

Using the knowledge or belief example above as the focus for this, the object here is simply to illustrate for the whole class a generally empathetic perspective to audience construction.

One student from each group takes on the role of the reader of the magazine being analysed (it helps if this is not a magazine they normally read).

In turn, they take the 'hot seat' (at the front of an oval arrangement with no desks to protect them). If you have a good enough relationship with your students, you can darken the room and shine an OHP on them at this point (although I should mention that I once made a student physically sick in a Film Studies class with this approach!).

The rest of the group fire questions at her, but not the questions already provided for the previous task. Instead, new questions thought up on the spot by students. This activity is amusing, participative, lively and entirely relevant to the study focus, which is to do with questions of readership, audience complicity and stereotyping. At this stage, the teacher is deliberately keeping things simple – we are making assumptions about the readership of magazines as fixed, stable types of people that we can second-guess in these ways. Clearly, this idea will be challenged later.

Male magazines, or 'lad mags' provide us with one of the most challenging, hotly debated areas for analysis. I have developed a case study on *Nuts* and *Zoo* (McDougall, 2004b) and a more sustained focus on *Men's Health* (in Harvey (ed.) 2002) to explore questions of audience and 'effects'. With the latter, I have asked students to consider the question of whether, for feminists, 'two wrongs make a right'. In other words, does the proliferation of male concern with body image and health reflect a maturing society within a wider discourse about the 'new man' or can we trace here a worrying objectification of men that actually reinforces that of women (a different kind of level playing-field)? Again, we get to this discussion through the 'legwork' of textual analysis, content analysis and study of journalistic approaches, as well as evaluating the advertising content (using the publisher's briefing notes as a starting point).

A comparison of *Nuts* with *Men's Health* gives students the change to consider different variants along a continuum. Whereas *Nuts* is explicit in its sexism and reduction of the male gender to its stereotype (undoubtedly in a playful way, as we shall discuss), *Men's Health* lays claim to a more sensitive, aspiring version of the male, yet the majority of its 'quick fix' approaches to everything from 'impressing the boss' to 'getting a six-pack' and 'making her beg for more' are based on a traditional hunter-gatherer discourse about male behaviour. There is little in the way of complexity in its pages, so whereas the mode of address is very different to *Nuts*, is the discourse so far removed?

At this point, then, having come to a developed understanding of how a range of magazines for both genders operate in textual and commercial terms, we can introduce a triangular approach to considering representation. Three questions should be asked of each text:

1. How does it represent its own gender to the reader?

2. How does it represent its own gender to the other gender?

3. How does it represent the other gender to its reader?

This pays attention to the importance of female readings of *Nuts* and male readings of *Sugar*, as this duality of representation serves to reinforce ideas of the other. Bring in discussions of sexuality and the 'secondary reader' (for example, the gay male reader of *Cosmo*, or the female reader of *Men's Health*) and things get more interesting, and remind us again of the complexity of representation. It is a fact that the cover models on *Men's Health* are always in black and white because the editors assume that the readership will be able to cope with a male cover model only on these terms (the black and white male torso becomes less sexual and more medical/muscular). And why do students think that, with a few exceptions, women's magazines feature female cover models and so do men's?

Finally, a consideration of rival perspectives.

Laura Barton (2004) asserts that:

'These days, the insinuation that all gents are satisfied by 29 cans of Stella and a slightly stained copy of *Razzle* is as quaintly outmoded as the suggestion that the lady loves Milk Tray. Nevertheless, *Zoo* and its brethren seem to act like some elaborate cultural muck-spreader, coating everything in an impermeable layer of tits and ass and porn and fighting. And the intimation is that any bird who can't handle that can feck off and take her scented candles with her.'

Barton, Althusser and Winship all offer a variation on the theme that gender magazines do some damage, and that there is a correlation between the representation of gender in their pages, the readers' acceptance of them and problems in society.

Another view that students absolutely *must* appreciate and take a stance on, is the growing idea that we 'pick and mix' our media and we similarly select in more or less regular ways how we form our identities in relation to media. Gauntlett (2002), through sustained audience research, describes readers' active negotiations in response to both women's and men's magazines:

'I have argued against the view that men's lifestyle magazines represent a reassertion of old-fashioned masculine values, or a "back-lash" against feminism. While certain pieces in the magazines might support such an argument, this is not their primary purpose or selling point. Instead, their existence and popularity shows men rather insecurely trying to find their place in the modern world, seeking help regarding how to behave in their relationships and advice on how to earn the attention, love and respect of women and the friendship of other men. In post-traditional cultures, where identities are not "given" but need to be constructed and negotiated, and where an individual has to establish their personal ethics and mode of living, the magazines offer some reassurance to men who are wondering "Is this right?" and "Am I doing this OK?", enabling a more confident management of the narrative of the self'. (Gauntlett, 2002: 180).

Kendall (2002) researched young people's reading habits and, predictably, magazines featured heavily. Kendall was concerned with readers' notions of themselves as particular kinds of readers, after all, young people are demonised for their lack of literacy, in conventional terms. She found that male readers adopted a less critical stance than their female counterparts:

'The magazines functioned, as for female readers, to offer prompts and possibilities for representing self through negotiation of symbolic codes. However, the male readers were characteristically less critical and more acquiescent to the identities inscribed through the modalities of their "hobby" magazines.'

Why this would be so is open to debate. Perhaps males take a less negotiated position in response to these texts, or perhaps the longer history of the woman's magazine is a factor. Either way, both Gauntlett and Kendall remind us that the only viable approach to these debates is, ultimately, audience research.

Gauntlett's last sentence is perfect for an old-fashioned academic essay, I think, reformed as: 'According to Gauntlett (2002), gender magazines 'enable a more confident management of the narrative of the self'. Discuss.' To answer this well, students would need to introduce the texts in their commercial contexts (circulation, publishers, etc.) and the big issues –

nature/culture, representation and broader debates about effects. They would move on to discuss the function of magazines, in terms of editorial policy and selling of audiences to advertizers. Next, they would approach, through textual examples, a range of theoretical positions, referring in particular to Winship and Gauntlett as alternatives. Next they would apply these positions to one example, and then, most important of all, describe their own audience research in this area. It is from this primary work that their conclusions should be drawn.

Audience, effects and censorship

There are several designated topic areas under this umbrella. Considerations of film censorship, children and television, audience research, media and violence, the effects model compared to others, and analysis of the effects of advertizing all demand (if they are to be done well) a sensible response to contemporary theories of media audiences (which involves considerably more than uses and gratifications, or the hierarchy of needs).

In the section on narrative in Chapter One I set out my views about students' dutiful yet bland application of Propp and Todorov to contemporary films. I want to make a similar case here against the BoBo Doll. I believe there is not much mileage for Media students in using dated behaviourist models from psychology to support an argument about media effects in the twenty-first century. As students will be aware of the media effects hypothesis from lived experience, it would be better to start with a variety of research on media audience and the more complex challenges to this orthodoxy. To this end, the sections on the effects debate in Dutton (1997), Barker and Petley (1997), Gauntlett (1998) and Buckingham (1995) are essential reading for students (or at least selected extracts from each), alongside the ITC 's 'Striking a Balance' report (Hanley, 2002), the most recent BBFC statements about how they rate films, the ASA code of practice for advertisers and Ofcom's website. From this range of reading (guided, through the kinds of class strategies offered throughout this book), students will encounter the history and nature of ideas about how audiences are 'effected', alongside some alternative perspectives, and the key policy criteria in use by institutions and regulators. Any one of the three paradigms in this triangle is meaningless in isolation from the other two. I also strongly suggest that you make links with other topics, so if students were looking at horror films, for example, they could usefully make a synoptic bridge to Dyer's work (1994) on action film pleasures, or they could return to Kermode's views on film censorship:

> 'It is very hard to maintain freedom of speech in a culture which has become terminally infantilised. We've allowed the censors to view us all as children, and we've handed over the reigns of responsibility for our viewing habits because we are not willing to accept that responsibility for ourselves.' (2001, in introduction to Channel 4 screening of *Bad Lieutenant*).

The important role for the teacher in managing this learning is to prevent students placing walls around different areas of Media study. It is common for the same student to deal with subtle nuances of audience pleasure when writing about a particular film genre, but then take a reductive, deficit-model approach when considering arguments for censorship. Another caveat is this – if you decide to use a case study like Barker and Petley's analysis (1997) of the moral panic arising from the Jamie Bulger case, make sure students are aware of the difference between general audience work and highly specific research. *Child's Play* was viewed on video, so it cannot be applied in work on children and television or film censorship, for example. To tackle audience work with confidence, you need to support students in their understanding of demographics, dominant readings and other possibilities, cultivation, moral panic, myth, reception theory and reader-response, research methods and theories of popular culture. I am setting up a sophisticated grasp of audience theory as a prerequisite for dealing with debates around censorship and effects for the obvious reason that there is a great danger otherwise of basing one's opinion (or demonstration of personal engagement) on a simplistic conception of how people read media texts.

To prepare students to write well about film censorship, I suggest you foreground the notion on protection within a broader discussion of 'concern' over popular culture:

> 'There is a continuous and necessarily uneven and unequal struggle, by the dominant culture, constantly to disorganise and reorganise popular culture; to enclose and confine its definitions and forms within a more inclusive range of dominant forms. There are points of resistance; there are also moments of supersession. This is the dialectic of cultural struggle'. (Hall, 1981: 228)

I utilise this sociological perspective from Stuart Hall because it reminds us that we cannot sensibly isolate the notion of the state censoring media content from power struggles over the function and limits of popular culture (and indeed all of Media Studies is negotiated within this contested terrain). Equally, students will often demonstrate, in free discussion, myths about 'the other' which are useful if they are reflected upon (i.e. we all do it, but knowing why we do it is helpful). Students will often admit to watching films and DVDs they are excluded from by classification, but will sometimes articulate the classic line that (unlike themselves) there are other people who wouldn't be 'suitable' for such illegal consumption. So again, discourse mapping is a sound methodology for dealing with the idea of protection. Going through some case study examples, such as *Crash* (not banned in novel form), *Clockwork Orange* (banned by its director), *Battleship Potemkin* (banned for some social groups, but not others), students can map the assumptions made against discourse categories. Alongside this work, it is interesting for students to consider the dilemma the 'cutter' faces and to analyse famous examples of problems with context (for example *Straw Dogs* where there is a view that the censor made the images more disturbing than before). To focus on the politics of censorious claims, films like *The Magdelene Sisters, Dogma* and *The Passion of the Christ* serve to highlight the ideological nature of such specific debates over faith, and this exercise is then useful for illustrating that actually all censorship is based on power-claims, there is no single text that is universally offensive. For example, as Kermode has argued recently, the BBFC (who, it should be noted, are funded by the film and industry rather than the government) appears more heavy-handed when dealing with English language films compared to subtitled art-house movies with controversial content. The assumption about audience is obvious. As always, I suggest that the most productive, active, strategy for student work in this area is audience research, not to try to 'prove' whether their peers or family are influenced negatively by film images, but to collect qualitative data through interviews and focus group discussions about films and censorship, so they can analyse the discourses articulated and where they come from historically and culturally. Students' own responses to shocking films will, naturally, be of great importance. Davey (2005) offers a really interesting student view:

> 'Films are a form of expression, and many forms of expression are prompted by sorrow and loss which, in many cases, are prompted by violence. Therefore, without violence, a vast number of films would never have been made. If violence has played a part in the making of a film, then it's understandable that in the content of the film, violence may play a part. We cannot distinguish between violence and film, because that would mean distinguishing between violence and life.' (2005: 30)

Class strategy – Critical discourse analysis

(Note – see also Role Play for Debate in Chapter Two)
For my research degree (McDougall, 2004a), I recorded nine hours of examiners' meetings, transcribed all of it, and then coded every statement made into three categories. This took a month. Students working towards a range of Level 2 or 3 qualifications have very little time, but this group activity is manageable and introduces them to a good strategy for discursive research.

In groups, students prepare a three-question interview and then choose one person as their research subject. Each group should have a strategic focus. For example, one group might interview a parent, another a film fan and another group a younger sibling. The questions must be the same for each group, and in this example we would expect them to be about the need for censorship, the type of films that need to be classified (which, of course, is not censorship but something related) and the kinds of people that need to be prevented from consuming some films.

Transcription is next, and students need to realize that every word must be transcribed accurately, for the researcher to avoid selection or poetic licence. If you have the funds, invest in some transcription software for this purpose.

The next stage is coding. I suggest differentiating between statements that are factual, statements that are based on assumption, those that are about specific films, those that are general and those that are about 'the other'.

Once statements are coded, and the ratio of each category calculated, the groups jigsaw, and you have a discourse analysis in operation. To make this critical, you then set up a more theoretical set of activities for students to work out:

- Where these discourses seem to come from.
- How they relate to competing claims to power/knowledge.
- What alternative discourses struggle to present themselves (the ways in which discourse delimits the sayable).

A note about resources – film magazines regularly devote whole issues to banned films, and documentary series regularly look into the history of censorship as well as the arising debates. In addition, *In the Picture* magazine, Film Education and the BFI produce study packs on this topic, and DVDs of controversial films usually contain documentary material or director's commentaries on these issues. The crucial role of the teacher, though, is to choose the resources to support the approach you already wish to take. On the one hand, content-driven Media learning can frustrate, and on the other, you will need to make decisions (and perhaps obtain parental agreement) that are sensitive to the cohort you are working with. Here are two responses to the film *Crash* to illustrate this point:

'A film, by an important director, of a book by a great novelist, which has generated much media heat (and of course, very little light) should be dealt with in the Media Studies classroom because if we're not doing it then sure as hell nobody else is.'

(Nick Lacey, quoted in Stafford, 1997: 7).

'Inevitably, trying to understand what people "do" with media products will involve discussing the issue of violence in moving image products. This does mean analysing the views of both those who maintain a direct "cause and effect" relationship between "violence" on screen and violence in society and those critics who reject such a crude model or way of describing the debate. There are enough examples from recent years to enable a thoughtful, intellectual debate. I just don't think a film about obtaining sado-masochistic sexual pleasure from car crashes is one of them. It is just too extreme for use with 16–18 year olds'.

(Graeme Kemp, quoted in Stafford, 1997: 7).

My own view is closer to that of the first respondent, but I have always played safe in this area and written to parents explaining the educational context of showing graphic scenes in class, and giving them an opt-out option. This has never arisen, but it means you need a back-up plan, perhaps even a different topic to run in tandem if necessary.

Researching children and television, students might again start with some contextual existing research in this area, most obviously Buckingham (2000), Livingstone (1999), and Hodge and Tripp (1986). This reading needs to be organized through a range of individual and collaborative tasks, but only in a few instances should it be isolated reading and note-taking. The key critical questions to address are:

1. How are children defined and by whom?

2. What research methods have been used to produce these findings?

3. What model of audience behaviour is evident?

Having asked these questions of some academic work, students should research media coverage of this debate and start to position articles and TV documentaries in relation to theoretical perspectives. Next, they can place regulators' practices (namely Ofcom, and previously, the ITC) in this context. Again, as for film censorship, we are establishing a triangular approach where academic theory, public debate and state intervention are understood only in relation to one another.

Primary research with parents and children is incredibly enlightening for students, as long as ethical issues are high on your agenda early on. Outcomes are only useful if students are aware that parents cannot be treated as objective subjects if they are asked questions about how much television their children watch, as this is an emotive area with an underlying subtext about parental neglect. Equally, children are great subjects for open-ended discursive work, especially in response to images. Students should be discouraged from trying to answer questions (such as, are children influenced by TV advertising – the answer is probably yes), and encouraged to find out about the range of different responses out there.

Some interesting examples of work I have supported students with in this area have been: In what different ways is *Teletubbies* considered to be educational? (note – *not* is it educational or not?); How do children understand the function of advertising; How do children and parents discuss the suitability of television? and What are children's responses to soap opera representations of family life? In each case, I had two objectives in discussing these projects with students. First, I had in every case to move them away from a 'headline' approach to research (they wanted to prove something negative). And second, my job was to present them with existing research, help them find a way of doing sensible, small-scale primary research with the people in question (and learn by making mistakes) and then relate the latter to the former. In this way, they were able to respond to a 'gap in the market': very little theory about children and television, until relatively recently, had included children in the debate!

'We need to begin by exploring what children make of the films and television programmes that they themselves identify as upsetting or indeed as "violent" – which, it should be emphasised, are not necessarily those that adults would identify for them. In a debate that is dominated by adults purporting to speak on children's behalf, children's voices have been almost entirely unheard'. (Buckingham, 2000: 73–74)

With this approach in mind, there follows a highly prescriptive framework for a student writing up a research exercise on children and television. Clearly, you may need to adapt this and differentiate the level of prescription for your own needs.

1. Research methods: describe the purpose of research, the different kinds of media research in operation, the kind of research you are doing, your broader topic and your micro-topic within it. Justify your hypothesis in terms of what it will add to the broader field of research in this area. What are you doing that is new, or specific, or local?

2. Literature review – how have you 'mapped the field'? What literature did you identify as central and why? Summarize and synthesize from these sources, and identify one

particularly useful source. Describe how your planning for the primary research relates to this secondary work.

3. Describe the research methodology for the primary work in detail, and any logistical and/or ethical issues you encountered.

4. Analyse the data you acquired, at a basic quantitative level and also a more discursive, qualitative and interpretive dimension. What were your research questions, and what are the answers? What further research can other people now undertake from your contribution to the field? How does your set of findings relate to the literature you started with?

5. Ensure all your sources are referenced correctly, and that you guarantee anonymity where needed.

I am choosing not to devote space here to the 'discrete' study of the effects debate or of media audience as an isolated topic, despite the appearance of such areas as 'stand-alone' options on various Media Studies specifications. Such an activity makes no sense without the kinds of case studies described here. Furthermore, I have argued that, conversely, no Media work on these case studies can begin without some serious attention to contemporary debates over audience behaviour. As always, the best way to get students into these debates is to get them talking to audiences. So for me, it goes without saying that any work on censorship or effects is really an audience research project.

British film and national identity

To prepare for the range of angles that awarding bodies might opt for in exams, or to give students a choice of focus for coursework, our teaching in this area should cover three perspectives:

1. The British Film Industry (changes over time, funding, relationship to America and Europe, dilemmas for producers, audience shifts, government agendas and the relationship of culture to commerce).

2. British Films as Texts (the range of commercially successful and critically acclaimed films on release at the time of the work, with regard to directors, styles and audience responses).

3. Representation of Britain (in particular, how different films do this in different ways, how this has changed as the notion of being British has changed, and the question of whether British cinema has always suffered, and still does, from a 'burden of representation').

Once again, here is a triangulation, and to focus on one at the expense of another is to skew the topic unnecessarily. Marking student exams in this domain, I have found that the conventional approach tends to be about social realizm and an unnecessary binary opposition between 'cultural' UK films and a homogenized description of Hollywood. This is problematic for all sorts of reasons, but to mention *28 Days Later* and *Sideways* as opposed to *Vera Drake* versus *Spiderman* illustrates the point.

With a film like *Vera Drake*, then, the questions to pose are about critical acclaim in relation to commercial imperatives, and the importance of cultural reflection alongside 'feelgood' depictions. But these questions cannot be answered without reference to the ways in which films get to be made and seen, in terms of co-funding, production scales, distribution and exhibition. For this reason my suggested starting point is a case study on the decline of Film Four, alongside some audience research on local cinema demographics. I would do this work before embarking on any textual analysis. Once students are familiar with the BFI categories for defining British films (in which Category A is an entirely British film, funded by UK finance, and staffed by a majority of British personnel; Category B is majority UK funded; C is the more common co-funding scenario and D describes US films with some creative input from the UK), they are not expected to decide that it is a 'bad thing' that, for example, people in the Dudley region get 80 per cent of their film culture from the West Coast of America. What they must come to realize is that sharing a language with Hollywood has been simultaneously a gift and a problem for British film, and your take on this will depend on whether you see film as cultural artefact, commercial product, or both. For example, while Nick Roddick asserts that 'every memorable achievement to come out of UK cinema since the war has come out of someone's desire to say something, not to sell it' (1999: 13), Roy Stafford reminds us that 'according to the usual flag-waving of the British press at Oscar time, we should all be excited by 'British' successes such as *American Beauty* (US) and *The Talented Mr Ripley* (US), on the grounds that their respective directors are British or by the 'British' contributions of Michael Caine and Phil Collins to other American movies'. (2000: 2). Actually, these are part of the same argument, that the media and government define success on the Hollywood model, and films funded by the Film Council and the National Lottery are expected to either compete with blockbusters or settle for low budgets and inadequate marketing.

You need at all times to be very careful not to set up simplistic arguments. While it might at first seem to be 'just plain wrong' that wholly British films have the lowest budgets and are in the minority, it must be said that the examples in this category that do well only make it because American distributors invest in them and many never get seen at all. Anyone making a film in the UK needs to be realistic – America shares our language and we are a tiny audience in comparison. So the temptation to go for the international market will always loom large. The problem is that this approach is untenable as occasional success cannot be sustained on smaller capital resources. Alongside these linguistic, geographical and financial elements, we have the cultural reality of audience expectations. Our students' film culture (alongside TV, games and to a lesser extent, music) is increasingly American. Simply telling them this is bad is not good enough. We have to get into the reasons for this (through reflective work on their part), and there are links here with Citizenship if you compare the elements of their culture that seem to be more or less American or European.

The Film Council, administrating lottery spend on films and lottery-funded franchises, have created under New Labour some more visible resources for UK production. However, the dilemmas faced by directors such as Shane Meadows are described here:

> 'The choices for British producers are: make low budget British films targeted at mainstream British audiences, hoping that the "peculiarly British" subject matter will attract oversees audiences who will see the films as "unusual". A low budget film could cover costs by careful sale of rights in the UK and Europe. Anything

earned in the US is then a bonus. Or make low budget films for a "niche" art-house audience in the UK and abroad. Or look for partners in Europe and/or America and aim more clearly for an "international audience". (Stafford, 2002: 6)

Students should start with the facts. What happened at Film Four was to do with a commercial and cultural mistake. In the 1980s, an editorial-driven approach had led to the production of many groundbreaking films reflecting social issues that, according to their directors, would not be made today. Following the success of the first wave of 'mockney' films in the late 1990s, the company attempted the factory-style approach to commissioning genre/format movies at great pace. When these flopped, the capital was not there to remain solvent (Hollywood players gamble, knowing the one major success will pay for nine losers). On the other hand, Lottery funding has led to increased production in other areas, and co-funding, particularly with European companies, keeps Mike Leigh going, with great success (for example, *Vera Drake*). The obvious comparative approach (which might be in danger of becoming dated) is to compare a film like *Vera Drake* with *Love, Actually* (ensuring textual analysis and consideration of representation of social class and gender is kept in dialogue with knowledge of funding and production). Alternatively, a case study on a range of internationally successful British films can work well, if the focus is on how producers' eyes on the international market can lead to particular representations of London that, as Morrissey has it, 'say nothing to me about my life'. Taking students to different kinds of cinema and focusing on them as an audience group is valuable.

I did some reflective work with my students at Runshaw College, by taking them to Cornerhouse in Manchester to see *My Name is Joe* and researching their responses (McDougall, 1999). When my students from Halesowen joined their counterparts from all over the country in Bradford for a study day on British film, they were shown clips from *The Land Girls, Sexy Beast, The Crying Game, Secrets and Lies, Brassed Off, East is East, Billy Elliot* and *Notting Hill*. Only the last example prompted a mass expression of disappointment when we moved back from clip to PowerPoint. What do we do with that response? The interesting work is to ask students what the reasons are and work from there (although others prefer to criticize them on teachers' e-lists!).

Dealing with the 'burden of representation' (the notion that UK film directors are weighed down by the legacy of 1950s social realism, Ealing Comedies and the longevity of Ken Loach), a case study on how recent British films have represented multi-cultural society in a variety of ways can offer an interesting departure from the Leigh versus Curtis, or Meadows versus Boyle approach. I have used *Bend it Like Beckham, East is East, Anita and Me, Bhaji on The Beach, Last Resort, Dirty Pretty Things* and *In this World* to this end. The three 'close study' texts within this range were *Beckham, East is East* (mainly because it overlapped with Film Studies, which some students were also taking) and *In this World*. Here we are setting up a comparison of a nostalgic and partly stereotypical depiction of British Asian life in the 1970s with a contemporary equivalent which has much more of an eye on the international audience, alongside a very different film which, despite being entirely about the nature of British citizenship, is largely set in Asia and Europe. Depending on the time and scale of the work, students can relate these films to the history of social realism, perhaps focusing on *Saturday Night and Sunday Morning* from the 'Kitchen Sink' period and *Raining Stones* from the Thatcher era. The important focus is always to ask these questions – who is being represented, by whom, for what purpose and with what range of responses? Albert Finney's portrayal of Arthur Seaton was all about putting new people on the screen within a wider discourse about working-class male ideology (as discussed in Chapter Two) Arthur understands his alienation, there is no false consciousness to sneer at, and this constructs his heroism, however laden with misogyny his world-view might be.

Two of the other films under scrutiny present themselves with this same kind of agenda, combining comedy with realism to depict the existence of 'kinds of people' previously absent from the screen (Asian youth in *East is East*, and a young empowered Asian woman in *Beckham*). But *In This World* stands alone in this study, as director Michael Winterbottom provides a partly documentary approach (he went to a refugee camp in Afghanistan and asked two of the residents to be filmed making the journey to London) to set up a more complex and troubling version of this 'representation of the new'.

> 'We see the characters "as is" – they are "ordinary" and "extraordinary" and we are forced to wonder what we would do in their situation. The drama comes from the situation and the way the characters struggle to respond to it. This is the classic neorealist approach – the opposite of a story "imposed" on the real world'. (Stafford, 2003: 16).

Without due attention to detail, students might well (and do, on the evidence of exam papers) lump together *In this World* with *Vera Drake* on the one hand, against *Notting Hill* and *Gosford Park* on the other. They shouldn't. Mike Leigh certainly *does* impose a fictional narrative, however authentic his approach might be. Equally, while looking like the kind of costume drama Americans love, at the same time *Gosford Park* is as sharp a deconstruction of social class relations as *High Hopes*. Our job here is to give students an understanding of how films relate to cultural identity and nationhood, within an analysis of media texts as sites of conflict between different discourses or world views. Once that is achieved, students can do good work, free from lazy categorization. As always, tasking students with the creation of their own British film, to be shot through with representational devices, is the best way to make this come alive.

There are countless other films that spring to mind if you want to explore the tension between challenging representation and stereotyping: *Billy Elliot*, *Trainspotting* and *The Full Monty* (and there are a plethora of good resources out there for teachers). However, once again the more complex and ambiguous texts provide richer analysis: *A Room for Romeo Brass*, *Ratcatcher* and *Wonderland* are essential, if only to remind us that British film is incredibly varied in its scope.

The more astute students will take the same approach to the notion of social realism as they will to genre – a sceptical scrutiny of the assumptions at work in the circulation of ideas about this kind of film. Comparing a film like *Secrets and Lies* to a TV documentary shows us that both texts make claims to realism, and Leigh's film certainly establishes a verisimilitude somewhat closer to most of our experiences than, say, *The Return of the King*, but the main narrative device employed is melodrama and the kinds of closure and pleasure offered by the later sequences are entirely constructed through neat conventions of plot and story. Real life is far less choreographically staged. Similarly, the 'Land of Hope and Glory' resolution and political resonance offered by the ending to *Brassed Off* is tremendously important cinema, in my opinion, but one suspects in real life the ground-down residents of Grimley would see their brass band come second or third in the grand final (see McDougall, 2000, for a more detailed account of the problems of social realizm).

Here is a framework for a scheme of work on contemporary British film:

1. Audience research and industry fact-finding. Local focus for audience – who goes where to see what, who owns cinemas, who distributes films seen, what alternatives are there which are not used, and why? Focus on audience reasons, not assumptions, and on students' own film culture. For industry, BFI categories, recent history of major and minor companies, lottery and Film Council, co-funding, UK tax breaks. *Sight & Sound*, Film Education and the annual BFI Handbook are good resources.

2. What are the most successful British films of the last year, in commercial terms and in cultural terms? With this in mind, students pitch for funding for a new Category A release. They need a contingency plan for Category B, which may lead to editorial changes.

3. The burden of representation – combination of reading (through collaborative approaches), lecture input and guided viewing. Three key films, from 'Kitchen Sink', Film Four in Thatcher era and contemporary. Attention to funding, production, distribution and exhibition.

4. Case study on representation of Asian British experience and asylum seeker/migrants. Key films: *East is East, Bend it Like Beckham, In this World* and *Last Resort*. Critical questions: who is being represented, by whom, for what purpose and with what range of responses? Attention to funding, production, distribution and exhibition.

5. Focus on range of British cinema over last twelve months to emphasize diversity. Explicitly avoid students reducing British film to 'gritty northern realizm' versus glossy London.

Working with students on the representation of asylum seekers, there are some relevant overlaps with News and Media/Politics. In this context, your students may hold views that are not your own. Your job is to get them reflecting on these views and where they come from in response to films, not to change their minds. Asking the following five questions as a context for screening *In this World, Last Resort* and *Dirty Pretty Things* establishes this reflective approach.

1. What is your view of asylum seekers, and where do these ideas come from?

2. How are these films British?

3. How are asylum seekers represented in different ways?

4. How are the films constructed in terms of style and narrative?

5. Have these films made you think differently about this issue?

In analysing *East is East* and *Bend it Like Beckham*, the interesting questions are around the blend of realizm/authenticity and stereotyping. Some Muslim critics of *East is East* have been concerned about the representation of 'traditional' Muslim values through the patriarch,

In this World: a contemporary representation of British identity?

George. *Beckham*, equally, represents Punjabi identity through the well-worn depiction of a wedding, and Jess is marked out as 'other' to this culture through her desire to play football (the most Western of activities, and traditionally male to boot, if you pardon the pun) on this day. The feelgood narrative, alongside the intertextual timing of the release (the World Cup and Beckham's super-celebrity) resulted in this film grossing ten times its production costs. The critical question for students is around the extent to which the film balances its shorthand representations of Punjabi life with a sensitive discourse about gender and identity.

Depending on the demographics of your cohort, they may be well served to answer this last question from experience. Could it be argued that the film avoids some of the more important issues about racism in the UK? But perhaps the most interesting angle to explore is the way in which this film seems to stand alone as one which bridges the 'culture or commerce' issue. On the one hand, the film is absolutely a reflection on contemporary British culture and is happy to carry the burden of representation (compared to, say, *Four Weddings*). But on the other, it was produced with America in mind, in the knowledge that soccer in the USA is a game played mostly by young women, the obvious audience for the product. Finally, with an Asian female director in Gurinder Chadha, *Bend It Like Beckham* offers an alternative to the tradition of social realist films about British housing estates made by white, middle-class men.

This leads me to a final point about British cinema that illustrates the tensions I have felt as a Media teacher (and which I researched for four years with teachers and examiners: McDougall, 2004a) between wanting to teaching Media from a 'student-first' approach to pedagogy, and the temptation to use the opportunity to show films I believe to be politically important. I have found this difficult, in so much as I personally believe that British citizens should encounter films like *Vera Drake*, *Sweet Sixteen* and *My Name is Joe*, as these films are politically and culturally important within my view of the world. But I can't have it both ways. If I don't think an English teacher should see it as her right to enforce a cultural position on students through suggesting they ought to 'appreciate' Shakespeare (or Toni Morrison, for that matter), then I can't abuse my position, either.

News, war and politics

Class strategy – Seemingly irrelevant, planned spontaneity

Sometimes, a change is as good as a rest for learning, and I have found that planning a seemingly 'on the spot' departure from the norm leads to activities that stick in students' minds. Here is an example, related to news and politics:

Bring in a newspaper (or rely on students having a copy of *Metro*).

Tell them you are abandoning the lesson but by the end of the school/college day, you want, in your pigeonhole, a word-processed report (one from the whole group) on how one political issue was reported on the day by a range of newspapers, television, online news provision and bloggers. If you can afford it from your budget, give the students £5 for resources and tell them you want copies of sources with the report.

There is a lot of trust at stake here, of course, and you need to have established ground rules and a collaborative learning ethos for it to work.

Although you will have scheduled this into your scheme or work, it tends to be most productive when you do it only with one group, and when you create the impression that you were going to teach this topic but then decided, on the spot, that the students are up to a task like this and that they will learn more through such an independent approach.

When Len Masterman (1985) wrote *Teaching the Media*, the most compelling case study through which to explore the divergent interests of media and state was the Falklands conflict. Masterman's words in response to that analysis resonate in our climate too:

'The media may not have emerged with much credit as champions of free speech during the Falklands, but it is too cheap and simple a shot to see the media as mere lackeys of the state machine. For one thing, we do need to recognise that the credibility of the media within democratic societies rests upon their ability to demonstrate *some* independence from government, big business and powerful interest groups'. (1985: 191).

Asking students to assess this statement in 2006 would in itself be a tremendously productive activity. After all, the Hutton enquiry and the coverage of the 2005 general election would seem to suggest a greater degree of media independence than was the case when Thatcher was in power, despite our paranoia about spin. But on the other hand, this independence is threatened by government, which students might see as being more concerned with control of news agendas than might be hoped for in a democracy.

What we must not do is assume our students understand democracy (or its alternatives) fully, or criticize them if they don't. Surely, if they are so comfortable in their freedoms that they sometimes lack an awareness of the struggles that have made them so, this is a good thing (presumably, the young people with the keenest understanding of freedom are those fighting for it). Either way, they need to gain a working understanding of the notion of a free press before any serious work on testing it out can begin.

A case study on the reporting on 9/11, the wars in Afghanistan and Iraq, the Hutton enquiry and the 2005 election can be used within a range of broader areas of study to do with news values, selection, construction and presentation, ideology and news agendas, news audiences, journalism, popular culture and cultural imperializm/globalization.

Class strategy – Matching tasks

A simple way of starting the process of analysing news agendas and journalistic styles that avoids either making assumptions or 'telling' s. is to ask students to bring in a range of newspapers from the same day. When an unforeseen event happens, the teacher needs to collect sources (as I did on September 12th 2001), but with a political event such as an election, students can be given the task of providing a particular newspaper, for example, on 7 May 2005 (the papers on 6 May were published too early for comprehensive coverage of the general election). They are then asked to select and cut out a range of headlines and sentences/paragraphs from the paper related to the events in question. Students are arranged strategically in small groups and each extract is copied for each group. How you ask students to match the examples will depend on where they are in relation to what learning outcomes, but here are some examples:

- Simply identify the newspaper, or type of newspaper.
- Match the statement to particular news agendas.
- Match the statement to particular categories of discourse (already identified in previous lessons).
- Group similar examples, or group conflicting examples.

Apart from the obvious advantage for kinaesthetic learners (if we can adopt such a simplistic logic), this activity is a good way of doing basic textual analysis, or for approaching more complex theoretical questions about discourse. An example from 12 September 2001 might be to do with degrees of simplicity/complexity in the immediate identification of heroes and villains, for example. Or, looking at 7 May 2005, students might consider the extent to which reporting of the election focused on personality or policy.

Clearly, to cover 9/11, two world wars, a major enquiry and an election is a lot to ask of students, but sensible selection of the 'highlights' of each within a scheme of work on Media and Politics is possible. In this context, it is not so much the reporting of war itself (for example the role of 'embedded' journalists) that we are concerned with, so much as the reporting of the political decision-making and discourse (in this example the key figures will be Bush and Blair, with Clare Short and Robin Cook in supporting roles). One really 'useful' thing about the coverage of the Iraq war in relation to how papers aligned themselves with politicians was the way in which *The Sun* and the *Daily Mail* took the opposite stance from the *Daily Mirror* while the *Daily Express* was more independent. This gets students away from over-stating the notion of the tabloid press as a collective, and makes them aware of how very different their news agendas can be, particularly when competing discourses are at work. For example, patriotism in war time overrides uncertainty about the political justification for *The Sun* (who have been pro-Labour since Tony Blair's famous strategic compromise with Murdoch), while the *Daily Mail*'s demonisation of Saddam took them closer to *The Sun* than the *Daily Express* at this time. The *Daily Mirror*'s stance was unrelenting in its portrayal of Bush and Blair's departure from the UN as illegal. Students should start from these obvious differences in tabloid response and then, through research and teaching, map out historical and current allegiances and agendas to consider questions about whether news agendas are stable, or whether they shift in response to single issues (albeit a pretty big one, in this case); and if the latter is true, whether these shifts in agenda are related to ethical stances (the editorial agenda) or second-guessing where public opinion will go (a commercial agenda).

Another area I make no apology for mentioning yet again is blogging. Salam Pax (meaning 'peace') offered the world a weblog account of being bombed in Baghdad, stating 'I am not anybody's propaganda ploy – well, except my own.' Media teachers (including Lewis, 2003, who offers a detailed analysis) seized on this as an example of the kind of war reporting we never got before the technology facilitated it. The blog in question created an opportunity for people to take a 'reality check' on the reports they were given by mainstream media by comparing these 'official' accounts to the internet diary of an ordinary citizen in the battle zone:

'Whatever the true identity of Salam Pax, his blog gave audiences another important perspective on the war – one which was apparently not controlled by the institutions of the Iraqi authorities nor by the US or British military.' (Lewis, 2003: 34)

In Chapter Five, I suggest a range of approaches to a case study on the Hutton enquiry and the subsequent charter agreement for the BBC. How the newspapers reported the results of the enquiry can again be assessed within this mapping out of allegiances and agendas. A very useful angle for Media students is that of journalistic sources. Newspaper law and ethics are not areas we often get into on general Media courses, but in my view, better theory arises on vocational courses where students are required to know about legislative and ethical considerations in news reporting than on apparently academic models, where a blander 'news values' approach is often taken. To consider a newspaper to be a neat collection of stories arranged around a set of coherent values is to misunderstand the pace and rhythm of news gathering and construction, as journalists will tell you. Any one set of reports on a major issue, like the lead-up to the war in Iraq, will be the result of a host of interactions with sources and editorial decisions about risk, law and protection. The Hutton enquiry and the death of David Kelly are best understood as narratives about a source and the ability of the government to seize upon an error in the management of news. For these reasons, I suggest that the best way of making a case study like this active is to ask a journalist to speak to students about working with sources.

Taking the example of the 2005 general election, the usual ways of analysing press coverage need adapting, as the Iraq war intervened in such a way that there were more ambiguities and departures from traditional agendas than usual. Students (if they are under 40) will have no experience of election campaigns and press coverage that were not 'presidential'. Their expectation is that newspapers will celebrate or demonise party leaders on the day of voting, and this time around the *Mirror*'s depiction of Michael Howard as Dracula (with the pun on what was at 'stake') was classic caricature, linguistics and mode of address. At the same time, the emergence of tactical voting as a serious strategy that the electorate could easily understand made the coverage of the lead-up more complex and less patronizing in other ways. So we could analyse this duality of cover images, with their straightforward mocking of the enemy, contrasting with guides to tactical voting on the inner pages, where most newspapers were encouraging readers to make an informed decision based on what MPs had voted for in the Commons in recent times. For this reason, I do not agree with the idea that this campaign was bland and dull, rather I think the electorate were more aware, from the media, of specific issues and how their local MPs were behaving than at any recent time. On the other hand, students need also to be aware of the dual nature of much journalism in these times of freelance and multi-contract practices, as Peter Preston illustrates here, in an excellent, snapshot example of how news agendas work:

> 'What goes around, comes around. Simon Jenkins in The Standard predicts a 'Tory meltdown', then tells his Times readers to "vote Conservative" before departing to The Guardian. Max Hastings writes off Michael Howard as "the Tories Michael Foot" in The Guardian one day, then Tony Blair as "Labour's principal liability" for the Mail the next.' (*The Observer*, May 9, 2005)

What this tells us, again, is that the enemy of the Media student is simplification. Illustrated in Chapter Seven, when considering 'staple' concepts like genre and narrative, we certainly know it about institutions and technologies in times of convergence. And we need to recognize it when teaching our students about news reporting. To say that news agendas and values are fixed and predictable is no longer satisfactory.

A rich area for analysis is the Conservative campaign, and the hiring of an aggressive Australian PR consultant to set up a series of issues around asylum seeking and immigration with which to attack the Government. Students could use this campaign to focus on representation, within a broader semiotic deconstruction of party political imagery which will involve considering how colour, iconic, indexical and arbitrary signs and framing add up to a range of cultural signifiers that are more or less persuasive (clearly, hindsight helps us here in the form of results from the ballot box).

In the first edition of *A2 Media Studies for OCR* (Harvey, ed., 2002) we offered a comparison of the 1910 Labour election poster, which featured a cartoon of a group of working-class males breaking into the House of Lords ('Labour clears the way') with the 2001 posters, which all featured the party leader, either posed to signify earnest intent (Charles Kennedy: 'I jump on injustice, not bandwagons') or caricatured for ridicule and suspicion (a 'pregnant' Tony Blair: 'four years of Labour and he still hasn't delivered').

Students could take this approach and update it to analyse the 2005 campaign. Interestingly, alongside the demonising of Howard and Blair, the latter smirking as the poster asks us if we can stand another four years of him (the most presidential approach imaginable, with the election reduced here entirely to annoying elements of Blair's image), the Conservative campaign did return to the depersonalized approach of 1910 to some extent. The 'Are you thinking what we're thinking?' campaign' featured no images of politicians, opting instead for a handwritten note (for example, 'I mean, how hard is it to clean a hospital?' and 'It's not rocket science.'). The attempt here is to signify, through the handwriting, a 'common-sense' rhetoric, as though the notes have been passed to the party by people on the doorstep.

These examples will always need to be worked through in the context of a broader debate – in this case usually around the selection and construction of news, news agendas, the free press and democracy or politics and the media. In order to make good sense of the debate and to demonstrate such understanding for assessment, students will need to form a narrative out of these 'micro' examples that is seen to test out (without assuming the answers beforehand) the hypothesis in the topic. Higher-level work of this kind will also include audience research: at the more simple, quantitative level this is to do with who reads what, and at the more complex end students will be evaluating (through the identification of dominant discourses) attitudes towards news and notions of truth and bias. For example, students might research their peers' responses to *The Sun*'s 'Tyrant's in His Pants' cover of 20 May 2005. With the

Students might research responses to *The Sun*'s mockery of Saddam

Muslim population of Britain in mind, this mockery of an enemy will be received in relation to a complex range of ideas about religion, offence, gender and culture.

Reality TV

This relatively new area for Media education tends to be looked at from the perspective of this kind of television's popularity, cultural value and contribution to forms of realizm. In each case, the debate will involve taking a stance on whether reality television lives up to its name. Is it more 'real' than, say, a soap opera? Is it democratic and interactive, as Peter Bazalgette claims when he compares young people's willingness to interact with the programme by voting and their disinterest in formal politics?

> 'As the world's academics piled into analysing *Big Brother*'s growing success, one of them had an unusual idea. Stephen Coleman is Professor of e-democracy at Oxford University, studying how new technologies can reinvigorate the democratic process. He isolated and polled two groups – political junkies (PJs) who were mostly older, more conservative and disliked or knew nothing of *Big Brother*, and *Big Brother* fans (BBs) who were younger and broadly not involved in organised politics. "The most persistent and overwhelming message from the BBs", concluded Coleman, "concerned authenticity. They regarded politics and politicians as somehow "unreal" and believed that opaque and devious construction of political imagery could be exposed through the lens of transparent media. . . The discourse of authenticity (who is a "real" person) and transparency (being "seen" to be who one says one is) may well offer significant clues to BBs' reasons for distrusting and disengaging from politics". Elsewhere this has been called the "death of deference" – that we no longer automatically believe and respect those in authority over us such as politicians, policemen, teachers and doctors. Whether politicians really have something to learn from the clash between idealism and cynicism is a nice debate.' (Bazalgette, 2005: 281–2)

Or is it a crass, dumbed down betrayal of the public service mission, as Germaine Greer said (and judgeing by her experience on *Celebrity Big Brother*, this is a view she is unlikely to depart from)? And what are the reasons for its popularity: is this a sign of our lapse into Americanised cultural decline, or is there something more culturally interesting and even empowering about ordinary people dominating the screens, and does the multi-platform, multi-schedule approach generated by *Big Brother* on E4 and the internet signal a paradigm shift?

To begin with, we should 'step up' the theory a little. If we are to judge a text by its proximity to 'the real,' we need to do a little philosophy. Clearly, any text with a claim to be realistic is making a false call. All it can do is attempt to reproduce an audience's dominant sense of reality, to match up as much as possible with phenomenology (point of view). So realistic texts transmit a socially convincing sense of reality. There is a continuum of realizm available for us to work with. A piece of German Expressionism is much more overtly 'playing' with the real than, say, *Celebrity Love Island*, but Media students will need to take a challenging position on this. If our notion of the 'most real' is that the presence of the camera is concealed to the subjects, then presumably *Wife Swap* is an anti-realist, even Brechtian intervention, and as such it deserves to be canonized as high culture?

Baudrillard's (1988) suggestion that reality lives at Disneyland, the postmodern condition described in terms of the knowledge economy and the suggestion in texts like *The Truman Show* and *The Matrix* that one could be perfectly happy in Plato's cave (as long as citizens never get to see the 'truth') all lead us to a pretty complex idea of reality, against which it is increasingly unsound to try to judge how close a TV show can get to it. The 'Lacanian real' is perfect for Media students:

> 'The signifier has an active function in determining certain effects in which the signifiable appears as submitting to its mark, by becoming through that passion the signified.' (Lacan, 1977: 284).

Language (by which we mean the symbolic order, all forms of representation) makes itself present through the lack of its reality. In other words, when we say the word chair, language stands in for the lack of the object itself and after learning the word we are unable to conceive of the 'thing in itself' without reverting to the representation of it in language. It is lost forever, absent in the wake of the presence of its signifier (the word for it). Can Media students usefully consider reality TV within this Lacanian sense of the real? I think they can, if we can find accessible ways in to this kind of stuff, like this application from Belsey (2005):

> 'Because we have no access to the real, visual realism is not truth, but a way of ordering the visible. . . realism positions objects in accordance with a point of view that makes them readily recognizable and, by this means, affirms the identity and confirms the knowledge of the viewing subject.' (2005:131)

So might we adapt Descartes: 'I watch, therefore I am'? Either way, we pretty quickly realize that audience reading of texts is where claims to reality stand or fall, as opposed to it depending on production techniques or aesthetic intent. That said, makers of documentary operate with a range of approaches that Sohn-Rethel (2001) describes as expository, observational and interactive modes. The expository mode describes documentary that, usually through voice-over, guides us to a particular point of view or opinion (in the same way as the classic realist text in fiction presents the world view of the hero as a privileged discourse). The observational mode is founded on non-intervention, an unobtrusive approach, often called the 'fly on the wall.' The interactive mode emphasizes the relationship between producer and subject. So students might start by relating a reality TV show to these modes, and they will usually find elements of all three at once. While *Big Brother* is clearly interactive to the extent that the observer speaks to the participants, it claims to be observational (the live stream on E4 is a classic example of a compromised version, as the sound cuts out so frequently, usually for corporate reasons). Setting students the simplest of questions will yield the most complex responses: 'How Real is *Big Brother*?'

To go further intro the conventions of realizm and documentary (a topic in its own right on some specifications), students can research (and, in balance, be taught about) Bazin and ontology (a big question, but fascinating for students); Soviet documentary (particularly Vertov and 'film truth'); Grierson; the British 'Mass Observation Movement'; and Free

Cinema (which Peter Bazalgette argues, persuasively, was patronizing in the extreme compared to today's offerings). In each case, the relationship between the director's voice, the subject/object positions of participants and the degree to which each is interactive are to be assessed. To what extent does reality TV in the twenty-first century draw on these legacies?

To explore debates around the cultural value of reality TV is, in my opinion, mandatory. Once again, critical discourse analysis is the most productive approach.

Class strategy – Critical discourse analysis

Set up Bazalgette's views (2005), which are clearly framed by his own commercial agenda as a hypothesis to be tested. Students, their peers, families and their teachers can all be interviewed and thrown into the 'statement bank' to be coded and analysed using the knowledge/belief formula previously described. The key questions are these:

1. What are the dominant discourses through which reality TV is described?
2. How often are people really making statements about their own cultural identity when talking about reality TV?
3. What discourses of 'the real' are articulated?
4. What descriptions of 'the other' are evident?

This activity is not just intended to discredit the views of those who don't like *Big Brother*! Instead, discourse analysis helps students understand how a debate such as this is constructed in relation to wider arguments about popular culture, television and citizenship and people's own sense of cultural distinction. Bourdieu's perspective on the politics of taste is useful:

'Taste classifies, and it classifies the classifier. Social subjects, classified by their classifications, distinguish themselves by the distinctions they make, between the beautiful and the ugly, the distinguished and the vulgar, in which their position in the objective classifications is expressed or betrayed. That is why art and cultural consumption are predisposed, consciously and deliberately or not, to fulfil a social function of legitimating social difference.' (Bourdieu, 2002: 7)

This is a fitting way to close a chapter on media realities, simply because all Media learning in this area is as much about the sense people make of media texts, within broader identity politics, as it is about how media products are made in the first place. Interesting Media learning of any kind, at any level, will not only deconstruct texts but start to deconstruct culture itself.

Further reading

Barker, M., and Petley, J., 1997, *Ill Effects: The Media/Violence Debate*, London: Routledge. Indispensable range of research and case studies in historical context.

Barker, M., 2002, 'Categories of Violence' in *Media Magazine*, 1, London: English and Media Centre.
Useful summary of Barker's work on how violence is understood by audiences and regulators.

Barton, L., 2004, 'It's all gone tits up' in *The Guardian*, January 17, 2004.

Bazalgette, P., 2005, *Billion Dollar Game: How three men risked it all and changed the face of television*, London: Time Warner.

Belsey, C., 2005, *Culture and the Real*, London; Routledge.
Interesting presentation of philosophical and psychoanalytical approaches in relation to contemporary (postmodern) debates over reality.

Benyahia, S., 2001, *Teaching Contemporary British Cinema*, London: BFI.

Bourdieu, P., 2002, *Distinction: A Social Critique of the Judgment of Taste*, London: Routledge.
For me, any discussion of media texts and their cultural value is framed by this account.

Branston, G., 1991, 'Audience', in Lusted, D. (ed.) *The Media Studies Book*, London: Routledge.

Buckingham, D., 1995, *Reading Audiences*, London: Edward Arnold.

Buckingham, D., 2000, 'Electronic Child Abuse: Rethinking the Media's Effects on Children' in Barker, M., and Petley, J., (eds.), *Ill Effects: The Media Violence Debate*, London: Routledge.

Davey, O., 2005, 'Pleasure and Pain: Why We Need Violence in the Movies' in *Media Magazine*, 12, London: English and Media Centre.

Dutton, B., 1997, *The Media*, London: Longman.
Excellent overview of the effects debate and contemporary approaches to audience.

Dyer, R., 1994, 'Action!' In *Sight & Sound*, October, London: BFI.
Fascinating analysis of action film viewers and codes of masculinity.

Gauntlett, D., 1998, 'Ten things wrong with the 'effects model'.' in Dickinson, R., Harindranath, R., and Linne, O., (eds.)., *Approaches to Audiences,* London: Arnold.

Gauntlett, D., 2002, *Media, Gender and Identity – An Introduction*, London: Routledge.
Indispensable for work on magazines in particular, but essential reading for anyone with an interest in gender representation.

Geraghty, C., 1991, *Women and Soap Opera: A Study of Prime-Time Soaps*, Cambridge: Polity Press.

Hanley, P., (ed.), 2002, *Striking a balance: the control of children's media consumption*, London: ITC.
Important regulatory body research report.

Harvey, R., (ed). 2002, *A2 Media Studies for OCR,* London: Hodder.
The chapter on Media Issues and Debates, while tailored to the OCR exam, is ideal for students doing work with debates and contains more detailed case studies on some of the material covered in this chapter.

Higson, A., 1995, *Waving the Flag: Constructing a National Cinema in Britain,* Oxford: Clarendon Press.

Hodge, R. and Tripp, D., 1996, *Children and Television,* London: Polity.
Australian research, describing children as active decoders of the TV they watch.

Kendall, A., 2002, 'The reading habits of 16–19 year olds – initial findings', Paper presented at BERA conference, University of Exeter.

Kirkup, M., 2005, *Contemporary British Cinema*: A Teacher's Guide, London, Anteus.

Lewis, E., 2001, *Teaching TV News,* London: BFI.

Lewis, E., 2003, 'True Lies: Reporting the War in Iraq', in *Media Magazine,* 5, London: English and Media Centre.

Livingstone, S., 1999, *Young People, New Media,* London: LSE report.
Research funded by the Advertising Association, BT, the BSC and ITV.

Martin, R., 2004, *Audiences: A Teacher's Guide,* London: Auteur.

McDougall, J., 2004b, 'Lads, Mags, *Nuts* and *Zoo*' in *Media Magazine,* 8, London: English and Media Centre.

McLuhan, M., 1994, *Understanding Media: The Extensions of Man,* London: MIT.
Interesting sociological 'future gazing' from the global village prophet.

Sardar, Z., and Van Loon, B., 2000, *Introducing Media Studies,* London: Icon.
Excellent resource for simple, illustrated introductions to key ideas in Media Studies. I have probably used this more than any other resource.

Sohn-Rethel, M., 2001, *Realism,* Unpublished conference presentation, London: BFI.

Stafford, R., 1997, 'Sex and Drugs and Rock n' Roll – Innoculate, Regulate or Celebrate?' in *In the Picture,* 31. Keighley: itp Publications.
Useful overview of questions, including teacher research findings, over the role of Media education in relation to controversial texts.

Stafford, R., (ed.), 2000, *Film Reader 2: British Cinema,* Keighley: itp Publications.

Stafford, R., 2002b, *British Cinema 1990–2002: Teacher's Notes,* Keighley: itp Publications.

Stafford, R., 2003, 'Nowhere to run to? Nowhere to hide for asylum?' in *In the Picture,* 46, Keighley: itp Publications.

Thompson, K., 1998, *Moral Panics,* London: Routledge.
Very useful sociological context for work on effects and audiences.

Winship, J., 1997, *Inside Women's Magazines,* London: Pandora.

See also the 'Top 40 Websites' section.

chapter nine

Managing Production and Research

Introduction

My premise here is from experience of working with students on long-term, largely independent forms of learning, leading either to the presentation of individual research findings or to practical group outcomes and artefacts. I think these areas of a Media course need the most 'hands on' control of any, but are often given the least. So this chapter consists of a set of strategies for supporting student coursework (individual research work and group production): work which tends to be assessed with reference to planning as well as outcome.

Class strategy – Meeting with client

Student production work comes alive if there is a client, either through a genuine contract or agreement with a media professional or another department in the college, or set up with a teacher 'in role'. A really good example is the commissioning by National Diploma Pop Music students of pop video production by a Media group.

So that both sets of students benefit, such meetings need to be well-planned and minuted, with an agenda like the one below. (In this example we are one month into the project.)

Agenda

Project manager: introduction, logistics and deadlines.

Band: presentation of ideas for video (PowerPoint).

Video group: presentation of ideas for video (storyboard, on projector).

Open discussion on creative options.

Project manager: agreement of production plan.

Note: if you treat students like creative professionals, their self-esteem increases and they get into role more readily. It is a good idea to provide tea and coffee for the meeting, just as you would if you were hosting an industry professional or an INSET event.

Class strategy – Research posters

This is just my opinion, but I think it is wrong to make assumptions about what students can and cannot do on the basis of the level of their course. When doing my research degree, I encountered academics presenting 'research poster' and I was immediately struck by how useful this would be for disciplining the early stages of research for Media students in further education.

To organise this coherently, arrange a conference (half a day) and provide a brief from which students can present (and then physically display) their poster. Rather than bidding for funding, what they will be doing is presenting to each other their ideas so they can team up and share the work in some cases, setting up sub-groups who collaborate on some aspects of their research, and later hold seminars.
In doing this you will:

- ensure that research is focused early on
- gain a visible understanding of what everyone is doing
- be aware of the collaborative opportunities
- do something a bit different
- raise students confidence by treating them as serious researchers.

Class strategy – Reflective logs

I am using the term 'log' here to describe the written evidence that accompanies production work. This might be more a narrative of the production process, or evidence of planning, research and evaluation, or it might be more of a theoretical analysis of students' own creative practice. Either way, the two fundamental requirements (that can be taught well) are reflective writing and micro/macro work.

It is good practice to provide a 'tight' structure for this kind of work and to set a series of deadlines for each stage of the writing that are in synch with the stages of production (this kind of evaluative work should not be produced in isolation at the end of the production process). For example, this kind of portfolio approach might be divided into:

- Response to brief and research
- Planning

- Creativity and construction
- Post-production
- Evaluation and reflective analysis

Clearly, you will tailor this to your own needs, but my advice is to provide a writing frame or detailed set of prompts for each element. This kind of work is really hard for students, and it is completely artificial, so we need to do all we can to make it easier, since the more important learning is in the production itself. Here is an example of a set of prompts that students can use during lesson 'down time' when they can't get into the edit suite or onto a Mac to finish production. In this example, it is assumed that students are in the last stages of both post-production and redrafting the production log.

- Make a list of all the creative decisions you made.
- Give examples that show the importance of pre-production.
- Explain how research into real media texts of this type led you to make certain creative decisions.
- Use text books to find quotes about genre, narrative, representation and audience and then for each one, write a sentence applying it to an aspect of your work.
- Cross reference any points made in your log to the appendix.
- Show your work to your class-mates and collect three strengths and three weaknesses from their responses.
- Go through your log and replace everyday language with technical terms wherever you can.
- Go through your log and make three connections with work from other units on the course.
- Write a short, clear statement about how you considered your target audience and their pleasures – one from pre-production, one from production and one from post-production.
- Make a list of the technical skills you already had, and ones you developed during this process.
- Write a short statement about the technology – what did it enable you to do creatively and what were the limitations?

Class strategy – Vocational roles/work experience 'in house'

Many Media teachers have problems organizing work experience, either for geographical reasons or because there are simply too many Media students competing for placements. An alternative is to create industry practice (or something like it) in-house. In this example (see McConnell, 2003 for a more detailed version), a colleague of mine organized a field trip to Cornwall for a group of AVCE Media students, where they filmed a TV drama.

Students applied for roles and went through an interview process. After appointments were made, students worked to job descriptions. By the time of the trip, everyone was perfectly clear on their role in the process. The drama was a great success and attracted some local media interest in itself. The teacher is one of those well-placed practitioners who has worked in the industry himself:

'Of course you don't actually have to travel far to do this. A mini-production can be undertaken in term breaks, or organised over a weekend. Working to a strict deadline does bring out the best in people. It also helps you to concentrate fully on what are at times very complex tasks. The production was remarkably similar to the experiences and work practices of a professional crew – we worked in the same manner and with comparable equipment. As a teacher it was one of the most valuable experiences I've ever been involved in; and as for the students: 'The best college trip ever!' (McConnell, 2003: 48)

Class strategy – Research seminars

When students are working on long-term research projects, your scheme of work should be structured around a series of group seminars, with a different chair each time, between students with similar research interests. My approach (not popular with the awarding body as it is in conflict with the 'spirit' of the specification, I should add) has been to prescribe the research topic for all students. This way, I can better manage the resources, library materials, intranet links and, equally, my own expertise. But from that highly prescriptive starting point, students have to form their own individual hypothesis, which I approve. My criteria for this approval stage is not only how appropriate the ideas are, but also how distinct each hypothesis is from one another. After research poster presentations (see earlier class strategy). I then group students into collaborative 'networks' and these sub-groups will hold the following seminars:

- hypotheses, hunches and plans for interventions
- methodologies
- literature reviews/mapping the field
- findings 1
- findings 2
- interpretations of data
- ideas for more research.

These are spread out, preferably monthly. Crucially, contributing to each of these is an assessed activity. If you are using a specification that requires only an essay or exam response to write up completed research, I advise that you mislead your students into believing that you will be assessing them for their planning, methodology and data acquisition, for obvious reasons!

Class strategy – Production mentoring

As you can only be in one place at a time, and production work is by nature fragmented and impossible to fit into neat timetables of contact time, appointing student mentors (and producing a college certificate to accredit them with, which they can use in job or HE applications) is a great idea. There are three options:

- previous students taking a year out or working part time can do this on a voluntary or paid basis (depending on your funds)
- students in their final year can support the new cohort
- students on vocational courses work with those on A Level.

In any of these ways, one student can cover up to four production groups, and they can have a technical brief or a more holistic framing agenda. For the latter, I have used Jenny Grahame's ten rules for ensuring production work provides the necessary evil of 'conceptual clout', which are as follows (from Grahame, 2001):

- Don't give free choice. Approve proposals within agreed criteria.
- Contextualise production work in relation to other texts.
- Identify a real target audience.
- Research for production, using industry practices.
- Check work in progress with the audience.
- Attention to detail – locations, *mise-en-scène*, graphics, layout and design, institutional details.
- Reduce use of, or manipulate, found images (although my advice is don't use them at all).
- Check work in progress against assessment criteria.
- Make sure sound is treated as seriously as image.
- Work on the written element at the same time (see the structure for this in the class strategy 'Reflective logs' on page 182).

If you appoint the right students for this work, in the role of 'critical friend' they can act as gatekeepers for you, so you can differentiate your support and your energies better.

Class strategy – Live simulation

A fairly common approach since the inception of Media Studies, this is an enjoyable, enlightening way to raise awareness of editorial agendas. Although no technology is absolutely necessary, the use of cameras and a mixing desk or a laptop for desk-top publishing does aid comprehension of the editorial/technological dynamic.

This pursuit is also tailor-made for some good differentiation practice, through sensible, strategic and sensitive allocation of roles. You need lots of preparation time, a three-line whip on punctuality, preferably a reward for motivation (perhaps a 'lesson off' if the activity works with no errors) and then a twist in the tale (for example, the football has gone into extra time so you have more preparation time but less broadcast time). Some examples in this area are:

- news bulletin (TV or radio)
- phone-in
- radio broadcast, combining presenter/DJ with pre-recorded material
- newspaper pages
- live internet broadcasting
- music programme featuring a live band.

If your institution has a radio station, of course, this will be everyday stuff. For less furnished departments, I advise you to do this at least once for each cohort, related to a theoretical area and a production activity. For example, you might host a live radio phone-in, with text and email inputs also, on the MP3 debate, and host it on a website for part of a production unit.

Class strategy – Production crisis management

This is the hardest of all to achieve in the heat of a lesson in the summer term when a group of anxious students tell you that their edited master has been wiped, their memory stick is corrupt, or someone has removed all their web files from the shared drive.

My suggested strategy is this: stop everything, get all the students in a horse-shoe arrangement or a circle, and ask them to help each other out. How can we manage this crisis for this group? What can we control and what is irretrievable? Draw up, formally or informally, a contract between everyone involved for redeeming the situation. This might involve you changing the timetable or requesting extra time from the moderator; it might involve students who have finished doing some extra acting or equipment carrying.

Whatever the situation, my experience is that forging collaborative approaches can make miracles happen in this context, as long as you assert early on that problem solving of this kind will definitely be a part of everyone's practical learning.

Class strategy – In-class data collection

There is one way in which Media Studies certainly *is* easier than other subjects. Students more often than not *are* themselves the audience that they need to study, and thus to access. So, for a piece of primary research on any quantitative area (for example, ownership of video phones or participation in weblogs), you can take a back seat and observe this activity.

- Appoint a manager and a scribe.
- The manager works out (through consultation) the quickest way to acquire the data.
- The interpreter does the calculating and expression of outcomes.
- The scribe produces the PowerPoint and presents the demographics.

Within a time limit, everyone, as a result of this exercise must have a clear paragraph starting with: 'I conducted some quantitative research with a sample of the target audience'.

Further reading

Clare, V., 2005, Researching Media and Film Studies: A Teacher's Guide, London: Anteus. A range of sensible guidance for supporting student research.

Fraser, P., 2002, 'Production Work Tips' in *Media Magazine*, 1, London: English and Media Centre.

Grahame, J., 2001, 'Being Creative with Minimal Resources', BFI conference workshop.

McConnell, S., 2003, 'A Trip to the Seaside' in *Media Magazine*, 5, London: English and Media Centre.
Summary of a residential project with students in vocational production roles.

Rayner, P., Wall, P., and Kruger, S., 2001, *Media Studies: The Essential Introduction*. London: Routledge.
Chapter 5 includes a very useful introduction to doing media research.

See also the 'Top 40 Websites' section.

chapter ten

Assessing Media Learning

Introduction

The outcome of my research into assessment and 'Subject Media' (McDougall, 2004a), was that there is clearly a tension between the 'spirit of the subject', with its claims to be an empowering, relevant, transgressive discipline, and the reality of its outdated assessment modes. Most explicitly, this tension shows in the confusion expressed by moderators over how they should be judgeing practical coursework and in the visible privileging of particular forms of written language within an agreed discourse through which media literacy can be presented and judged. To put it bluntly, being able to write a conventional English/Humanities essay is still by far the most important skill a Media student on an 'academic' course can acquire (although these skills are largely already in place, I would argue). Vocational learners, however, are harnessed by the need for written evaluations and evidence of planning, which distracts from the work itself. Generally, there is an anxiety over letting creative work stand alone as evidence of learning, and this is what still distances Media from Art and annexes it to English, in my opinion.

Ultimately, as Foucault helps us understand, judgement (or subjects' will to be judged) is bound up with claims to legitimate knowledge, and thus power, as Ki's research into GCSE Media students' evaluative work illustrates:

'Although producing a media text is not considered as an end but as a means to understand the ways in which a range of media texts are produced and how they are read and interpreted by different audiences, the institutional requirement for *evidence* of learning in the form of discursive writing often leaves behind what really happens in the production process. What teachers and examiners alike finally see and eventually look for is nothing but what students (choose to) present or demonstrate for the purpose of assessment in writing. I wondered and I am still wondering to what extent this formalised practice could tell me about what students have achieved and acquired, or even understood, and how far I could take what they have presented or demonstrated in their evaluative commentaries as *evidence* of their learning. In this respect, the practice of evaluation is the very place where I can tackle the questions and issues that I have raised but not quite resolved so far. It also serves as a very useful lens through which I can detect the tensions between legitimate knowledge and illegitimate knowledge and the ambiguities in determining power or legitimacy over whose knowledge counts within this subject discipline.' (Ki, 2004:8)

Once again, this book must return to the 'state we're in' and offer suggestions for good practice within these constraints. First, we need to look at assessing for learning in general. There are a number of reasons for assessment, and being clear about your motives in each case is really helpful for students and teachers. There are differences between assessing with external criteria for moderation, assessing to aid progression, to guide improvement, diagnose problems and offer solutions, test out our teaching, add variety or, crucially, to motivate students (Brown, Race and Smith, 1996: 16). Equally, the power relations in each form of assessment vary, between students assessing themselves for the teacher, students self-assessing on their own, examiners assessing students, students assessing each other, students assessing teachers and, most commonly, teachers assessing students (Meighan and Siraj-Blatchford, 2003: 170).

In addition, we should be transparent when telling students what is being assessed (by which I don't mean Bloom's (1984) taxonomy, though this might be useful). Often, students really do not know what it is you are looking for in simple content terms (for example, can you criticize a student for not using examples without checking they know what you mean by an example?). Although this involves educational compromise (reducing everything to assessment), you might do well to accept that today's teenagers have been assessed so intensely since they started school that they have become 'cue-conscious' (Miller and Parlett, 1974). This means they are concerned at all times with what counts for assessment and what does not. Those that are not so 'cue-aware' on the other hand, struggle with this crucial aspect of the 'hidden curriculum'.

Meighan and Siraj-Blatchford (2003) distinguish three ideologies of education within which we can locate assessment modes. The transmission ideology privileges identifiable knowledge which is given and acquired, and usually evidenced in written exams. The interpretation ideology assesses the reshaping of knowledge by the learner throughout the course of study, and the autonomous ideology allows assessment to be controlled eventually by the learner. Analysing the kinds of assessment that a) you carry out and b) the awarding body use, might well be a sobering experience if you have a sense of your work as liberating.

Trainee teachers are encouraged to use 'Assessment for Learning' wherever possible, as this form of 'feeding forward' allows greater student autonomy:

'Assessment for learning must involve students, so as to provide them with information about how well they are doing and guide their subsequent efforts. Much of this information will come as feedback from the teacher, but some will be through their direct involvement in assessing their own work. The awareness of learning and ability of learners to direct it for themselves is of increasing importance in the context of encouraging lifelong learning'. (Black et al., 2002: 7)

A really good example 'from the patch' is offered on the English and Media Centre's KS3 resource video for Media in English (2004). It features Stephen Connolly from Haydon School skilfully drawing out a discussion about news manipulation from students' still images. Connolly chooses to let the creative work set up the theoretical discussion, asking questions about how the work seems to reflect news practices.

The 'rub' of course, is that exams tend to be the 'end-game', still. However, Media education, perhaps more than other subjects, allows for this kind of 'feeding forward.'

The remainder of this chapter will consist of a set of strategies for assessing Media Studies work.

Class strategy – Feed-forward lesson

Rather than giving students work back at the beginning or the end of lesson time, it is a good idea to include in schemes of work regular feed forward lessons. To facilitate this, I recommend using an assessment template across the Media department which includes no marks or grades, but has four boxes. In the first two boxes a student notes what they are particularly pleased with about the work, and an area they struggled with. At the start of the course, you should produce a list of the kinds of things that might appear in these spaces, related to the assessment objectives. These boxes are complete at the time of submitting the work to you. There is also a space for the student to note, at the time of *starting* the work, a negotiated target from the previous assessment. You have just two boxes to complete – specific credit and areas for improvement. The final space is for the next negotiated target (which, of course, is then repeated on the next front sheet). In the regular feed-forward lesson, through a variety of open discussion, small group reflective work and individual tutorial time, you get to monitor the degree to which your students are able to understand and take ownership for making progress. A final point: I have noticed that students prefer to have marks or grades, but it is harder to get them to focus on the formative work if you give in to this.

Class strategy – Students as examiners/Standardized self or peer assessment

This simple activity recreates the format of an awarding body standardization meeting for students. If done well, it empowers students with the ability to accurately self and peer assess. From then on, you have a range of productive, labour-saving opportunities available to you. I have genuinely found that students very easily arrive at an accurate level of self and peer assessment. Generally, they start by being too harsh on themselves and too generous with one another. This means you have to informally 'scale' the feedback you get if you want to make any real sense of it. With this in mind, it is better to train students as awarding bodies train examiners, so that eventually you can be confident that you are getting accurate judgements from them. Then, all you need to do is check a sample, just as a Team Leader for an exam board does.

Step 1

Produce an honest mark scheme that really reflects how you mark. In my experience, this includes things like how easy it is to read, whether the language is academic or technical, the number of examples and how useful they are, and the accuracy of any factual content. But we have to admit the degree of 'gut instinct' and find a way of conveying to students how this works. This is all about establishing a criteria for presenting themselves to you as an enthusiastic, critical, informed person (they do not have to be so, of course). I have tended to finally pick five criteria and for each of them have a 2-mark scale (0 = not at all, 1 = a bit and 2 = yes).

Step 2

Provide an exemplar essay which is worth half marks. Present this and ask students to scale their original mark up or down accordingly.

Step 3

Put students into teams and ask them to moderate each other's marking.

Step 4

Check whether everyone has managed to scale and achieve a rank order in their group.

Once you have done this two or three times, students' accuracy will improve. Every time you do this you are increasing their ability to play the assessment game. I would go as far as to say that while at first it might seem negligent to foreground self and peer assessment (after all it means you do not do the marking), in reality it is negligent not to do it, as you may unintentionally reinforce students' feelings of alienation from the assessment process if you exclude them from experiencing it as a social practice.

Class strategy – Individual presentations

I have often heard teachers from a variety of subject areas explaining why it is impossible to use individual presentations as an assessment mode, because they have thirty students in a class. I would have to agree (and I have tended to go for the group model), if the objective is for every student to give a detailed and similar presentation on the same topic. It can be pretty soul-destroying for teachers and students listening to thirty similar presentations over three lessons. So you have to plan this activity well, and stagger it. If you see a group three times a week, simply devote fifteen minutes each lesson for a couple of weeks to presentations, and give every student a different focus. Stagger your assessment so that those who go earlier have less criteria (or differentiate by giving your 'gifted and talented' students less time – after all, everything else is on their side in life!), and crucially, make sure that every student can benefit from every other. For example, if students need to research their local newspaper, give every student a different (and strategically differentiated) research question and activity for acquiring the data. This will range from the more ambitious (interviewing a reporter) to the more straightforward (finding out circulation figures and revenue streams). The objective is for each student to summarize (an advanced skill) their findings into five minutes and a maximum of one slide per minute. Arranged this way, presentations are varied, mutually beneficial and 'punchy'.

Class strategy – Tutorials

I once had a timetabled tutorial session with A2 students on a Friday afternoon. The idea was that they would turn up with their media research and see me in a supervisor role. To make this more productive, they had appointments every other week. They never turned up. At first, I went into the usual 'sluggish sixth former' discourse ('When I was their age. . .' etc.), but when I asked them about this I found out it was usually because they didn't know what to do in order to be prepared for the meetings (and there was the Friday afternoon thing, as well). This was the starting point for the integrated approach, which turned out to work so well (we realized that we should reduce the distinction between different kinds of lessons so that we didn't end up with such variance in attendance).

Having a research lesson where students provide the material is hard enough in higher education, I have since found, so we need more structure. This form of interaction with students works best if you set it up as a carrot, rather than a stick. Rather than insisting that students come to you with work, tell them that they should come to you with a 'wish list' for support, which might include helping them find source material, helping them with 'silly questions' or (and hopefully this is the outcome), checking through what they have written.

The shift in emphasis from teacher as judge (of how much work they have done) to tutor as a friendly, supportive resource, provides a more accessible, productive atmosphere for individual tutorials. But this only works if you remove your services in this area from other lesson time, as students will try to impose their preferred timetable on you, otherwise. If a student brings you some work or asks you a research question in the corridor or during a production class, you have to be consistent and arrange a tutorial instead.

Class strategies – Memory games

It is still a sad and ugly reality of our educational system that memory is of such great significance in determining life chances. Asking students to articulate their anxieties about doing exams, they tend to mention fear of 'going blank'. Although Media Studies has a higher ratio of 'soft' exams compared to other subjects, offering scenario questions, case studies, unseen stimulus, the use of notes and reasonably predictable questions, the revision/exam dynamic is still largely to do with finding strategies for remembering things. In this context, Derren Brown may be more valuable than Roland Barthes if you are looking for inspiration!

So we need to accept this, and provide a range of strategies to allow students to practice recall. Examples mentioned elsewhere include the collaborative essay (where students write a sentence and pass on their paper clockwise – see Chapter Seven). Another option is the 1-3-5 game, where, under time pressure, students recall one example alone, then pair up and share to make 2 and then team up with another pair to make 5 (the first group to have five examples is rewarded). Another is a straightforward quiz, or a Millionaire activity (described in more detail in Chapter Seven). Or, you might award a prize for the best mnemonic on a particular topic. Reveal games offer an entertaining context for memory recall (you can use A3 paper or you can buy a set of wipe clean boards and pens for not much expense). If I can assume you remember the television programme *Blankety Blank*, no further explanation is required. This game is useful for simple, one-word answers, like the names of companies, writers, theories or texts – the kinds of things that students get wrong or forget under pressure.

Finally, an offering based on 'insider knowledge'. Having worked for an exam board in the past as a Subject Officer, and as a Senior Examiner still, I have, on occasion, offered a set of 'tips' for preparing students for external assessment (which have tended to go down very well) at INSET meetings. I must make it clear that these are *not* official recommendations from any exam board. That said, here are a dozen suggestions from my experience:

1. Accept that assessment objectives are vital. Make them explicit and memorable for students, translate them into their own language and return to them constantly.
2. Translate terms like limited, minimal, competent, proficient, sophisticated and personal engagement into what they really mean and display them on the wall.
3. Accept that writing skills are paramount, and teach them.
4. Play safe with theory – train students to use simple ideas, on their own terms, well. Although some examiners are impressed by inaccurate name-dropping, they are not supposed to be!

5. Integrate as much as you can. Although this may appear to narrow down your course, and there may be statements in the specification suggesting that using the same texts across units is against the 'spirit' of the units, a counter argument to this is that learners become more expert and make more synoptic connections.

6. Teach the context of research and provide resources. Make sure students each have a different specific angle, but you can teach the broader topic, again, even if the 'spirit' of the specification says otherwise.

7. Understand the power of 'spin' in writing up research, if the examiner has not been on the journey. One person's 'chat with friends' is another's focus group.

8. Unlike other subjects, finding information the night before the exam is really useful for Media. So don't tell students 'if you don't know it now, you never will'. An opportunistic bit of internet work hours before the exam may yield the most topical, contemporary example imaginable (about, say, a new technology, an institutional merger or a piece of breaking news).

9. Moderators are not looking to downgrade students' work. It is more work and bad PR. They work within a 'tolerance', so if in doubt, be generous.

10. Media awareness is not innate, it can be taught, and it is 50 per cent of the job description of a good Media student.

11. Understand how the awarding process works. Panels, accounting to QCA, make horrible assumptions (if more FE colleges are taking the exam, we would expect lower achievement; if more independent schools, the opposite). The outcomes are 'norm referenced' with the aim of avoiding too great a change in performance from the previous year. This means a student could take the same exam and perform equally well two years running and get different grades (and the same goes for coursework). Essentially the correct analogy is a race: where you finish depends on the ability of the other runners, not just your own pace. With this in mind, if you are working with students who are not the beneficiaries of the unequal distribution of cultural capital, you are doing them down if you don't play the system. With this in mind, make strategic decisions about when to enter particular units.

12. Become an examiner, and you get to attend the standardisation meeting for the exam or coursework unit. This is more useful than this book or a hundred INSET meetings if you want an accurate sense of the board's expectations, and to meet the people who, ultimately, decide your students' fates! The insight you will get from this is invaluable. Whilst awarding body mark schemes are undoubtedly valid documents that provide a textual account of how examiners should interpret student responses, human nature dictates that examiners construct a sense of the 'ideal student'. The student who can position herself closely to this construct is destined to succeed.

I hope this is helpful and that you have, or continue to have, as interesting a time teaching Media as I have. Nothing stands still for long with a subject like this. As Bob Dylan says, 'There is nothing so stable as change'.

Further reading

Black, P., Harrison, C., Lee, H., Marshall, B. and William, D., 2002, *Working Inside the Black Box: Assessment for Learning in the Classroom,* London: Kings College Publications.

Bloom, B., 1984, *Taxonomy of Educational Objectives,* Boston, MA: Allyn and Bacon.

Brown, S., Race, P. and Smith, B., 1996, *500 Tips on Assessment,* London: Kogan Page.

Clare, V., 2005, *Researching Media and Film Studies: A Teacher's Guide,* London: Anteus.

Ki, S., 2004, 'The Evaluation of Practical Production as the Process of Legitimation in GCSE Media Studies', London: unpublished PhD dissertation: Institute of Education.

McDougall, J., 2004, 'Subject Media: A Study in the Sociocultural Framing of Discourse', Unpublished PhD thesis: University of Birmingham.

McDougall, J., 2004, *Judging Media Learning,* in *In the Picture,* 50, Keighley: itp Publications.

Meighan, R., and Siraj-Blatchford, I., 2003, *A Sociology of Educating,* London: Continuum.

Miller, C. and Parlett, M., 1974, *Up to the Mark: a study of the examination game,* London: S.R.H.E.

Sefton-Greene, J., and Sinker, R. (eds.), 2000, *Evaluating Creativity: Making and Learning by Young People,* London: Routledge.

See also the 'Top 40 Websites' section.

Glossary: 100 Key Ideas

AESTHETIC
In Media education, usually understood as one type of code among several, the aesthetic domain describes visual language in cultural context. I have used the term in contrast to technical considerations, arguing that digital technology allows the Media teacher to focus less on operational tuition and more on the language of film, for example.

ANALOGUE
A variable signal, as opposed to a digital one, which is discrete. Essentially, the difference is that an analogue signal will be effected by small fluctuations in the quality of sound and/or image.

ANCHORAGE
The 'pinning down' of meaning through image being placed in relation to text, or vice versa. The shipping metaphor suggests a wild sea of potential meaning, with the sign (boat) needing to be motivated through grounding.

ASSESSING FOR LEARNING
Formative assessment, as described by the Assessment Reform Group (see Black *et al*, 2002), seeking to raise standards through improving teachers' use of questioning and feedback strategies.

AUDIENCE
An umbrella term for the person or people reading any media text. Digital technology has led to increasing uncertainty over how we define an audience, with general agreement that the notion of a large group of people, brought together by time, responding to a text, is outdated.

AVATAR
An on-screen icon or representation of the user/player in a computer game.

BINARY
Western thought is framed by a tendency for us to think in opposites, for example good/evil, rather than embrace ambiguity and difference. In digital coding, binary describes the coding of digits as noughts and ones.

BLOGGING
Web logs, published by anyone, which can offer an alternative to conventional forms of news.

BRECHTIAN
Referring to the dramatist Bertolt Brecht, whose key intervention was to make the audience 'ultra-aware' of the artifice of theatre, as opposed to the classic realist tradition of suspending their disbelief.

BROADBAND
High speed, thicker cable transmitting a powerful digital signal that can deal with complex data such as moving images, music and games.

CITIZENSHIP
My use of the term is not related to the National Curriculum subject. Rather, I am referring to the potential of Media education to foster in students reflective consideration of their place in contemporary democracy and the role of the media in constructing us as modern citizens.

COMPRESSION
Simply, getting more data into less space and sending it from one place to another, through encoding data using fewer units in digital coding.

CONVENTIONS
The repeated, normative practices expected within a culture. In the context of Media learning, we are concerned with the normative elements of a particular type of media text.

CONVERGENCE
Hardware and software coming together across media, and companies coming together across similar boundaries, to make the distinction between different types of media and different media industries increasingly dubious.

CULTURAL CAPITAL
From Bourdieu and Passeron (1977). Symbolic acquisition that can be exchanged, including qualifications, knowledge, family background, taste, values and other non-material forms of status. Our articulated responses to media texts are sensibly understood within this 'taste-market', I would argue.

CULTURAL IMPERIALIZM
Alongside broader discussions of globalization, the practice of dominant groups and nations imposing their cultural preferences and claims to legitimate knowledge on other people and nations. Hollywood is the classic example. The assumption tends to be that corporate power is simultaneous with cultural dominance.

DATA
Original information acquired in learning, usually through research activity. This might be from interviews, surveys, observation or case study work. It is unique information brought into the classroom by students, self-originated.

DECONSTRUCTION
From Derrida (1977). A philosophy of extended textual analysis, in which it is accepted that we cannot find meaning. Instead we investigate intertextuality and ways in which texts can only be understood in relation to other texts (including ourselves).

DEMOCRACY
Society founded on equality, in which the decision-making powers are elected and are thus representative and accountable. Whether the media is democratic is a very different question, as we do not elect newspaper owners, for example.

DEMOGRAPHIC
Breaking down society or a sample of people by characteristics such as age, gender, ethnicity, occupation, income and socio-economic status (quantitative means).

DIALECTICAL
An exchange of points of view, or propositions (theses) and counter-propositions (antitheses) resulting in an attempt to reduce the dissensus through the creation of new ideas, which are then new propositions to be countered (so dialectical thinking is infinite). See Lunenfield (2000) for discussions around the 'digital dialectic'.

DIEGESIS
Describes what is present in the world of a text, as opposed to the extra bits (e.g. soundtrack or voice-over) that exist only for the audience.

DIGITAL
Information broken down into noughts and ones, leading to a digitisation of culture and convergence.

DISCOURSE
A way of speaking, thinking and understanding, in language. Systematically organized ways of talking, from Foucault (1988).

DOWNLOAD
The practice of choosing and receiving digital information (as opposed to sending it, which is uploading).

e-LEARNING
Participating in education through a computer without physical access to a tutor or other students.

ELLIPSIS
What is left out of a narrative, but remains in the story.

e-MEDIA
Electronic media, such as websites, with integrated functions and a degree of adaptability in terms of systems and time.

ETHICS
Issues of morality (always 'up for grabs'). Often different to legal considerations, an important distinction for students to grapple with.

FALSE CONSCIOUSNESS
Marxist term describing a state of being in which individuals are happily distracted from the truth (by ideology) and are thus convinced, or at least prepared to accept, that things are as they have to be. See Strinati (1995), Chapter 4.

FEMINISM
Often misunderstood as an 'extreme', militant politics, for us feminism is nothing more outrageous than the belief that we should oppose media texts that represent women as unequal to men, or as mere unthinking objects for male scrutiny.

FRANKFURT SCHOOL
Marxist school of thought, featuring Adorno and Marcuse, concerned mainly with ideology and the role of mass media (the culture industry) in reinforcing hegemony and manufacturing consensus. See Strinati (1995), Chapter 2.

GATEKEEPING
The role played by editors, producers, owners and regulators in opening and closing, to greater and lesser extents, the flow of media information through processes of selection and construction.

GLOBALIZATION
The proliferation of digital technology, deregulation and convergence combine to allow multinational and cross-cultural media production and consumption within a global economic system founded on the free market.

HIDDEN CURRICULUM
The set of behavioural codes, practices and additional support needed to be successful in an education system, outside of formal curriculum and institutional policies. From Bowles and Gintis (1976). See Bartlett, Burton and Peim (2001) for an application to contemporary education.

HORIZONTAL DISCOURSE
From Bernstein (1990): a discourse which is 'fed into' by a number of different communities, and is thus spread out, evolving and complex. Media Studies began in this way, I think.

HTML
Hyper Text Mark up Language: a structuring language for electronic text interfaced with links to other supplementary texts, for websites.

HYPER-REALITY
A state in which images and simulations take on more reality than the state they represent, so that the distinction between reality and representation is no longer sustainable. From Baudrillard (1988).

HYPOTHESIS
A statement to be tested out through research, arising from a hunch.

IDENTITY
Culture and discourse construct subjects (Foucault, 1988), so for Media Studies the task is not so much to consider the relationship between texts and identities taken on by individuals as to analyse the plurality of identities that subjects play with and the ways in which these are mediated and increasingly virtual.

IDEOLOGY
A dominant set of ideas presenting itself as common sense or truth. Power relations are reinforced through ideology. For Chomsky (2003), the recent military practices of the USA are an example of a super power acting without establishing a traditional ideological consensus.

INFORMATION ECONOMY
In our post-industrial society, it is suggested (see Lyotard, 1984) that information is the key resource from which wealth can be generated, as opposed to land, raw materials or the means of production.

INTERACTIVE
Media texts which offer audiences the opportunity to shape the text in some way. Choosing from a menu is not interactive if the choices are preconstructed. Voting for a winner or loser is interactive, but we should distinguish between mass interaction (where you are one of millions making choices) and individual interaction (perhaps a computer game can offer this).

INTERPELLATION
The misrecognition of oneself in a media text (from Althusser, 1971): for example, women recognizing a sense of their gender which was not their construction.

INTERTEXTUAL
The chain of signification, in which texts always make overt or more subtle references to one another. All language is intertextual, and as all experience in culture is languaged, hence reality becomes intertextual by nature.

KINAESTHETIC
Tactile, physical activity. Some types of learners are assumed to learn more through such practices, but I would advise caution against overstating this, the danger of which is stereotyping and mistaking a preference for an enabling intervention.

LIFEWORLD
The network of experiences of families, hobbies, social gatherings, leading to culturally transmitted ways of understanding the world. In education, there is a tension between the hidden curriculum of schooling and students' life worlds, for the majority of people.

LINEAR
In a clear, logical order, moving in one direction.

LITERACY
The ability to read and write. Media education extends such a notion of competence to recognize all forms of writing (for example, taking photographs) and all forms of reading (for example, listening to music), and activities which may combine them (for example, playing a computer game).

LOGOCENTRIC
From Derrida (1977), referring to the Greek word 'logos' (word, speech or reason). Western thought and culture is logocentric as it privileges speech over writing (since Aristotle and his scribe Plato) and sets up as core beliefs the idea that we can strive for a central set of truths and origins as universal principles.

MALE GAZE
From Laura Mulvey (1975), an analysis of media images which suggests that the camera represents a male perspective, and as such casts men as subjects and women as objects.

MARKET FORCES
This discourse likens the 'natural' flow of capitalism (competition leading to consumer choice and selection and hence the survival of the fittest) to the laws of nature. Increasingly, this discourse is impermeable and all aspects of life, including education, are described in this way. To offer an alternative view is considered 'outdated' within such a hegemonic discourse (less 'sayable').

MARXIST
All theory derived from the works of Marx, founded on a belief that the ruling classes in any time and place maintain their economic and systematic power through controlling not only the means of production but also culture and ideology. Marxist theory, traditionally, seeks to expose the falsity of dominant ideology and reveal the truth previously obscured, and as such it has empowerment of the alienated as its primary objective.

MEDIA ACCESS
Describes the degree of ease with which citizens can be seen and/or heard in the media, respond to the media and be provided with a dialogue with institutions, and the amount of opportunities evident for people to produce media texts themselves and for them to be distributed.

MEDIA LANGUAGE
An umbrella term to describe the ways in which audiences read media texts through understanding formal and conventional structures (for example, the grammar of film editing). Media literacy describes our ability to read and write in this extended sense of language.

MISE-EN-SCÈNE
Everything that is put into the frame (considering the paused moving image as a still image). Includes set design, location, costume, actors and make up, non-verbal communication, colour and contrast, lighting and filter. Primarily an aesthetic practice.

MODE OF ADDRESS
How a text, in any media, speaks to its audience, and with what assumptions.

MORAL PANIC
Media and/or political paranoia over, and scapegoating of, an individual or group, leading to over-stated fear and perceptions of subversive behaviour. See Cohen (1980).

MULTIMEDIA
Fairly self-explanatory, a text created in a variety of media.

MULTIMODALITY
See Burn and Parker (2003). A form of semiotics, attempting to find general principles that underpin all forms of communication (for example, rhythm in film editing, or aesthetic principles in computer game avatar perspectives).

NEWS AGENDA
The simple realization, and subsequent analysis, that a particular news provider will select and construct news within a framework influenced by political, corporate, cultural and commercial objectives. I suggest avoiding news values, which over-simplify news practices and treat them as homogenous.

PARADIGM
A framework of understanding scientific or cultural phenomenon. All messages, of any kind, are selected from paradigms. A 'paradigm shift' describes the point at which the usual ways of comprehending culture become outdated.

PARODY
A text which does not simply imitate the style of another (pastiche) but instead, is transformative in that it either mocks or shifts in some way the original text's conventions.

PEDAGOGY
Learning and teaching methods, developed from ideas about how learning takes place. Different to curriculum, which describes content, pedagogy is concerned with the how, rather than the what, of teaching, and hence this book is much more pedagogical.

PEER-TO-PEER
The sharing of media material between two parties in an equal relationship (as opposed to the traditional, hierarchical and commercial seller-buyer interaction).

PHENOMENOLOGY
Theoretical considerations of the relation between consciousness and 'reality', involving analysis of language, culture and being. Embracing phenomenology leads us to depart from assumptions about the nature of reality as existing outside of perception. Much media theory is now, I would argue, a form of phenomenology, especially if the concept of representation is foregrounded.

PIRACY
Distribution of media material that infringes copyright law.

PLEASURE
All forms of engagement with media texts. Crucially, a rejection of judgemental responses to audience choices.

PODCAST
Uploading an MP3 playlist over the internet for others to access.

POPULAR CULTURE
See Strinati (1995). Any attempt to define popular culture is situated within a particular theory of it. However, as a way in to more complex questions, we can say that texts which are consumed by a wide range of people, as opposed to a smaller group, configured in some way as an elite, tend to be described as popular and that this implies a derogatory view of tastes. Popular culture has been studied and analysed since the 1960s, and Media Studies is now a 'classic' example of this attention, hence the discourse of derision around it.

PRE-PRODUCTION
All forms of idea generation, planning and research in response to a brief.

POST-PRODUCTION
The editing stage, where material is manipulated using software and transformed into a finished media product.

PUBLIC SERVICE
Founded on principles of democracy as opposed to profit. We should avoid overstating binary oppositions between public service and commercial media, however.

REALIZM
A variety of ideas about the degree to which, and the variety of ways in which, media texts represent an idea of reality.

RECEPTION THEORY
Contemporary audience theory is concerned with audience response and reaction and subsequently our understanding of a text's meanings emerge more from attention to audience interpretation than producer intent. Or a variant of the 'death of the author' thesis (Barthes, 1983).

REGULATION
The surveillance and the threat of action by organizations and quangos, sometimes governmental, sometimes from industry, leading to a degree of self-regulation on the part of media institutions, and actual punitive measures in response to self-regulation breaking down. Regulation is sometimes economic, sometimes cultural and always political.

REFLEXIVE
A way of working that demands not only reflecting on one's practices through evaluation, but changing such practice constantly, and ultimately empowering oneself by recognizing the 'conditions of possibility' for the work one does.

REITHIAN
Lord Reith's (Director General during the BBC's inception) rationale for the BBC was that it should offer the public information, entertainment and education, in equal measure. Opinion is now divided over whether Reith was a bastion of democracy or a patronizing elitist.

SCHEDULING
The strategic positioning of media texts within broadcasting time. Digital television is increasingly disrupting this approach, since viewers can choose more easily than before when to watch.

SEMIOTICS
The science of signs and symbols. From Saussure's linguistics (1974), and Barthes' structuralism (1973), as I use the term. Essentially, the study of the sign, in terms of its connotations within cultural myth system (the symbolic order). See Masterman (1984) for an application to television texts.

SOCIO-CULTURAL
Describes considerations of how our social experiences and cultural choices combine in our life worlds. When discussing media texts, the onus is on paying attention to ways in which meanings will be constructed by audiences through experience as much as through any fixed, intended, preferred messages from producers' points of view.

SPECTATORSHIP
How a reader of moving images behaves, which will be culturally specific. Reminds us that, for example, watching a film is not a practice that can be described as though it is a common experience.

SYMBIOSIS
Two forms arranged in an interactive, organic relationship. Used to describe relationships between different media products in commercial terms.

TEXT
All media products are texts. But we can extend this term to include people, ourselves and others – anything that is made up of a range of signs that are decoded and interpreted by people.

TRANSGRESSIVE
A practice which transcends conventional approaches, and either subverts these existing ways of working, or challenges their value.

VERISIMILITUDE
The logical, seemingly authentic world of a text. Not the same as 'realist', because every text has a logical, sensible world constructed through continuity, detail and recognition. So while we might not believe that aliens are ready to invade, *Independence Day* is believable because it constructs a coherent verisimilitude.

VERTICAL DISCOURSE
From Bernstein (1990). A discourse which is organized hierarchically and coherently, so it can be 'handed down'. My research (McDougall, 2004a) suggests that Subject Media is developing from a horizontal to a vertical discourse, primarily through its modes of assessment.

VIRTUAL LEARNING
Participating in education without access to other students or a tutor, usually through computers and online facilities.

WAP
Wireless application protocol – the internet and email on a phone of personal device without the need for cables or wires.

WE MEDIA
See Gillmoor (2004). Ordinary people deciding that they want to create media, through easily accessible technologies such as blogging, digital video, podcasting and v-logging. Wikipedia is a great example – I use this every day as a reference tool, despite the fact that I have no way of knowing who has provided its content. See also sites like Ourmedia.org.

Bibliography

Alden, C., 2005, *The Media Directory 2005,* London: Guardian Books.

Althusser, L., 1971, *Lenin and Philosophy and other essays*, London: New Left Books.

Altman, R., 1982, *Genre: The Musical*, London: Routledge.

Altman, R., 1999, *Film/Genre*, London: BFI.

Arrey, D., 2005, Unpublished: Huw Weldon lecture.

Arroyo, J., 2001, 'Mission Sublime' in Arroyo, J. (ed.), *Action/Spectacle*, London: BFI.

Baker, J., 2003, *Teaching TV Sitcom*, London: BFI.

Bakhtin, M., 1981, The Dialogic Imagination, Austin: University of Texas Press.

Balvanes, M., Donald, J., and Donald, S., 2001, *The Global Media Atlas*, London: BFI.

Barker, M., 2002, 'Categories of Violence' in *Media Magazine*, 1, London: English and Media Centre.

Barker, M., and Petley, J., 2000, *Ill Effects: The Media/Violence Debate,* London: Routledge.

Barthes, R., 1973, *Mythologies*, London: Paladin.

Barthes, R, 1983, *Selected Writings,* London: Fontana.

Bartlett, S., Burton., D., and Peim, N., 2001, *Introduction to Education Studies*, London: Paul Chapman Publishing.

Barton, L., 2004, 'It's all gone tits up' in *The Guardian*, 17 January.

Bates, S., 2003, 'You and Your Media: New Media Technologies and Audience Consumption' in *Media Magazine*, 6, London: English and Media Centre.

Bates, S., 2005, 'Squashed Out – Money, the Media and Minority Sport' in *Media Magazine*, 11, London: English and Media Centre.

Baudrillard, J., 1988, (ed. Poster, M.), *Selected Writings,* Cambridge: Polity.

Bazalgette, P., 2005, *Billion Dollar Game: How three men risked it all and changed the face of television*, London: Time Warner.

Beetlestone, F., 1998, *Creative Children, Imaginative Teaching*, Buckingham: Open University Press.

Bell, E. and Alden, C., 2004 *The Guardian Media Directory*, London: Guardian Books.

Belsey, C., 2005, *Culture and the Real*, London: Routledge.

Bennett, J., 2003, 'How to create a Simple Website' in *Media Magazine,* 3, London: English and Media Centre.

Benyahia, S., 2001, *Teaching Contemporary British Cinema,* London: BFI.

Berners-Lee, T., 1999, *Weaving the Web: The Past, Present and Future of the World Wide Web*, London: Orion.

Bernstein, B., 1990, *The Structuring of Pedagogic Discourse*, London: Routledge.

Bignell, J., 1997, *Media Semiotics: an introduction*, Manchester: MUP.

Black, P., Harrison, C., Lee, H., Marshall, B. and William, D., 2002, *Working Inside the Black Box: Assessment for Learning in the Classroom*, London: Kings College Publications.

Bloom, B., 1984, *Taxonomy of Educational Objectives*, Boston, MA: Allyn and Bacon.

de Bono, E., 2000, *Six Thinking Hats*, London: Penguin.

Bourdieu, P., 2002, *Distinction: A Social Critique of the Judgment of Taste*, London: Routledge.

Bourdieu, P., and Passeron, J., 1977, *Reproduction in Education, Society and Culture*, London: Sage.

Bowles, S., and Gintis, H., 1976, *Schooling in Capitalist America*, London: Routledge.

Branston, G., 1991, 'Audience' in Lusted, D. (ed.) *The Media Studies Book*, London: Routledge.

Brown, S., Race, P. and Smith, B., 1996, *500 Tips on Assessment*, London: Kogan Page.

Bruce, C., 2002, 'Analyse This!' In *Media Magazine*, 2, London: English and Media Centre.

Buckingham, D., 1987, *Public Secrets: EastEnders and its Audience*, London: BFI.

Buckingham, D., 1995, *Reading Audiences*, London: Edward Arnold.

Buckingham, D., 2000, 'Electronic Child Abuse: Rethinking the Media's Effects on Children' in Barker, M., and Petley, J., (eds.), *Ill Effects: The Media Violence Debate*, London: Routledge.

Buckingham, D., 2003, *Media Education: Literacy, Learning and Contemporary Culture*, London: Polity.

Burn, A. (*et al.*) 2001, 'The Rush of Images: a research report into digital editing and the moving image' in *English in Education*, 35(2), Sheffield: Nate.

Burn, A., Carr, D., Oram, B., and Horrell, K., and Schott, G., 2003, 'Why Study Digital Games?' in *Media Magazine*, 5 and 6, London: English and Media Centre.

Burn, A., and Parker, D., 2003, *Analysing Media Texts*, London: Continuum.

Caldwell, J., and Everett, A., 2003, *New Media; Practices of Digitextuality*, London: Routledge.

Carr, D., Buckingham, D. and Burn, A., 2005, *Computer Games: Text, Narrative and Play*, London: Polity.

Chomsky, N., 2003, *Doctrines and Visions*, London: Penguin.

Clare, V., 2005, *Researching Media and Film Studies: A Teacher's Guide*, London: Auteur.

Clark, V., 2005, *Media Briefing: The Global Picture & Teaching Notes*, London: BFI.

Cohen, S., 1980, *Folk Devils and Moral Panics*, Oxford: Martin Robertson.

Creeber, G. (ed.), 2001, *The Television Genre Book*, London: BFI.

Curran, J., 2002, *Media and Power*, London: Routledge.

Davey, O., 2005, 'Pleasure and Pain: Why We Need Violence in the Movies' in *Media Magazine*, 12, London: English and Media Centre.

Derrida, J., 1977, *Of Grammatology*, London: John Hopkins.

DfES/English and Media Centre, 2004, *Media Objectives in the KS3 Framework for Teaching English Years 7–9*, (Book and Video), London: DfES.

Dutton, B., 1997, *The Media*, London: Longman.

Dyer, R., 1994, 'Action!' In *Sight & Sound*, October, London: BFI.

Dyja, E., (ed.), 2005, *BFI Film and Television Handbook*, London: BFI.

Edwards, C., 2001, *Radio for Media Studies*, London: Auteur.

Feldman, T., 1997, *Introduction to Digital Media,* London: Routledge.

Fiske, J., 1987, *Television Culture*, London: Methuen.

Foucault, M., 1988, *Technologies of the Self: A Seminar with Michel Foucault*, Amherst: University of Massachusetts Press.

Fraser, P., 2001, *Teaching Music Video*, London: BFI.

Fraser, P., 2002, 'Production Work Tips' in *Media Magazine*, 1. London: English and Media Centre.

Fraser, P., and Oram, B., 2004, *Teaching Digital Video Production*, London: BFI.

Gauntlett, D., 1997, 'Another crisis for Media Studies' in *In the Picture*, 31, Keighley: itp Publications.

Gauntlett, D., 1998, 'Ten things wrong with the 'effects model', in Dickinson, R., Harindranath, R., and Linne, O., (eds.), *Approaches to Audiences,* London: Arnold.

Gauntlett, D., 2002, *Media, Gender and Identity – An Introduction*, London: Routledge.

Gauntlett, D., 2004, *Web Studies: Rewiring Media studies for the Digital Age,* 2nd edn., London: Arnold.

Gee, J., 2003, *What Video Games have to teach us about Learning and Literacy*, New York: Palgrave MacMillan.

Geraghty, C., 1991a, 'Representation and popular culture', in J. Curran and M. Gurevitch (eds.,) *Mass Media and Society*, London: Edward Arnold.

Geraghty, C., 1991b, *Women and Soap Opera: A Study of Prime-Time Soaps*, Cambridge: Polity Press.

Gillmoor, D., 2004, *We, The Media*, California: O'Reilly.

Grahame, J., 1994, *Production Practices*, London: English and Media Centre.

Grahame, J., 2001, 'Being Creative with Minimal Resources', BFI conference workshop.

Grant, L., 1996, 'Plays for Today' in *Guardian Weekend*, December 21, London: Guardian Newspapers.

Habermas, J., 1985, 'Modernity – An Incomplete Project' in Foster, H. (ed.), *Postmodern Culture*, London: Pluto.

Hall, S., 1981, 'Cultural Studies: Two Paradigms' in Bennett, T. *et al.* (eds.), *Culture, Ideology and Social Progress*, London: Batsford.

Hanley, P., (ed.), 2002, *Striking a balance: the control of children's media consumption*, London: ITC.

Hartley, J., 1999, *The Uses of Television*, London: Routledge.

Harvey, R., (ed.), 2002, *A2 Media Studies for OCR*, London: Hodder.

Hegel, G., 1996, *The Philosophy of Right*, London: Great Books in Philosophy.

Higson, A., 1995, *Waving the Flag: Constructing a National Cinema in Britain,* Oxford: Clarendon Press.

Higson, A., 1995, *Dissolving Views*, London: Cassell.

Hirschorn, A., 2003, 'Sitcoms and Absurdism', in *In the Picture*, 46, Keighley: itp Publications.

Hodge and Tripp, 1996, *Children and Television*, London: Polity.

Holland, P., 2000, *The Television Handbook*, London: Routledge.

Horrocks, C., and Jetvic, Z., 1999, *Introducing Foucault*, Cambridge: Icon.

In the Picture, 2003, 47, *Institution*, Keighley: itp Publications.

Irvine, S., 2004, 'Media in FE; How Things Stand Today' in *In the Picture*, 50. Keighley: itp
Publications.

Izod, J., 1984, *Reading the Screen*, London: Longman.

Jencks, C., 2005, *Culture,* London: Routledge.

Johnson, S., 1997, *Interface Culture*, California: Basic Books.

Johnson, S., 2005, *Everything Bad is Good for You*, London: Penguin.

Joseph, A., 2004, 'Identity Crisis: How to Create Your Own Digital Identity' in *Media
Magazine*, 8, London: English and Media Centre.

Kabir, N., 2001, *Bollywood: The Indian Cinema Story,* London: C4 books.

Kendall, A., 2002, 'The reading habits of 16–19 year olds – initial findings', paper presented
at BERA conference, University of Exeter.

Kermode, M., 2001, Introduction to Channel 4 Screening of *Bad Lieutenant*, London:
Channel 4.

Ki, S., 2004, 'The Evaluation of Practical Production as the Process of Legitimation in GCSE
Media Studies', unpublished PhD dissertation, London: Institute of Education.

Kirkup, M., 2005, *Contemporary British Cinema: A Teacher's Guide*, London: Auteur.

Krug, S., 2000, *Don't Make Me Think! A Common Sense Guide to Web Useability*, New York:
New Riders.

Lacan, J., 1977, *The Four Fundamental Concepts of Psycho-Analysis*, London: Hogarth Press.

Lacey, N., 2000a, *Narrative and Genre*, London: MacMillan.

Lacey, N., 2000b, *Image and Representation*, London: MacMillan

Lacey, N., and Stafford, R., 2002, 'Cut or Move the camera? Framing the Action', in *In the
Picture*, 45, Keighley: itp Publications.

Lacey, N., 2004, *Media Institutions and Audiences*, London: MacMillan.

Levan, S., 2000, *York Film Notes: Fargo*, London: York Press.

Lewis, E., 2001, *Teaching TV News*, London: BFI.

Lewis, E., 2003, 'True Lies: Reporting the War in Iraq', in *Media Magazine*, 5, London:
English and Media Centre.

Livingstone, S., 1999, *Young People, New Media,* London: LSE report.

Luhrs, G., 2002a, 'Why Convergence Matters' in *Media Magazine*, 1, London: English and
Media Centre.

Luhrs, G., 2002b, 'New Media Technologies: a Glossary' in *Media Magazine*, 2, London:
English and Media Centre.

Luhrs, G., 2005, 'The Future Will be Blogged' in *Media Magazine*, 12, London: English and
Media Centre.

Lunenfield, P., 2000, *The Digital Dialectic*, Massachussetts: MIT.

Lyotard, J., 1984, *The Postmodern Condition*, Manchester: MUP.

Lyotard, J., 1992, *The Postmodern Explained to Children*, London: Turnaround.

Martin, R., 2004, *Audiences: A Teacher's Guide,* London: Auteur.

Masterman, L., 1984, *Television Mythologies*, London: Comedia.

Masterman, L., 1985, *Teaching the Media*, London: Routledge.

Masterman, L., 2004, 'Visions of Media Education; The Road from Dystopia' in *In the Picture*, 48. Keighley: itp Publications.

McConnell, S., 2003, 'A Trip to the Seaside' in *Media Magazine*, 5, London: English and Media Centre.

McDougall, J., 1999, 'My Name is Joe: Reverberations in the Audience', in *In the Picture*, 36, Keighley, itp Publications.

McDougall, J., 2000, 'Finding the Ism of the Real', in *In the Picture, Film Reader*, Keighley: itp Publications.

McDougall, J., 2003, 'Games in the Classroom – Whatever Next?' in *Media Magazine*, 6, London: English and Media Magazine.

McDougall, J., 2004a, *Subject Media: A Study in the Sociocultural Framing of Discourse*. Unpublished PhD thesis: University of Birmingham.

McDougall, J., 2004b, 'Lads, Mags, *Nuts* and *Zoo*' in *Media Magazine*, 8, London: English and Media Centre.

McDougall, J., 2004c, 'Judging Media Learning' in *In the Picture*, 50, Keighley: itp Publications.

McKay, J., 2000, *The Magazines Handbook*, London: Routledge.

McLuhan, M., 1994, *Understanding Media; The Extensions of Man*, London: MIT.

McNair, B., 2003, *News and Journalism in the UK*, London: Routledge.

McQueen, D., 1998, *Television: A Media Student's Guide,* London: Arnold.

Medhurst, A., 1994, *The Magnificent Seven Rides Again*, London: The Observer.

Medhurst, A., 1996, *Dissolving Views*, London: Cassell.

Meighan, R., and Siraj-Blatchford, I., 2003, *A Sociology of Educating*, London: Continuum.

Meigs, T., 2003, *Ultimate Game Design: Building Game Worlds*, London: Osborne McGraw-Hill.

Miller, C. and Parlett, M., 1974, *Up the Mark: A Study of the Examination Game*, London: SRHE.

Mottershead, C., 2001, *How to Teach Narrative*, London: BFI Media Studies Conference Workshop.

Mulvey, L., 1975, Visual Pleasure and Narrative Cinema in Screen16, no. 3.

Musburger, R., and Kindem, G., 2004, *Introduction to Media Production: The Path to Digital Media Production*, Oxford: Focal Press.

Neale, S., 1980, *Genre*, London: BFI.

Neale, S., and Turner, G., 2001, *What is Genre?*, in Creeber, G. (ed.) *The Television Genre Book*, London: BFI.

Nelmes, J., (ed.), 1996, *An Introduction to Film Studies*, London: Routledge.

Newman, J., 2004, *Videogames*, London: Routledge.

Nock, D., 2004, 'Confessions of a B-Movie Writer' in *Media Magazine*, 8, London: English and Media Centre.

O'Brien, W., 2003, 'Key Media Concepts Courtesy of Big Brother 4', in *Media Magazine*, 6, London: English and Media Centre.

Ofcom, 2005, 'Media Literacy Bulletin', 1 and 2. London: Ofcom.

Ofsted, 2001, *Common Inspection Framework*, London: HMI.

Peim, N., 1995, *Critical Theory and the English Teacher*, London: Routledge.

Peim, N., 2000, 'The Cultural Politics of English Teaching' in *Issues in English Teaching*, London: Routledge.

Phillips, N., 1996, '*Genre*' in Nelmes, J., (ed.), *An Introduction to Film Studies*, London: Routledge.

Priestman, C., 2001, *Web Radio*, Oxford: Focal Press.

Propp, V., 1968, *Morphology of the Folktale*, USA: American Folklore Society.

QCA, 2005, 'Media Matters: a review of Media Studies in schools and colleges', London: QCA.

Raynor, P., Wall, P., and Kruger, S., 2001, *Media Studies: The Essential Introduction*, London: Routledge.

Readman, M., 2001, *Teaching Scriptwriting, Screenplays and Storyboards for Film and TV Production,* London: BFI.

Reid, M., 2001, *Teaching Genre*, unpublished conference presentation, London: BFI.

Reid, M., Buin, A. and Parker, D., 2002, *Evaluation Report of the BECTA Digital Video Project*, London: BECTA.

Robinson, P., 2002, *The CNN Effect*, London: Routledge.

Roddick, N., 1999, 'Show Me the Culture' in *Sight and Sound*, 8.12, London: BFI.

Sampson, A,. 2004, *Who Owns this Place?*, London: John Murray.

Sardar, Z., and Van Loon, B., 2000, *Introducing Media Studies*, London: Icon.

Saussure, F., 1974, *Course in General Linguistics,* London: Fontana.

Sefton-Greene, J., 1999, 'Media education, but not as we know it; digital technology and the end of Media Studies?' in *English and Media Magazine*, 40, London: English and Media Centre.

Sefton-Greene, J., and Sinker, R., (eds.), 2000, *Evaluating Creativity: Making and Learning by Young People,* London: Routledge.

Selby, K., and Cowdery, R., 1995, *How to Study Television*, London: MacMillan.

Shannon, C. and Weaver, W., 1949, *Mathematical Theory of Communication*, USA: University of Illinois Press.

Sohn-Rethel, M., 2001, *Realism*, unpublished conference presentation, London: BFI.

Spraggon, L., 2004, *Into Animation*, London: BFI Education.

Stafford, R., 1997, 'Sex and Drugs and Rock 'n' Roll – Innoculate, Regulate or Celebrate?' in *In the Picture*, 31, Keighley: itp Publications.

Stafford, R., (ed.), 2000, *Film Reader 2: British Cinema*, Keighley: itp Publications.

Stafford, R., 2002a, 'Formats and Genres across Media' in *In the Picture*, 44, Keighley: itp Publications.

Stafford, R., 2002b, *British Cinema 1990–2002: Teacher's Notes,* Keighley: itp Publications.

Stafford, R., 2003, 'Nowhere to run to? Nowhere to hide for asylum?' in *In the Picture*, 46, Keighley: itp Publications.

Stafford, R., 2003, 'Ofcom is Up and Running' in *In the Picture,* 47, Keighley: itp Publications.

Stafford, R., and Branston, G., 2004, *The Media Student's Book*, London: Routledge.

Strinati, D., 1995, *An Introduction to Theories of Popular Culture*, London: Routledge.

Tapscott, D., 1998, *Growing Up Digital: The Rise of the Net Generation*, McGraw Hill: New York.

Tasker, Y., (ed.), 2005, *Action and Adventure Cinema*, London: Routledge.

Taylor, N., 2005, *Search Me: The Surprising Success of Google*, London: Cyan.

Taylor, P., 1999, *Hackers: Crime in the Digital Sublime*, Routledge, London.

Thompson, K., 1998, *Moral Panics*, London: Routledge.

Thusso, D., 2000, *International Communication*, London: Hodder.

Todorov, T., 1971, 'The Two Principles of Narrative' in *Diacritics*, vol. 1, no. 1.

Toland, P., 2004, 'What are you Playing At?' in *Media Magazine*, 7, London: English and Media Centre.

Tyrell, H., 1988, *Bollywood in Britain* in *Sight & Sound*, August 1998, London: BFI.

UK Film Council, 2004, *Film Theft in the UK*, London: Film Council.

Vygotsky, L.S., 1962, *Thought and Language*, Cambridge, MA: MIT Press.

Walker, C., 2004, 'Are MP3s Killing the Music Business?' Birmingham: unpublished undergraduate dissertation, Coventry University.

Watson, J., and Hill, A., 2003, *Dictionary of Media and Communication Studies*, London: Arnold.

Winship, J., 1997, *Inside Women's Magazines*, London: Pandora.

Withall, K., 2000, 'Exploring Documentary Truth?' in *In the Picture*, 40, Keighley: itp Publications.

Wolf, J., and Perron, B., 2003, *The Video Game Theory Reader*, London: Routledge.

Zimmerman, E., and Salen, K., 2003, *Rules of Play: Game Design Fundamentals*, Massachusets: MIT Press.

Top 40 Websites

The following list of URLs, at the time of writing, offers you a pretty comprehensive range of organizations that offer in some cases excellent resources and INSET opportunities and in others facilities for you to network, share ideas or raise issues.

BFI Education – www.bfi.org.uk/education
The British Film Institute's education resources are wide ranging and very popular with Media teachers working on moving image analysis and production. The BFI also organize a conference for A Level teachers, held once a year each in Bradford and London. The BFI runs an accreditation scheme for Media and Film teachers – the Associate Tutor Scheme, and a range of continuing professional development and INSET options.

In the Picture – www.itpmag.demon.co.uk
The website of the excellent magazine for Media teachers, edited by Roy Stafford and Nick Lacey. A range of very good teaching resources and study materials is available from this site, as is subscription to the magazine and information on a range of INSET events and continuing professional development opportunities.

BBC online – www.bbconline.org.uk
The most used web presence in the world.

Google – www.google.com
Now more than a search engine (see Chapter Five), Google is starting to seriously mediate information as well as just provide access to it.

Film Education – www.filmeducation.org.uk
Essential site for teaching film.

Screen Online – www.screenonline.org.uk
BFI's site for British Film and TV history resources, with an option to register and access video/audio material.

Internet Newspaper Directory – www.discover.co.uk/NET/NEWS
Global newspaper access facility.

Daniel Chandler's Media and Communications site – www.aber.ac.uk/media
Very useful academic site.

Media Zoo – www.mediazoo.co.uk
Discussions on contemporary UK media.

Theory.org – www.theory.org.uk
David Gauntlett's excellent website, with a cultural theory focus.

Media and Culture Journal – http://journal.media-culture.org,au/index.php
Academic journal, fairly self-explanatory.

Popcultures – www.popcultures.com
A collection of articles on TV and popular culture generally.

OCR e-mail forum and resource site –
http://community.ocr.org.uk/community/mediastudies-a/home
I was involved in setting this up while at OCR and I am quite proud of this, since it has become a daily resource for those teaching OCR specifications. A great example of how technology can increase community experience, rather than reduce it. Usually features some lively debate.

Media UK – www.mediauk.com/directory
A gateway to websites of all the main media institutions.

Media Channel – www.mediachannel.org
USA media directory with a variety of global links.

English and Media Centre – www.englishandmedia.co.uk
This organization offers a range of high quality resources and INSET events, as well as the wonderful *Media Magazine* and the *MoreMediaMag* webiste, which your students can subscribe to through your centre. Pioneering in publishing A Level student work.

Long Road Sixth Form College Media site – http://www.longroadmedia.com/
Great Media department doing cutting edge production work, on view here. Exemplary.

Long Road Sixth Form College Media blog – http://longroadmedia.blogspot.com
Student blog and podcast resource. Have a look, and make your own.

The Radio Site – www.i-way.co.uk/~stunova
Links to global stations and organizations.

Media Magazine – www.mediamagazine.org.uk
See English and Media Centre.

UK Film Council – www.ukfilmcouncil.org.uk
Essential for facts and figures, as well as the recent research on piracy.

OFCOM – www.ofcom.org.uk
The regulatory body with a media literacy agenda as well as their surveillance remit.

Advertising Education Forum – http://www.aeforum.org/
Interesting range of educational perspectives on contemporary ads.

Media Education – www.mediaed.org.uk
Another online forum, but not affiliated to any awarding body. An essential resource for those feeling isolated. Tends to be less focused on 'questions for the board' than the OCR list, and hence more interesting in a pedagogic sense at times.

The Internet Movie Database – www.imdb.com
Printing out details about any film is now a five-minute job.

CCEA Moving Image Arts pilot – www.ccea.org.uk/movingimagearts
Pilot specification for new qualification in Moving Image Arts, in Northern Ireland.

Campaign for Press and Broadcasting Freedom – www.cpbf.org.uk
Very useful for student research around the free press.

Game Culture online journal – www.game-culture.com
Academic journal offering a range of theoretical responses to video and computer games.

Skillset – www.skillset.org
The National Training Organisation for broadcasting media. Increasingly agenda-setting given the 14–19 reform's focus on employer engagement.

National Museum of Film, Photography and Television – www.nmpft.org.uk
Museum in Bradford with an IMAX cinema, offering a great day trip for Media students and a range of study days and INSET opportunities.

New Media – www.newmediastudies.com
Really useful for up-to-date facts and figures, such as global internet usage statistics.

Indymedia UK – www.indymedia.org.uk/
Voice of the people, potentially subversive website. Excellent for student research on media access.

OFCOM Watch – www.ofcomwatch.co.uk/
The watcher watched. The panopticon subverted?!

Our media – www.ourmedia.org
Offers easy ways to upload and distribute 'DIY' media.

Centre for the Study of Children, Youth and Media – www.ccsonline.org.uk
Institute of Education's research centre – loads of very interesting audience research going on here. To avoid assumptions about children's media consumption, this is essential. Also offers a lot of very useful links to other research, especially related to computer games.

Robert Smyth School Media Studies Blog – http://rssmedia.com
Another student blog. Again, have a look and then make your own.

Media Guardian – www.media.guardian.co.uk
Online version of the Monday supplement.

Blogger.com – www.blogger.com
You can create your own blog for free in minutes here.

Transom – www.transom.org
This site enables you to make your own internet radio programme.

Art Lab – http://www.artlab.org.uk/
Very interesting – this might inspire some interesting media arts work.

Wikimedia – http://en.wikipedia.org/wiki/Wikimedia
Great 'we media' resource. If you can't find a definition, you get to write it yourself. What the internet was supposed to be like.

Index